EDITOR
Susan E. Laemmle

MANAGING EDITOR
Hara E. Person

BOOK REVIEW EDITOR
Laurence Edwards

POETRY EDITOR
Adam Fisher

***MAAYANOT* (PRIMARY SOURCES) EDITOR**
Daniel F. Polish

EDITORIAL BOARD
Mona Alfi, Lawrence Bach, Leah Berkowitz, Daniel Fink, Joshua Garroway, Paul Golomb, Elaine Rose Glickman, Evan Moffic, Jason Rosenberg, Mark Dov Shapiro, Kinneret Shiryon, Donald M. Splansky

PRODUCTION
Publishing Synthesis, Ltd.

COPY EDITOR
Michael Isralewitz

CCAR ELECTED OFFICERS
Richard A. Block, President
Denise L. Eger, President-elect
David E. Stern, VP Organizational Relationships
Elaine Zecher, VP Leadership
Samuel Gordon, VP Financial Affairs
Deborah Bravo, VP Programs
Stephen Einstein, VP Member Services
Jonathan Stein, Past-President

CCAR RABBINIC STAFF
Steven A. Fox, Chief Executive
Deborah Prinz, Director of Program and Mentor Services
Alan H. Henkin, Director of Placement
Hara E. Person, Publisher and Director of CCAR Press
Dan Medwin, Publishing Technology Manager

Arnold I. Sher, Director of Placement Emeritus (1989–2008)
and Interim Executive Vice President (2005)
Paul J. Menitoff, Executive Vice President Emeritus (1994–2005)

PAST EDITORS
Abraham J. Klausner * (1953–58), Joseph Klein* (1958–64),
Daniel Jeremy Silver* (1964–72), Joseph R. Narot* (1972–75),
Bernard Martin* (1975–81), Samuel E. Karff (1981–84),
Samuel M. Stahl (1984–90), Lawrence Englander (1990–93),
Henry Bamberger (1993–96), Rifat Sonsino (1996–2000)
Stephen Pearce (2000–2003), Jonathan A. Stein (2003–2009)

*Deceased

CCAR Journal
The Reform Jewish Quarterly

Preparing for the New Machzor *and the High Holidays*

Contents

FROM THE EDITOR
At the Gates — בשערים 1

ARTICLES
Preparing for the New *Machzor* and the High Holy Days:
   An Integrated Approach 3
Elaine Zecher, Guest Editor

SECTION ONE: FROM THE EDITORS OF THE NEW MACHZOR
The New Reform *Machzor* Is a Solution, but What
   Is the Problem? 8
Edwin C. Goldberg

What Happens When We Use Poetry in Our Prayer
   Books—and Why? 16
Sheldon Marder

The End of Liturgical Reform as We Know It:
   Creative Retrieval as a New Paradigm 29
Leon A. Morris

SECTION TWO: FROM PROFESSORS OF LITURGY AT HUC-JIR
"Lu Yehi": High Holy Day Liturgy and Experience
   in Israel 35
Dalia Marx

Machzor: **The Poetry of Truly Awe-Inspiring Days** 40
Richard S. Sarason

CONTENTS

A Tale of Three *Machzorim* 45
Richard N. Levy

Doing It Right or Doing It Well? 50
Lawrence A. Hoffman

SECTION THREE: FROM OUR COLLEAGUES

When I Hear the Shofar I Taste Chocolate: Seeking the
    Synesthetic on the High Holy Days 63
Evan Kent

Love, Liturgy, Leadership 71
Elyse D. Frishman

The Yamim Nora'im: Concentric Circles of Liturgy
    and Relation 81
Lawrence A. Englander

The Calves of Our Lips: The Inescapable Connections
    between Prayer and Sacrifice 92
Leon A. Morris

"Baavur Sheani Noder Tzedakah Baado" 103
Margaret Moers Wenig

Visions for a New/Old Reform Yizkor Service 115
Donald B. Rossoff

We, the *Avaryanim*, Chant *Kol Nidrei* 126
Donald P. Cashman

The *Un'taneh Tokef* Prayer—Sealing Our Faith,
    Not Our Fate 135
Y. Lindsey bat Joseph

Viewing *Un'taneh Tokef* through a New Lens 144
Amy Scheinerman

Mystical Journeys and Magical Letters: The *Y'rushalmi's*
    Cosmology in the *Machzor* 153
Judith Z. Abrams

The *Machzor* before the *Machzor*: Interpreting the
    High Holy Days during the Second Temple Period 164
Aaron D. Panken

CONTENTS

Yom Kippur in Moab: Reflections on the Setting of the *Parashah* 175
Elsie R. Stern

MAAYANOT (PRIMARY SOURCES)
Maimonides' *T'shuvah* to Ovadyah the Proselyte 185
Philip Matoff Posner

RESPONSES TO THE FALL 2012 SYMPOSIUM
Kenneth D. Roseman 203
Jeff Marx 204

POETRY
Stretching toward S'lichot 207
Ruth Lerner

Rosh HaShanah in the Pines, 2011/5772 209
Hara E. Person

What If 210
Donald B. Rossoff

Kol Nidrei 212
Jenni Person

Yom Kippur, The Essence Does Not Change 213
Yehoshua November

The Ankle of the High Priest 214
Joseph R. Black

The Wilderness of Tishrei 216
Barbara AB Symons

Join the Conversation!

Subscribe Now.

Engage with ideas about Judaism and Jewish life through essays, poetry and book reviews by leading scholars, rabbis, and thinkers.

A Journal for All Jews
The CCAR Journal: The Reform Jewish Quarterly
$100 for one year subscription
$150 for two year subscription

For more information and to order, go to:
www.ccarpress.org or call 212-972-3636 x243
CCAR | 355 Lexington Avenue | New York, NY 10017

At the Gates — בשערים

The Dodgers moved to Los Angeles during my college years, and I still remember hearing about Sandy Koufax's decision not to pitch Game One of the 1965 World Series when it fell on Yom Kippur. This memory played a role in my reply to the inquiry of a young professor shortly after my arrival at USC Hillel in 1992: Could he install his art in the university's gallery on Yom Kippur, as the schedule called for? At that point, this fellow's observance was minimal. I took a deep breath and replied "no."

Years later when Professor Ken Goldberg, now of UC Berkeley, asked me to officiate at his wedding to Tiffany Shlain, both he and I recalled the incident. Indeed, I have often told this story to make the point that sometimes it's important to draw a clear line—to say "no." In recent years, Ken and Tiffany have made a series of films about social issues, including *The Tribe* and *Connected*. Jewish values palpate through their work and lives.

Like many rabbis, I look for opportunities to underscore the centrality of Shabbat in Jewish life. But there's no denying that the High Holy Days function as a clearer litmus test of Jewish identification than Shabbat. Although "twice a year" Jews get criticized, the pull that brings them back into the fold each year is something to be taken seriously—something to build upon in creating and renewing our liturgy. Thus comes the new Reform *machzor*, as well as this symposium issue of the *CCAR Journal: The Reform Jewish Quarterly*.

Within this important issue you will find, somewhat surprisingly, two references to Sandy Koufax, both in poems that were submitted in response to a special Call for Poems. Jenni Person pictures a modern couple experiencing *Kol Nidrei*, not in shul but via their bedside laptop as their young children drift asleep. Tuned in to their television and accessing an iPhone at the same time, this multi-platform couple compares a baseball player who's "Jew/Half-Jew" to Koufax: "He did what Sandy Koufax/swore he'd never do/But never needed to." The poem concludes on two legs: baseball's "lineage is long" and "*Kol Nidrei* is live online."

The second poem in which Sandy Koufax appears is by Yehoshua November, who has published and been reviewed in these pages (unlike Person, whom we welcome a newcomer). In "Yom Kippur, The Essence Does Not Change," November parallels (1) the way in which "though he knew little Torah,/Sandy Koufax gave up what is unthinkable to give up" to (2) "young Jewish boys—kidnapped from the *cheder* and raised/in the Russian army—/[who] took off their shirts/at the last hour of Yom Kippur" as they asked for God's blessing. We can imagine gates of *t'shuvah* and *b'rachah* opening for these tender and abused youths, whose margin of freedom was severely limited but whose spiritual imagination was huge.

Searching online, I learn that as a youngster Sandy Koufax was constantly at the Jewish Community Center in Brooklyn shooting baskets or playing with a team; also, that his stepfather took him and his stepsister Edith to Yiddish theatre in New York City. Who's to say what portion of Koufax's capacity to swim against the current derived from the Jewish cultural and communal settings to which he was exposed.

The *CCAR Journal* sees itself as such a setting. This special issue should help rabbis and congregants understand the intellectual and religious underpinnings of the new *machzor*. Elaine Zecher, chair of the *Machzor* Advisory Group and of the CCAR's Liturgy and Practices Committee, has done a splendid job of attracting and inviting authors. Her Introduction presents them to you individually and within the larger context. It has been a particular pleasure for me to work with Elaine since she was the first guest editor I encountered when becoming editor of the *Journal*. Then, she helped me along with great generosity. As I now move toward the conclusion of my term, it's meaningful to round back by once again joining hands with Elaine.

I hope that readers enjoy the articles and poems in this issue, as well as the fourth piece to appear within our new *Maayanot* (Primary Sources) rubric. Philip Posner's introduction to and translation of Maimonides' T'shuvah *to Ovadyah the Proselyte* connects nicely to High Holy Day themes: openness to change, human and divine compassion, and reaching out to God from within the Jewish People.

Susan Laemmle, Editor

Preparing for the New *Machzor* and the High Holy Days: An Integrated Approach

Elaine Zecher

In order to begin to speak about the new *machzor*, I first turn to the subject of medicine. Many years ago, I learned from my physician husband about a particular concept that I believe informs an approach to liturgy—especially *Mishkan T'filah* and the new *machzor*. It was and continues to be referred to as "integrative medicine."[1] The idea arose from the consistent and widespread use of medical approaches not widely practiced in established medical institutions like hospitals and doctors' offices. Common examples include acupuncture, herbal remedies, massage, and mindfulness-based meditation, to name a few. Their practice was widespread but they were deemed alternative or complementary as they were not part of the mainstream. Following a scientific survey documenting the widespread use of these practices[2] and continued studies of their safety and efficacies, the medical establishment slowly began to explore how best to incorporate them into medical settings like academic health centers and medical schools. Over the course of two decades, these modalities turned from having an exclusively complementary role in the practice of medicine to being more commonly integrated and part of routine treatment protocols. Side by side with traditional medical modalities like prescription drugs, surgery, radiation therapies, and other modern methods, the juxtaposition of these treatments created a potential synergistic relationship aimed at preventing, treating, and managing diseases. Each treatment method could stand on its own, but combined they could have a more powerful influence on the health

---

ELAINE ZECHER (NY83) has served as rabbi at Temple Israel, Boston, since 1990. She serves as chair of the Liturgy and Practices Committee of the CCAR. She also chairs the *Machzor* Advisory Group and is a vice president of the CCAR Board.

and well-being of an individual. The goal wasn't necessarily to create a hybrid treatment but rather to apply these multiple medical modalities in a coordinated fashion in conjunction with each other so that a stronger result could potentially ensue.

Understanding the concept of integrative medicine has led me to see parallels in the way we utilize a similar protocol through *Mishkan T'filah* and the new *machzor*—though our intention is to affect the soul more than the body. As a member of the Editorial Committee for the New Prayer Book, now called *Mishkan T'filah*, I remember the conversation we had on how to arrange a page of liturgy so that it contained multiple modalities of expression with traditional and other creative approaches. In the beginning of putting together the prayer book, Elyse Frishman, the editor, worked diligently to ensure each page could reflect more than its traditional counterpart. She presented what has become an integral part of the Reform liturgical experience: two pages facing each other based on the theme of the prayer. In that moment she opened up the possibility to enter different voices, perspectives, and understanding into prayer. It was transformative. Poetry, psalms, creative interpretations, spiritual commentary, and source explanations could complement the traditional prayer, the faithful translation, and transliteration.

Through organizing and reorganizing the two-page spread, a design emerged, but something else happened as well. Most of the historical, traditional prayers we use refer to God as omnipotent, omnipresent, and most often, in a hierarchical framework. With the advent of the two-page spread, we could also include varied expressions of the Divine. In the same way that integrative medicine seeks to combine different therapeutic approaches, both "conventional" and "complementary," to treat an individual, we began to see how an individual could experience the sacred through the exposure and employment of different approaches to God. Unlike *Gates of Prayer*, which has different services each expressing a different theological view of God, *Mishkan T'filah*, as designed by Elyse Frishman with the Editorial Committee, could create a synergistic understanding of God. I call this an integrated theology. As such, an integrated theology juxtaposes and places different theological ideas in close proximity allowing them to stand alone but also to combine for a stronger concept of God. Take most pages of *Mishkan*

T'filah and it is possible to find different voices rising from the page together.

The editors of the new *machzor* have taken the concept of an integrated theology but have applied it to the unique complexities of a High Holy Day prayer book. The new *machzor*, like *Mishkan T'filah*, will provide us new and innovative approaches and will certainly reflect the thoughtful work of these editors.

As we began to think about the introduction of the new *machzor*, we wanted to utilize this *CCAR Journal* symposium as a resource with which to consider new ideas and concepts, some of which will be reflected in our new High Holy Day prayer book. All of the articles, however, provide thoughtful consideration for this important season of the year. Whether we lead the prayers, offer words of Torah, interpret the liturgy through music, organize and administer all details, or find ourselves sitting among the community, this time of year calls upon us to prepare. Each year, the *machzor* invites us to plummet the depths of our souls, to be lost in the search, and then to find our way back.

It is an honor to introduce this symposium issue of the *CCAR Journal* focusing on the *machzor* and its myriad components. Though we may only use it during a brief time during the Jewish calendar year, its influence reaches much further beyond time and space. The articles that follow integrate many of the ideas that the *machzor* presents.

This issue is divided into three sections. The first one is made up of articles by the Editorial Core Team, whose efforts have helped to shape the new *machzor* in profound ways. Edwin Goldberg shares the *machzor* Vision Statement created by the editors as a vision to guide the process and provides commentary of it. Shelley Marder offers a beautiful understanding to the role of poetry not only in the new *machzor* but also its important place in liturgy as a whole. Leon Morris considers how to mine our traditional resources as a dynamic and vibrant process in creating innovative and meaningful worship. Although Janet Marder has not submitted her own essay, her influence is contained throughout.

We are grateful to have the voices of a professor of liturgy from each of the four HUC-JIR campuses, which make up the second section of the symposium. Whether through a personal experience with her Israeli students as Dalia Marx describes or Richard Sarason's wonderful concept of "music inside the text" or Richard

Levy's analysis of the three major *machzorim* utilized by our movement or Larry Hoffman's foundational explication of the power of liturgy done well, each of these professors continue to guide us with their wisdom in order to increase and to deepen our own understanding and thinking.

The third and final section's collection of articles by colleagues in diverse Jewish settings further complements our preparation. We begin on a conceptual level taking a broader and more general perspective and then move closer in to specific sections and prayers. Cantor Evan Kent, whose contributions have been invaluable to the Editorial Core Team, introduces the concept of synesthesia and analyzes the importance of the senses to the liturgical experience. Elyse Frishman beautifully synthesizes the role of the *machzor* as a tool to the greater endeavor of High Holy Day worship. Lawrence Englander explains his concept using concentric circles to describe how relationships on multiple levels inform our understanding of the *machzor*. Leon Morris offers an example of creative retrieval and uses the "inescapable link between sacrifice and prayer" as an example. Margaret Moers Wenig and Donald Rossoff help us make the transition into specific sections of the *machzor* with a focus on the *Yizkor* service. Wenig delves into the inherent significance of the experience and Rossoff analyzes its structure and its impact, presenting additional possibilities to be included. Donald Cashman demonstrates how *Kol Nidrei* can be offered through the involvement and direct participation of the congregation. Lindsay Bat Joseph weaves a personal story around *Un'taneh Tokef* and Amy Scheinerman examines this same prayer through the lens of process theology.

This section and the symposium's concluding three articles ground us with the influence of other important texts. Judith Abrams exposes the *Y'rushalmi*'s mystical influence on the *machzor*. Aaron Panken shares his scholarship of the Second Temple Period and how texts from that time inform our understanding of the *machzor*. And finally, Elsie Stern focuses her attention on the Deuteronomy sources that make up the Yom Kippur Morning Torah Service as an intriguing perspective from Moab.

This year in particular, as 5773 turns to 5774, we want to help position ourselves to enter into the Days of Awe with intention and introspection. As we prepare to receive a new *machzor* in the near future, we wanted to provide a forum to consider the many themes and ideas provided by the worship experience itself, the liturgy, and the vast array of ideas and themes that stem from it to create an integrated and well-informed platform.

One more note: Many of us, as members of the Central Conference of American Rabbis, benefit in known and unknown ways from the work of the professionals at the CCAR. I want to express our profound gratitude to Hara Person, who works diligently on our behalf to develop, foster, and steward the many publications. Her contributions, in particular, to secure the strength and quality of the new *machzor* has enabled the kind of creative and innovative work being offered to produce this important piece of liturgy for our movement. We thank her immensely.

Notes

1. Ralph Snyderman and Andrew T. Weil, "Integrative Medicine: Bringing Medicine Back to Its Roots," *Archives of Internal Medicine* 162, no. 2 (2002): 395–97.
2. David M Eisenberg, Ronald Kessler, et al., "Unconventional Medicine in the United States—Prevalence, Costs, and Patterns of Use" *New England Journal of Medicine* 328 (1993): 246–52.

Section One: *From the Editors of the New* Machzor

The New Reform *Machzor* Is a Solution, but What Is the Problem?

Edwin C. Goldberg

Introduction

Creating a new *machzor* for the Reform Movement is a daunting task and, speaking on behalf of the editorial committee, we are humbled by the challenge. Effective worship is difficult enough to create under normal Shabbat circumstances. The theological, sociological, and logistical trials wrought by the Days of Awe (or Days of Fright, in Lawrence Hoffman's felicitous translation) are formidable. Of course, the challenge is a holy one, and a problem that reflects the greatest reason for our rabbinic *raison d'être*. Meeting this task head on, we are guided by a clear vision of what we wish to produce, as well as aided by the outstanding work of those who prepared earlier *machzorim* and siddurim. Indeed, we are honored by the position we have been given in the chain of American Reform Jewish continuity.

Shortly after beginning work on the *machzor* I came across an original 1895 *Union Prayer Book II*, which I had forgotten I owned. My great-grandfather's name is inscribed inside. I enjoy imagining Lewis Wessel praying with this book at Shaaray Tefila on the Upper West Side. Our new book will be quite different, of course, but if we succeed it will seek to solve the same essential problem: how do we help ourselves return to our sacred path, in a world that continually seduces us away from the work that we must do?

EDWIN C. GOLDBERG, D.H.L. (C89) is the incoming senior rabbi at Temple Shalom of Chicago.

THE NEW REFORM *MACHZOR* IS A SOLUTION, BUT WHAT IS THE PROBLEM?

This question has been at the forefront of the editorial team of the upcoming CCAR *machzor*. We are not creating a book, per se, so much as a sacred tool that is part of the solution to a problem (or set of problems). Therefore, before any decisions could be made concerning the book itself, we needed to make sure we accurately defined the problem. After all, as the late Stephen Covey used to teach, it doesn't matter how efficient you are chopping down trees if you are actually in the wrong forest.

The desire to make sure we were addressing the right challenge led us to create a vision statement before we began producing the *machzor*. This statement not only reflects the solution we would be proposing in the form of a sacred book but also the challenges such a book would seek to address, with the understanding that the book itself could only be a part of a larger assemblage of sacred worship tools.

At the end of the article is the full vision statement we produced. In this article I want to focus on the central bullet points of the statement and include some personal commentary. For the sake of clarity I am putting into italics the key terms that are featured in the commentary. These italics do not appear in the actual vision statement.

Bullet Points of Vision Statement

We envision a twenty-first-century *machzor* that . . .
- provides meaningful liturgy to those who pray regularly, and welcomes those who are new to Jewish spirituality and practice;
- *inspires Reform Jews* to participate in the multifaceted experience of the Yamim Noraim—from feelings of awe to moments of solace, from the solitude of contemplation to the solidarity of song and worship;
- draws from the deep wellsprings of Jewish liturgy, history, thought, music, interpretation, and creativity;
- guides worshipers, in accessible ways, through the journey of *t'shuvah* and *cheshbon hanefesh*;
- *values continuity and incorporates the outlook of the twenty-first-century* Reform Jewish community of North America;
- bridges the personal and the communal, the ritual and the ethical dimensions of the Yamim Noraim.

Commentary

"Inspires Reform Jews"

In order to inspire the worshiper we must begin by defining who that worshiper is and who the worshiper is not. In this case, although we value the prayer experience of the rabbi and cantor, we are clear in our desire to fashion a prayer book for *amcha*. In other words, we are the first to admit that the book will not be the most user-friendly option out there. As with *Mishkan T'filah* it is highly likely that the clergy who use this book initially will find it less enjoyable than the congregants they serve. We know that the book will take plenty of forethought and will call upon a balance between offering directions and allowing the congregation to have their own experience. No one said that leading effective worship should be easy, and we believe that the goal is not to offer simple worship. Having said that, we want worship that is complex rather than complicated and we are striving to meet that goal as best we can.

The *machzor* is not just for *amcha* (or "Jews in the pews"); it is for specific Jews, Reform Jews. One might argue that we would be better off producing a book that we could market to all Jews. Nevertheless, our committee understands the principle that we cannot create a *kol bo machzor* for all people, so we are better off making sure the *machzor* reflects the sensibilities of Reform Jews. In our era, such a group is diverse enough to present many challenges.

"T'shuvah and Cheshbon Hanefesh"

In designing a *machzor* we find it helpful to begin with the end in mind, another useful insight from the late Stephen Covey. Specifically, what do we hope to have realized by the worshipers at the end of *N'ilah*? How will their lives have changed? What will be different? The simple answer is to suggest that *t'shuvah* will have occurred, but what does this mean? Certainly it seems impossible to measure the inner life of a person, so would we even know if we had succeeded? Such is the work of rabbis that we will never know for sure if the experiences we provide lead to the results we desire. Nevertheless, even if we cannot know for certain where people end up, we most assuredly should design the best "map" possible. Hence our *machzor* will be designed to lead the worshiper through a process that we label the "i-axis," in which the various services build up to a climax where painful truths are realized, change is considered and adopted, and the individual leaves with a plan for self-improvement.

A little more explanation of the "i-axis": If you imagine a graph with an x-axis and a y-axis, representing horizontal and vertical points, one can also speak of the actual flow-line of the graph, which ends up in a different place from where it starts. We are designing the *machzor* with a vision in mind in which the worshiper will end up in a different place on Yom Kippur afternoon than where one began on Rosh HaShanah eve (or better yet, on Rosh Chodesh Elul). We hope that an inner-process of *t'shuvah* will have occurred, including the difficult work of examining oneself, finding faults, and beginning to correct such faults.

This i-axis manifests itself in the selection of *Avinu Malkeinu* verses and *Al Cheit* confessions we choose for various parts of the service, as well as the decision to focus in particular on Musar material for Yom Kippur afternoon. By that point in the Days of Awe we hope that *amcha* is ready for "building themselves back up" through Musar meditation and learning, as well as prayer, in order to greet the end of the day with not only renewed hope but also a new direction.

"Values Continuity and Incorporates the Outlook of the Twenty-first Century"

During the course of our work we often consider the various Friday night services in the *Gates of Prayer* and how each one reflects a different theology. Then there is the *integrated theology* of *Mishkan T'filah*. Our approach is to build on the integrated theology while at the same time understanding that, to put it mildly, the theological stakes are higher on these Days of Awe. In other words, on a given Friday night one might very well focus on a non-dualistic image of God or perhaps the theology of human adequacy. The High Holy Days cannot be treated in the same manner. Somewhere a more traditional theology of hierarchy has to be offered if we are to be true to the essential message and tone of these days. Therefore we know the greatest challenge of the book will most likely be how to reflect this tradition while at the same time not turning off all those who cannot reconcile such views with the God in which they want to believe.

I call this the "Singing in the Rain" factor. The popular song was eventually slated to be a movie. Asked about it, its future star, Gene Kelly, said he had no idea what the movie would be about but he was sure of two things: "There will be rain and I will be singing in it." We know as editors that there is going to be some form of *Un'taneh Tokef* in the book, even if during our investigation we discovered how relatively minor this *piyut* (actually a *siluk*) was in its initial incarnation. In addition to the more traditional approach to God, we will offer, especially on the left side of the two-page spread, various images of God that challenge the hierarchical model, especially making use of poetry and well-chosen metaphor.

The purpose of having a two-page spread throughout most of the book is not to provide variety, per se, but rather to ensure that there are different theological positions mingling together so that each service can be—if the leaders choose—different every time, offering a mix of theologies in an effort to reflect the diversity of our God perspectives.

Conclusion

Harvard professor Clayton Christensen likes to tell the story of the fast food chain that found that about half of milkshake sales occurred in the morning. These buyers came into the restaurant by themselves, bought a milkshake and nothing else, and drove away with the milkshake rather than consuming it at the restaurant. Looking deeper, researchers learned that the buyers were commuters, and the job of the milkshake was to provide distraction on a long commute and to tide them over until lunch. For this job, the milkshake competed with bananas, donuts, breakfast bars, and coffee. Commuters bought milkshakes over the competition because milkshakes take a long time to consume, don't slosh or leave crumbs, and can be held in one hand or be put into a cup holder during the drive.

Most of us don't think of milkshakes as solution to a problem (i.e., hunger, boredom, need for convenience) but it turns out they are a solution and happy is the fast food establishment that knows the problem its product seeks to address.

Likewise, although milkshakes and the Days of Awe are not a natural pairing (*alas*) there is an important lesson: Our new *machzor* will be judged on how it looks and its content, but our visioning process began from a different place: what problem should the *machzor* set out to solve, and therefore what are the challenges we must face? Our vision statement reflects our working through this question in an effort to make sure that our sacred book will not only be sacred but also relevant.

A VISION STATEMENT FOR A NEW REFORM *MACHZOR*

T'shuvah is the chief goal of the Yamim Noraim, and a *machzor* is our indispensable manual and guide. We aim to create a *machzor* that will serve Reform Jews as they seek repentance, new direction, and a sense of return to God and the Jewish people.

We envision a twenty-first-century *machzor* that . . .

- provides meaningful liturgy to those who pray regularly and welcomes those who are new to Jewish spirituality and practice;
- inspires Reform Jews to participate in the multifaceted experience of the Yamim Noraim—from feelings of awe to moments of solace, from the solitude of contemplation to the solidarity of song and worship;
- draws from the deep wellsprings of Jewish liturgy, history, thought, music, interpretation, and creativity;
- guides worshipers, in accessible ways, through the journey of *t'shuvah* and *cheshbon hanefesh*;
- values continuity and incorporates the outlook of the twenty-first-century Reform Jewish community of North America;
- bridges the personal and the communal, the ritual and the ethic

We embrace the rich liturgical voices of the Jewish past and the aspirations of our people today. Among those aspirations is the wish for a *machzor* whose words, tone, and theological range are uplifting, inviting, and challenging. We seek metaphors and images of God that will speak to our time, as the prayers of *Union Prayer Book II* and *Gates of Repentance* spoke with depth and authenticity to theirs. We seek an integration of tradition and innovation, prayer and music, speech and silence, the struggle with God and the struggle with being human.

Most important to our work are the people for whom this book is intended: the members of a dynamic, ever-changing, and diverse Reform Movement who gather in community to experience awe and forgiveness and hope. Some call themselves classical

Reform; some seek to recover and reinterpret the broader Jewish heritage. Some resonate with traditional views of God; others find it hard to believe in God at all. One can hardly overstate the challenge before us, as we strive for a liturgical message that illuminates and inspires.

We are open to exploring the use of early *piyutim* and modern poetry, visual art used as text, commentary that is intellectually engaging and spiritually provocative, music that we already cherish as well as musical innovation. We will attempt to frame with sensitivity texts that are painful or disturbing. Translations and original materials must be beautiful and evocative, conveying to worshipers an appreciation of our inherited liturgical tradition, as well as Judaism's relevance to their lives. We seek a balance between the creative retrieval of classical texts and the present-day sensibilities of Reform Jews.

Mishkan T'filah is our base text, and a great deal will flow from the structure it provides. At the same time, the historical *machzor* is central to our efforts, as it has been to Reform liturgists of the past. Our work will be informed by the various *minhagim* developed by Jews over many centuries in response to their circumstances and their faith.

What do we mean by "base text"? *Mishkan T'filah* provides us with fundamental principles and a carefully crafted framework and design. The specific requirements of a *machzor* may lead us to expand on *Mishkan T'filah*'s paradigm, but our plan is to create a book that is a fitting companion to *Mishkan T'filah*.

Mishkan T'filah's right-side/left-side format encourages diversity, choice, and the inclusion of many "voices"; the use of counter-text; and a stimulating balance of *keva* and *kavanah*. It allows for midrashic creativity and the presentation of different ideas about God, in order to reflect contemporary realities of Reform Judaism and the Jewish world. The dialogue—or confrontation—between the two facing pages also seems particularly suited to the themes of *s'lichot, t'shuvah,* and *cheshbon hanefesh*, which are fundamentally relational and dynamic in nature.

We will take seriously the diverse opinions about gender language for God. Ours will be more than a superficial "He said, She said" approach; gender is far more profound and complex than substituting one noun or pronoun for another. We look forward to an exploration of gender that leads Reform Jews to encounter and experience God in interesting, meaningful ways.

The Editorial Core Team will oversee a process involving diverse working groups of rabbis (assigned to such tasks as translation, commentary, and poetry); consultation with cantors and educators to assure that music and learning are integral to the book; consultation with academic experts in related fields; and responders who will evaluate our work and offer critique. Self-evaluation will be ongoing. We are committed to creating an efficient review and piloting process that will result in the timely production of the book.

We believe the Reform nature of this *machzor* will be most evident in its respectful yet fresh approach to tradition; in its unwavering commitment to the equality of men and women; in its attention to the present-day concerns, fears, and hopes of the people who will pray from its pages; in its faithfulness to the ethical dimension of Judaism; in its embrace of the universal and the particular; and, perhaps, most of all, in its effort to deal with the tension between the historical theology of the High Holy Days (God's sovereignty and judgment) and more contemporary beliefs, such as the "theology of human adequacy."

We are mindful that the High Holy Days are a time of change and challenge for each person; yet also, profoundly, a time of memory—a time when a familiar smell, sound, or *ta'am* can make all the difference for many of us; and a time when families and communities take stock and grow closer. We take seriously the feelings associated with holiness, as we envision a *machzor* that encourages and activates these significant levels of experience.

(The Vision Statement was created by Edwin Goldberg, Janet Marder, Shelly Marder, Leon Morris, Elaine Zecher, and Hara Person.)

What Happens When We Use Poetry in Our Prayer Books— and Why?

Sheldon Marder

In memory of Rabbi Scott Corngold (1962–2011)

1

One of my teachers, West African writer Kofi Awoonor, always began his poetry workshops with an enthusiastic pronouncement like this one: "Poetry is life! I could not live without it." Kofi knew better than to use the word "spirituality" in a college classroom in 1969; but thirty years later Edward Hirsch could give full expression to the true motivation behind Kofi's exuberance:

> Reading poetry is a way of connecting—through the medium of language—more deeply with yourself even as you connect more deeply with another. The poem delivers on our spiritual lives precisely because it simultaneously gives us the gift of intimacy and interiority, privacy and participation . . . I understand the relationship between the poet, the poem, and the reader not as a static entity but as a dynamic unfolding. An emerging sacramental event. A relation between an I and a You. A relational process.[1]

Hirsch unlocks my teacher's enigmatic pronouncement: poetry is life because it is "a way of connecting . . . a relational process." And, for a number of reasons, which we will explore in this essay, poetry is uniquely suited to the task of bringing the gifts of connection and "dynamic unfolding" into the Jewish worship experience.

SHELDON MARDER (NY78) is the rabbi and director of the Department of Jewish Life, Jewish Home of San Francisco.

2

Current discussion on the use of poetry in the prayer book is indebted to years of public discourse on the subject. In 1981 Herbert Bronstein wrote a proposal entitled "Suggested Program for T. Carmi on Prayer Book Enhancement/Revision." T. Carmi (whose major anthology, *The Penguin Book of Hebrew Verse*, appeared in print that year) would be given the task of providing the CCAR with liturgical and nonliturgical Hebrew poetry—evocative texts to encourage "engagement, aspiration, quest, searching, [and] affirmation." T. Carmi's extant files include Hebrew poems related to all of the major rubrics and themes of the Shabbat liturgy, as well as some translations by members of the CCAR. The project was meant to be didactic (informing liberal Jews of our "spiritual treasury"), preservationist (saving the *piyutim* of modern Hebrew writers), and, most of all, liturgically creative (using Hebrew poems in translation to "open up or develop" the siddur's motifs and themes). T. Carmi's contribution would be noted posthumously twenty-six years later on the Acknowledgments page of *Mishkan T'filah*.[2]

Early examples of modern poetry in Reform prayer books can be seen in the CCAR's *A Passover Haggadah* (1974) and in *Gates of Prayer* (1975); in *Gates of Repentance* (1978) Chaim Stern placed the poems most prominently in *Avodah*—for example, Jacob Glatshteyn, Avraham Shlonsky, Haim Lensky, Chaim Nachman Bialik—though several poems appear elsewhere (e.g., Rainer Maria Rilke, Anthony Hecht). IMPJ's 1982 *Ha'Avodah Shebalev* made significant use of modern poetry (both Hebrew and Yiddish), inspiring a generation of creative liturgists, and laid the groundwork for the recent *Siddur Erev Shabbat* of the Tel Aviv community Beit T'filah Yisraeli (2011).

The Reconstructionist Movement made a strong statement about the value of poetry by choosing a professional poet (Joel Rosenberg) to translate the liturgy for its *Kol Haneshamah* series (1996, 1998, and 1999), which included poems by non-Jewish as well as Jewish writers.

The CCAR's *On the Doorposts of Your House* (1994) also includes non-Jewish works in its nearly forty pages of poems: pillars of English and American literature like Wordsworth, Shelley, Dickinson, and Stevens are side by side with superb Hebrew and Yiddish writers such as Abba Kovner and Kadya Molodovsky. The editorial team for *Doorposts* envisioned Reform Jews enhancing their home rituals and personal spiritual practices with world-class poetry.

By the time Elyse Frishman led the CCAR's creation of *Mishkan T'filah*, decades of discourse and experimentation had laid a strong foundation for the pervasiveness of modern *piyutim* in Reform prayer books. With *MT*'s publication in 2007, the poetry of Bialik, Lea Goldberg, and Yehuda Amichai was now fully at home among the works of Solomon Ibn Gabirol, Yehuda Halevi, and the Psalmists. Some rabbis expressed the fear that worshipers would prefer the twentieth-century Yehuda to his Spanish namesake.

When the Rabbinical Assembly published *Mahzor Lev Shalem* in 2010—with an A to Z (Amichai to Zelda) thoroughness, including poets as varied as Admiel Kosman and Denise Levertov—the Conservative Movement completed a trajectory that began with Jules Harlow's inclusion of poems by Nelly Sachs, Hillel Zeitlin, and other modernists in his groundbreaking 1972 *machzor*.

It is clear that all three major liberal movements have advanced the use of modern *piyutim* to reframe and reinvigorate worship along the lines foreseen by the Carmi Project. A box of T. Carmi's files now resides (temporarily) in my office: a symbol, for me, of modern poetry's importance in our spiritual lives. Further, those files encourage us to ask what kind of public dialogue should precede liturgical innovation.

3

Innovation is one of the core ideas in Jewish prayer—from the concept of *chiddush bit'filah* to the religious creativity of the great medieval poets. Why did the *payetanim* innovate in the ways they did? How does one explain the impulse to incorporate their poems in the prayer books of our people? Although these questions are beyond the scope of this essay, a few words on this subject by Jakob Petuchowski are most useful as we begin:

> Theology is compelled to rely on intimations. When we speak of something *of* which we only have hints and intimations, we can speak of it likewise only *in* hints and intimations. We can allude to it, and we can suggest it; but we can hardly formulate it in propositions which will pass muster before the bar of logical rigor. We had, therefore, best express it in the images and the nuances of poetry.[3]

Guided by the idea that poetry—the genre of image and nuance—is the literary mode best suited to theology, I will take an essentially literary approach to the question I have posed in the title: "What happens when we use poetry in our prayer books—and why?"

4

Let's turn first to metaphor, one of the most compelling reasons why poetry "works" in a prayer book. Jorge Luis Borges provides our first example:

> There is a Persian metaphor which says that the moon is the mirror of time. In that phrase, *mirror of time* is the fragility of the moon and also its eternity. It is the contradiction of the moon, so nearly [translucent], so nearly nothing, but whose measure is eternity. To say *moon* or to say *mirror of time* are two aesthetic events, except that the latter is the work of a second stage, because *mirror of time* is composed of two unities, while *moon* give us, perhaps more effectively, the word, the concept of the moon. Each word is a poetic work.[4]

Think of the word "moon" as the faithful translation of a Hebrew prayer in our *machzor*. And think of the beautiful Persian metaphor "mirror of time" as a poem on the opposite page. How does the poetic "mirror of time" function in relation to the original prayer, "moon"? What does it accomplish?

For the sake of argument, imagine that, inexplicably, we have lost all reason to pay attention to the moon—the way Jews sometimes lose their appetite for God, angels, and messiah. The metaphor "mirror of time" invites us to reconsider the moon and ponder its place in our lives from a fresh, new perspective: its dynamic and visible relationship to time. So, too, evocative poetry, with interesting and surprising metaphors for God, can wake up our theological reflection.

Or consider a metaphor spoken by novelist David Grossman in a newspaper interview in 2010:

> [Grossman's] younger son, Uri, was killed in combat in the final hours of the 2006 Lebanon War . . . "You have to understand," he said, a photo of Uri—uniformed, eyes laughing behind glasses—on a shelf to his right, "that when something like this happens to you, you feel exiled from every part of your life. Nothing is home again, not even your body."[5]

Grossman's metaphor says that losing a child is an extreme form of *galut* in which feeling "at home" is no longer possible; for this bereaved father, the emotional reality of home no longer exists as it did before his son's death. Could a Jewish writer have chosen a more poignant, transformational metaphor to describe the death of a son? Metaphor has worked its mysterious alchemy: since the death of his son Grossman is not the same anymore; and, having read his words, neither are we.

5

Philosopher Ted Cohen presents metaphor as an effective way to cultivate and achieve intimacy.[6] Cohen's insight is remarkable and eye-opening. Let's use Grossman's metaphor to illustrate Cohen's idea. Notice, for example, how the metaphor instantly draws us into Grossman's inner life and shows us how it feels to be a grief-stricken father. Through one word, "exile," we feel close to a man we have met only through a newspaper interview. How does this happen? Edward Hirsch, excited by the poetic implications of Cohen's idea, describes it this way:

> Cohen argues . . . that the maker and the appreciator of a metaphor are brought into deeper relationship with one another. That's because the speaker issues a concealed invitation through metaphor which the listener makes a special effort to accept and interpret. Such a "transaction constitutes the acknowledgment of a community." This notion perfectly describes how the poet enlists the reader's intellectual and emotive involvement and how the reader actively participates in making meaning in poetry. Through this dynamic and creative exchange the poem ultimately engages us in something deeper than intellect and emotion. And through this ongoing process the reader becomes more deeply initiated into the sacred mysteries of poetry.[7]

Nothing proves Ted Cohen's point better than the poetry of Yehuda Amichai. In "My Mother on Her Sickbed" Amichai invites us into his mother's room, where we find ourselves face to face with a dying woman he loves. She has "the lightness and hollowness of a person/Who has already said goodbye at the airport/In the beautiful and quiet area/Between parting and takeoff."[8]

Now consider the following words, which the poet spoke to an interviewer: "The impulse to compare your inner world to the world around you is very natural, and this is how a metaphor is born . . . The right metaphor is the core of my poem."[9] Following his impulse, Amichai discovers in his mother's illness a connection between the airport's "quiet area" (where the passengers have stepped beyond our reach) and the liminal state of a loved one who is actively dying—in transition and inaccessible to her family. The two things linked in this metaphor resonate like notes in a musical chord; and, in the making of metaphor, Amichai had perfect pitch.

Again, we hear the resonance when the poet likens his tallis to a wedding canopy, a parachute, the cocoon of a butterfly—and, in the end, in Hirsch's words, "engages us in something deeper than intellect and emotion":

> Whoever has put on a tallis will never forget.
> When he comes out of a swimming pool or the sea,
> he wraps himself in a large towel, spreads it out again
> over his head and again snuggles into it close and slow,
> still shivering a little, and he laughs and blesses.[10]

That "something deeper" is the spiritual core of our lives. And I suggest that the poet gives us a spiritual thrill in this poem by means of a complex metaphor in which he invites us to join him not only in the act of wrapping a tallis, but also in the religious experience of immersion (*mikveh*). I think, perhaps, Amichai laughs between the shiver and the blessing because of the dizzying beauty of the image he has wrought.

Our tradition is rich in beautiful metaphors for God. The use of modern poetry does not trump the value of an arresting phrase like *Atik Yomin* or the High Holy Days' defining metaphor, *Avinu Malkeinu*. Tradition is the heartbeat of our liturgy. At the same time, the metaphors we discover in nonliturgical sources matter a great deal for reasons we have now put forth: metaphor awakens and refreshes perception; it cultivates intimacy by encouraging connection, community, and "a relational process"; it opens the door to a poet's inner world—and therefore can encourage us to open the doors to our inner worlds.

6

But those doors do not open easily. Religious language—prayer language—can be a barrier. For Diaspora Jews, that includes the additional barrier posed by Hebrew. As we think about offering the Reform Movement a new *machzor* that speaks to our many constituencies at once (including those who do not know Hebrew, and especially those who struggle—or worse, have stopped struggling—with belief in God), we need to build bridges across the many streams of twenty-first-century liberal Judaism. Poetry can be a bridge.

In making a case for the use of poems in pastoral care, theologian Donald Capps speaks of the affinity between poets and pastors:

> The tendency of poets to be explorative, questioning, and tentative, though not spineless or without conviction and a passion for truth, has a natural fit with the kinds of human experience that have been of greatest concern to pastoral care, and with the ways that pastors, in confronting these situations, have found themselves responding to them.[11]

We learn from Capps that poems are helpful in pastoral settings because they raise more questions than they answer. Poems do not preach or dictate to us—they are not dogmatic; rather, they are suggestive, evocative, and open-ended. A poem can turn a statement of belief into a question for our consideration. Writing about one of Robert Frost's most evocative lines ("And miles to go before I sleep"), Jorge Luis Borges writes:

> Anything suggested is far more effective than anything laid down. Perhaps the human mind has a tendency to deny a statement . . . But when something is merely said or—better still—hinted at, there is a kind of hospitality in our imagination. We are ready to accept it.[12]

These qualities, which make poetry useful to the pastoral caregiver, also make it a bridge between traditional liturgical language and a worshiper for whom that language is a barrier to prayer because it has the sound of unyielding, dogmatic truth. Poetry in the prayer book can make our liturgies more pastoral, more inviting, and more intimate.

7

In her poem "*Panim*" Israeli poet Sivan Har-Shefi shows us how modern verse can function as modern *piyut*: a bridge between a challenging biblical/liturgical image and contemporary life.

Though a faithful translation of *Birkat Kohanim* need not (perhaps should not) include the word "face," we cannot deny that the word *panav* refers literally to God's face—illumined and lifted up in blessing. Consider what this poem might add when juxtaposed to the priestly benediction.

Face[13]

Your face, from finery
from miracles that do not stop one's breath
from moist darkness in the niches of all creatures
from the ash of humanity stirred up in the winds
with great mercy I will gather

Your face, from constant kindnesses
from the man who envelops me at night
from my daughter falling asleep at the shore of the milk river
I'll seek

Your face,
for the face of the soldier has become distorted
the face of my father has dispersed
and my face is an idol in my sack

but You exist as does Your face

פָּנִים

אֶת פָּנֶיךָ, מְסַדְקִית
מִנִּסִּים שֶׁאֵינָם עוֹצְרִים נְשִׁימָה
מֵחֲשֵׁכָה לַחָה בְּגֻמְחוֹת הַבְּרוּאִים
מֵאֵפֶר אָדָם נִטְרָד בָּרוּחוֹת
בְּרַחֲמִים גְּדוֹלִים אֲקַבֵּץ

אֶת פָּנֶיךָ, מֵחֲסָדִים קְבוּעִים
מֵאִישׁ עוֹטֵף לִי בַּלַּיְלָה
מִבִּתִּי נִרְדְּמָה עַל שְׂפַת נְהַר הֶחָלָב
אֲבַקֵּשׁ

אֶת פָּנֶיךָ,
כִּי פְּנֵי הַחַיָּל הִתְעַוְּתוּ
פְּנֵי אָבִי הִתְפַּזְּרוּ
וּפָנַי תְּרָפִים בְּאַמְתַּחְתִּי

וְאַתָּה הוּא וּפָנֶיךָ

In Donald Capps's terms, this is a poem for a pastoral encounter: "explorative though not without conviction." It is, as well, a poem for our liturgy because, in the right circumstances, the pastoral texture and ambiance of a modern poem can give theological language a human face, as it were.

A seeker of God's face, Har-Shefi knows well the Psalmist's cry, "How long will You hide Your face from me?" (Ps. 13:2). Here she first describes the experience of seeing God's face almost everywhere: in fine clothing and acts of kindness, in the ordinary "miracles" of daily life, in her husband's embrace, and in her daughter nursing at her breast. She gathers these "sightings" together as though creating a composite sketch of God's multifaceted presence. But then we hear urgent echoes of Psalm 13 as the poet notes the places where she has felt threats to God and perhaps even God's absence: the face of war, the face of a parent no longer available to her, her own face (that is, vanity and the modern cult of self-worship). In the end, like the author of Psalm 13, the poet affirms the truth of her experience: God exists and God's face exists—both the idea of God and, more important, the living reality of God in the world: source of protection, grace, and peace.

What's more, by exploring the word *panecha* in a very personal way, and with disarming simplicity and honesty, Har-Shefi (an Orthodox Israeli) might even make non-Hebrew readers curious about the wording of the original prayer and pry open the Hebrew text to those for whom it would otherwise be a barrier or, at least, a mystery.

8

Is a poem like "Face" too confusing for worshipers? Writes Yochanan Muffs:

> Every poem is a challenge to our total being: our senses, our intelligence, and our soul. We are afraid to confront the poem head-on (or at all) because we may be found lacking in the balance. Poems are written in a special language, and even though we instinctively know this, to defend ourselves, we dismiss poems as "only poetry." Thus, most people act in one of two ways: they either reject poems as silly or they read them literally. However, to read them literally is to overlook the fact that every poetic statement is a compromise between what is seen and what can be said in the limit of words.[14]

"Face" may well be a challenging poem for many worshipers. But is it any harder to decode than, say, the familiar words *"ya-eir Adonai panav eilecha vichuneka"*? What does that sentence actually mean? There are a great many things in our prayer books that require enormous effort to explain or defend; but often we allow the claims and assertions of our liturgy to wash over us without giving them the thought they deserve.

I suggest that poetry in the prayer book is an invitation to greater mindfulness—thought, reflection, and contemplation. But, most of all, a poem invites us to join the poet in the act of imagining and wondering. For example, what might the image "God's face" mean? What does it suggest to us, as a Jewish idea or on a personal level? "Every poem," says Muffs, "is a challenge to our total being." Instead of fearing that our interpretation of a poem will be wrong or inadequate, we can learn from poets to be playful and inventive—discovering in metaphor, rhyme, and alliteration ways to expand the territory between what we see and what we are able to say with words. That territory, it seems to me, is the very place where we experience what we call spirituality and God.

9

I can look
At my body
As an old friend
Who needs my help,
Or an enemy
Who frustrates me
In every way
With its frailty
And inability to cope.
Old friend,
I shall try
To be of comfort to you
To the end.[15]

I think about the prayer *Asher Yatzar* as I read these lines by May Sarton. Their brevity encourages us to slow down and focus closely on each word or phrase: the sweetness of "old friend"; the harshness of "enemy"; the soft, slant rhyme of "help" and "cope"; the modesty of "I shall try"; the poignancy of "to the end." The prayer, too, is a "close reading" of the body, suggesting that we focus and reflect on every wondrous detail of our physicality: the openings, the arteries, the organs.[16]

The prayer *Asher Yatzar* views the human body with wonder, appreciation, and gratitude. The poet sets forth a view of the aging body that is marked by tenderness, compassion, and forgiveness. Each work, in its own way, presents a countercultural perspective that challenges the message we receive from the secular world—that beauty resides only in the youthful and "perfect" body.

The poem, of course, differs from the prayer in a most significant way: the poet addresses her body, not God. And yet Sarton's poem strikes a deeply spiritual chord as she considers the choice that is entirely hers to make—and then makes it with humility and dignity. The prayer attributes the body's grandeur to its Divine Maker. The poem emphasizes, instead, the crucial function of human attitudes and perceptions in determining our view of the body. Thus it honors the idea of human adequacy and initiative that is a counterweight to the traditional theology of Jewish prayer.[17] Both *Asher Yatzar* and the poem offer, in the words of poet Seamus Heaney, "a glimpsed alternative, a revelation of potential that is denied or constantly threatened by circumstances."[18]

Sarton's poem puts human flesh on the theological bones of *Asher Yatzar*. In a sense, this is a central task of all poetry in the prayer book: to help us make the language of prayer, which can be abstract, alienating, and remote, into something concrete, inviting, and deeply personal. The Torah promises that God's teaching is "not too baffling for you, nor is it beyond reach . . . No, the thing is very close to you, in your mouth and in your heart, to observe it" (Deut. 30:11, 14). Poetry can bring the teachings of Jewish tradition close to us. Through compelling, evocative language that is "experience-near," the right poem helps us open our hearts to the ineffable.[19]

What's more, poetry offers us an opportunity for *tikkun* (an act of healing, repair, and perhaps even transformation). May Sarton's words show us a woman, entering her ninth decade of life, who is powerfully resisting the social forces that tell her that old age is an enemy and her body a source of frustration. Here she beautifully exemplifies Wallace Stevens's famous definition of poetry as "a violence from within that protects us from a violence without." Seamus Heaney elaborates: "It is the imagination pressing back against the pressure of reality." It is the power of the imagination, says Heaney, that provides the "redress of poetry"—its ability to heal and make whole, "to place a counter-reality in the scales—a reality which may only be imagined, but which nevertheless has weight."[20]

Writers like Sarton, Amichai, Har-Shefi, and Grossman show us how *tikkun* happens in real life—not suddenly and not perfectly, but as a result of thoughtful reflection, choice, the force of imagination, and will. At its best, poetry celebrates the gift that allows human beings to see things differently, to remake the world and reinterpret received ideas and traditions. This "glimpsed alternative" can be poetry's greatest contribution to our Jewish books of prayer.

Notes

1. Edward Hirsch, *How to Read a Poem* (New York: Harcourt Brace, 1999), 4–5.
2. Elyse D. Frishman, ed., *Mishkan T'filah* (New York: CCAR, 2007), xiii.
3. Jakob J. Petuchowski, *Theology and Poetry: Studies in the Medieval Piyyut* (London: Routledge & Kegan Paul, 1978), 3.
4. Jorge Luis Borges, "Poetry," *Seven Nights*, trans. Eliot Weinberger (New York: New Directions, 1984), 78.
5. Ethan Bronner, *The New York Times*, November 17, 2010.
6. Ted Cohen, "Metaphor and the Cultivation of Intimacy," *Critical Inquiry* 5, no. 1 (Special Issue on Metaphor, Autumn 1978), 3–12.
7. Hirsch, *How to Read a Poem*, 15.
8. Yehuda Amichai, *Yehuda Amichai: A Life of Poetry 1948–1994*, selected and trans. Benjamin and Barbara Harshav (New York: HarperPerennial, 1995), 368.
9. Esther Fuchs, *Encounters with Israeli Authors* (Marblehead, MA: Micah Publications, 1982), 88.
10. Yehuda Amichai, *Open Closed Open*, trans. Chana Bloch and Chana Kronfeld (New York: Harcourt, 2000), 44.
11. Donald Capps, *The Poet's Gift: Toward the Renewal of Pastoral Care* (Louisville: Westminster/John Knox, 1993), 3.
12. Jorge Luis Borges, *This Craft of Verse*, ed. Calin-Andrei Mihailescu (Cambridge, MA: Harvard University, 2000), 31.
13. Sivan Har-Shefi, *Galut Halivyatan* (Tel Aviv: Hakibbutz Hameuchad, 2005), 78. Translation: David C. Jacobson, *Beyond Political Messianism: The Poetry of Second Generation Religious Zionist Settlers* (Brighton, MA: Academic Studies Press, 2011), 133–34.
14. Yochanan Muffs, *The Personhood of God: Biblical Theology, Human Faith and the Divine Image* (Woodstock, VT: Jewish Lights, 2005), 106–107.

15. May Sarton, "Friend or Enemy," *Coming into Eighty: Poems* (New York: Norton, 1994).
16. From the translation of the prayer *Asher Yatzar* in *Machzor Lev Shalem*, ed. Edward Feld (New York: The Rabbinical Assembly, 2010), 35.
17. See David Hartman, *A Living Covenant: The Innovative Spirit in Traditional Judaism* (Woodstock, VT: Jewish Lights, 1997).
18. Seamus Heaney, *The Redress of Poetry* (New York: The Noonday Press—Farrar, Straus and Giroux, 1995), 4.
19. The phrase "experience-near" is from Capps, *The Poet's Gift*, 3.
20. Heaney, *Redress of Poetry*, 1, 3–4, which includes the statement from Wallace Stevens's essay "The Noble Rider and the Sounds of Words."

The End of Liturgical Reform as We Know It: Creative Retrieval as a New Paradigm

Leon A. Morris

Prayer book reform was always one of the most significant and defining features of Reform Judaism in both Europe and America. While some reforms of the liturgy were driven by practical concerns, such as abbreviating the service or removing passages that were deemed to be inconsistent with the practice of most Reform Jews, most major reforms of traditional Jewish liturgy were ideologically based. Liturgical reform overwhelmingly was grounded in the notion that our prayers should be consistent with our theology. Reforms of this type are reflected in the deletion of phrases that reference a return to Zion, the resurrection of the dead, and the desire to rebuild the Temple in Jerusalem (and even phrases recalling that we once *did* offer sacrifices there). As Jakob Petuchowski wrote, "Prayer, it was argued, demands absolute honesty; and the corollary was understood to imply that the prayerbook can contain only such statements as are factually correct, literally true, and historically verifiable."[1]

Such criteria seem out of place in twenty-first-century religious life. Does our prayer book really need to be consistent with our theology? Must we believe literally the words we recite? Is our prayer book intended to be a catechism of Jewish belief? A new generation's answers to these questions may differ sharply from those who wrote or edited *The Union Prayer Book, Gates of Prayer*, and even *Mishkan T'filah*.

Our Reform forbearers had a posture of certainty, both about what God is and what God is not, about what God can do and what God cannot. In contrast, our theological perspective tends

---

LEON A. MORRIS (NY97) is the rabbi at Temple Adas Israel in Sag Harbor, New York.

to be marked by great uncertainty. We are suspect of almost all absolute truth claims, including those that emanate from our own denominational camp. For many of us, contemporary Jewish theology is less about what we know with certainty to be true and much more about religious ways of organizing and conceiving the world. If medieval and modern Jewish theology were prose, ours is a theology of poetry. So, the expectation that any prayer book, itself an anthology of texts reflecting multiple theological positions, must be in line with our own contemporary theology now seems inappropriate, unachievable, and outdated.

In addition, our comfort with "text study" and its centrality in our religious lives has changed dramatically, and such changes impact directly on how we relate to the words of the prayer book. For the past twenty years, there has been a renaissance of Jewish learning that has impacted the entire American Jewish community, including our Reform Movement. The phrase "lifelong learning" has become standard. There are increased opportunities for serious text study in our synagogues, on retreats, and at institutions solely devoted to Jewish learning. Events like Limmud have proliferated to most major cities, and numerous online offerings are available to anyone with a computer.

There is today, inside and outside of Reform synagogues, a strong interest and deep love for primary Jewish texts and the rich and varied conversations that emerge from a meaningful encounter with them. Among these primary Jewish texts are surely the classic siddur and the classic *machzor*. Widespread positive experiences with text study have resulted in an appreciation even for texts that are difficult and challenging in light of contemporary attitudes. Increasingly, twenty-first-century American Jews value opportunities to confront such texts directly and to play a role in trying to derive relevance and meaning from them. The history of reforming the prayer book embraced an approach that assumed that laity would be put off by such texts or simply would not know what to do with them. Such passivity regarding the texts was part of a wider context for Reform worship in which worshipers were largely observers in a service that was mostly read to them by their rabbis. In contrast, today's Reform Jews would privilege interpretation over revision. They would want to struggle with, and make meaning from, the classic words themselves, rather than have it done for them by others.

Influenced, consciously or not, by the postmodern turn and deconstruction, contemporary Jews are comfortable reading on several levels simultaneously. They intuit that reading is a generative process and are less concerned about authorial intention: "And so one can state that the meaning of a text—if it is a great text—not just occasionally but always escapes its author: that is why understanding is not simply a reproductive attitude but is always a productive one."[2]

Contemporary American Jews know that the words of the siddur and the *machzor* are poetry and metaphor. They could not conceive of taking its words literally. More than reforming its words, they would desire the tools to help them appreciate the multi-vocality of the text, with commentary that speaks to the intellect as well as to the soul. While it might be argued that study and worship are entirely different modes, learning as a spiritual practice and meaningful prayer experiences share much in common.

In many ways, then, the age of liturgical reform as previously understood and implemented is over. The guiding principle of a twenty-first-century Reform prayer book must now be the notion of "creative retrieval." I first encountered this term in this journal by our colleague, Herbert Bronstein. He defined it as "the retrieval from our own traditional sources and our own roots, from the design of our own liturgy, of meaningful elements relevant to our own time."[3] In the same article, he also borrowed the term "ressourcement" from the Nouvelle Theologie, a mid-twentieth-century school of Catholic theology. "Ressourcement" refers to a return to the sources, in their case to Scriptures and writings of the church fathers. Creative retrieval or ressourcement represents an approach to Reform liturgy that is committed to mine the classic words of our sources to see how they might be used or transformed for our own context. Applying this approach to the writing and editing of a prayer book would require each prayer book to begin with the classic text itself as the primary referent and touchstone. Yes, the liturgical decisions of previous generations of Reform Jews may be noteworthy, but each generation needs for its own response to come directly from the inherited texts of our tradition. The sacred task of shaping Reform liturgy must never be seen as creating a prayer experience from scratch, any more than it is our task to write a new Torah or a new Talmud. A commitment to the project of creative retrieval means that the class prayer book is seen not as the "Orthodox" prayer book, but as our own, to draw from, to explain, and to adapt.

While such an approach may seem somewhat radical in Reform Judaism, similar ideas were expressed over a century ago in the Reform synagogue by Rabbi Judah L. Magnes. In a Passover sermon delivered in Manhattan's Temple Emanu-El in 1910, Magnes urged the abandonment of the *Union Prayer Book*:

> Far be it from me to underestimate the struggles endured in the creation of this book of prayer and the benefits that a modernized, uniform service has conferred upon numerous congregations. But I cannot be blind to the fact that the Union Prayer Book, as at present constituted, has done its work and has lived out its day. The one prayer book that can ever be the Book of Common Prayer for the Jewish people is the traditional Jewish prayer book, hallowed by the sufferings and the hopes and the religious yearnings of countless generations of our ancestors.[4]

Creative retrieval requires of us a shift from a "hermeneutic of suspicion" to a "hermeneutic of embrace." We are well aware that the prayer book is a compilation over many centuries. We know that it is the work of human beings who in many cases were responding to the issues of their time. At the same time, a hermeneutic of embrace urges us to see the classic siddur and *machzor* as the poetry of the Jewish People. A hermeneutic of embrace begins with a love for the classic liturgy and a firm belief that it can be mined for contemporary meaning and relevance. A hermeneutic of embrace is rooted in the idea that the classic text has a great deal to teach us and that our primary task is to realize how it might be reframed, explained, or translated in such a way as to allow it to live in our Reform synagogues.

Of course, there will be parts of the liturgy that will cause pain or offend and that even the most robust commentary will not be able to rescue. In these cases, the best choice may indeed be to remove it from our prayers. But such instances are few and far between, and liturgical reforms such as these represent a miniscule number of changes Reform has made to the prayer book. As Richard Rubenstein wrote in 1966:

> Our attitude in approaching the liturgy ought to be one of extreme conservatism, not for the sake of conservatism, but rather because the harm we can do by making the wrong decision af-

fects the continuity of Jewish history and of Jewish religious sentiment itself. There is nothing necessarily sacred about any given liturgical form. What is impressive, however, is the extent to which both conscious and unconscious themes tend to intersect creatively in any liturgical mode.[5]

A hermeneutic of embrace rejects claims that "we Reform Jews don't say this," or that "this is the authoritative Reform *nusach*." Such closed determinism has no place in a twenty-first-century approach to liberal liturgy. Equally important, a hermeneutic of embrace shifts the burden of proof away from the classic prayer needing to argue its worthiness for inclusion, to we who must defend why a prayer was not included, why we changed the words, or why we chose to translate it metaphorically. A hermeneutic of embrace argues against apologizing for wanting to restore the traditional text if it can be restored in ways that allow it to inspire, to teach, and or elicit creative interpretations.

Finally, a hermeneutic of embrace raises the bar for the work of liberal liturgy. It is much easier to delete and to change than to explain, to "translate" (understood narrowly and broadly), or to use in new ways. The growing phenomenon of groups reviving *piyut* through song and study, here and in Israel, and the number of new recordings of medieval *piyutim* by contemporary Israeli musicians present us with paradigms of allowing old texts to live and flourish in new ways.

A hermeneutic of embrace with respect to liturgy urges us to expand our understanding of prayer as *avodah*. Most commonly, we explain that prayer is *avodah* because it is a form of service, *avodah sh'balev* (service of the heart). However, the understanding of *avodah* as "work" might be apt as well when we consider the interpretive labor required of us when trying our best to bridge the gap between the inherited words of the classic siddur and our contemporary lives. It is hard work to make meaning from these words.[6] Simultaneously, such work is a privilege, a blessing, and an opportunity for connection and continuity.

Notes

1. Jakob J. Petuchowski, *Prayerbook Reform in Europe: The Liturgy of European Liberal and Reform Judaism* (New York: World Union for Progressive Judaism, 1968), 353.

2. Marc-Alain Ouaknin, *The Burnt Book: Reading the Talmud* (Princeton, NJ: Princeton University Press, 1995), 59.
3. Herbert Bronstein, "Yom Kippur Worship: A Missing Center?" *CCAR Journal* (Summer 2004): 7–15.
4. Arthur A. Goren, ed., *Dissenter in Zion: From the Writings of Judah L. Magnes* (Cambridge, MA: Harvard University Press, 1982), 113.
5. Richard L. Rubenstein, *After Auschwitz: Radical Theology and Contemporary Judaism* (Indianapolis: 1966), 108.
6. This notion of *avodah* as "work" as it relates to the interpretative process of making meaning from the words of the siddur is that of Dr. Elie Holzer, assistant professor of education at Bar Ilan University.

Section Two: From Professors of Liturgy at HUC-JIR

"Lu Yehi": High Holy Day Liturgy and Experience in Israel

Dalia Marx

Our cups of coffee were almost empty. Galit, an Israeli rabbinical student, and Amnon, a student in our prayer leaders course, sat in my living room to prepare for their High Holy Day student pulpits. They felt that they were almost ready. We went over *Kavvanat HaLev*, the Israeli Reform *machzor*, and discussed the different considerations when leading services in a young congregation of people who have very little liturgical background. They were a bit anxious but also very excited. They were filled with a sense of the mission of making the services meaningful and accessible to people who normally shy away from any kind of organized religious activity in the city of Holon.

After going through the bulk of the service, we reached the end of the *N'ilah* service. The question we weighed was how to conclude the day. We discussed the importance of the concluding note. How should the worshipers, most of whom are not regular shul goers, leave the service? Galit and Amnon decided to end with "HaTikvah," the Israeli national anthem, which appears at the end of our *machzor*. But then what should introduce the shofar blowing? We had a few ideas but none of them seemed to be the right fit. We paused for a moment, closed our eyes, and tried to think about the essence of the day. And then, from afar, an old and beloved tune trickled into my mind: Naomi Shemer's "Lu Yehi." One of us began softly humming the tune, and all of us immediately said:

RABBI DALIA MARX, Ph.D. (J&C03) is associate professor of Liturgy and Midrash at the Jerusalem campus of HUC-JIR. She has been teaching in HUC-JIR since 2002. She thanks Rabbi David Ariel-Joel, Rabbi Naamah Kelman, and Ms. Julie Mendelson for their helpful comments on this article.

"That's it." Both Amnon, who was drafted to the army shortly after this song was composed, and Galit, who was not yet born then, thought that it would be perfect pitch!

What was there in the song that made it the "right" ending note for the service? "Lu Yehi" is a sublime expression of Israeli concerns and hopes. It talks about the personal but also about the national home; it talks about the comfort in simplicity and normality; and it is a song about redemption: *"od yesh mifrash lavan ba'ofek mul anan shachor kaved"* (there is still a white sail in the horizon facing a heavy black cloud). It is so Israeli and at the same time it is universal. The song expresses the idea that every human being has similar wishes and fears regarding the safety of loved ones and the yearnings of the heart.[1] Naomi Shemer (1930–2004), a beloved musician and songwriter, said that initially she decided to write an Israeli version of "Let It Be" to the Beatles' tune shortly before the Yom Kippur War (1973).[2] When the war broke out, Shemer actually sat down to compose the Hebrew lyrics for her friend, the singer Chava Alberstein. It was during the days of the terrible shock and trauma caused by the war, the days between Yom Kippur and Sukkot. Shemer understood that this was going to be a fierce and harsh war, and the fears of these days are reflected in the words of "Lu Yehi." She explained that when her husband returned home from the war and heard the song, he urged her to compose her own music to it. And so she did.

"Lu Yehi" to Shemer's tune was played again and again during those difficult days. I was seven years old during the war, and like many of my friends, I still feel a chill down my spine whenever I hear it. In a way it not only became a symbol of the Yom Kippur War, but it offered the experience of the solemnity of the day to Israelis not necessarily sitting in synagogue. Only when I spend the High Holy Days outside of Israel do I realize that there is something unique and incomparable in the way they are experienced back home—especially in the case of Yom Kippur. If you ask Israelis for the first thought that pops into their minds when they hear the words "Yom Kippur," I believe that many of them will say without hesitation: *Milchemet Yom Kippur* (the Yom Kippur War). Even now, four decades later, the war, which began with the surprise attack coordinated by Egypt and Syria on the afternoon of Shabbat Yom Hakippurim, October 6, 1973, remains a painful remainder of the fragility of the young State of Israel.[3]

For many Israelis, there is no clear-cut division between the mental, spiritual, and emotional demands of the Day of Atonement and the social and national ones that arise from memory of the Yom Kippur War. In both cases the day is an invitation for *cheshbon nefesh* (personal and communal soul searching). It is so evident to us in Israel that we actually feel it only when we are away from home, spending the Holy Day with fellow Jews for whom Yom Hakippurim is something similar and yet so different. Apart from memories of the war, there are some other matters that inform the special situation of non-Orthodox Israeli experience of the High Holy Days and its liturgy. Here is a list, which is by no means an exhaustive one, of the unique Israel experience:

1. Not unlike many North American Jews, the so called "secular" Israelis are insufficiently acquainted with the liturgy. Yet their feeling of inadequacy may be even more disturbing than that of their siblings in the Diaspora. I am referring to the fact that the language of the prayers is also our vernacular (albeit in a higher register).[4] Israeli worshipers recite the prayers "as they are." They cannot use an ideologically adequate translation as a coping device with difficult theological and ideological issues; this cannot be done in Israel because they understand the actual words of the liturgy, which are always challenging, and during the High Holy Days even more so.
2. Regardless of their liturgical proficiency, Israelis have a readymade organized High Holy Day experience: unsatisfactory as it may be, the kindergartens and the school system expose children to the holidays, and the media offers holiday programs. In a way, the entire country pauses and honors the holiday, especially Yom Kippur. When I served in a small North American community as a student rabbi, my biggest surprise was the daily city rush that did not stop when I opened the temple gates and went out to the street. Whether Israelis desire it or not, the car-free streets and the dramatic quality of Yom Kippur's stillness create an incomparable atmosphere for the High Holy Days. You do not need to enter a synagogue to experience the solemn nature of these days. This public structure and atmosphere allows people to bypass the liturgy and the synagogue. It absolves them of the

need to take the time to seriously respond to the challenges these days pose in a personal, cognizant manner.
3. It is not only the difficult content of the *machzor* that causes Israelis to shy away from the synagogue, but also their discontentment with Orthodox and ultra-Orthodox religious coercion. In the eyes of many, religion, in and of itself, is connected with the way the religious establishment requires people to submit to a stringent and outdated form of religiosity. It is a well-known fact that the ultra-Orthodox minority in Israel has much greater power than their share in the population, and at the same time, their contribution to economic and social life in Israel is, at best, insufficient. This situation drives many people away from synagogue, any synagogue. Indeed, it is quite common that people allow themselves to experience meaningful Jewish experiences only when they are outside Israel, where prayer and religion are not associated with extremism and inequality. What a paradox—you need to leave the Jewish state in order to be actively Jewish!
4. Surprisingly there is still a suspicious sentiment toward non-Orthodox forms of religiosity in Israel, albeit less than in the past. Many still maintain an "all or nothing" attitude and will tell you that if you do it, do it "properly" or do not do it at all. The Reform and Conservative movements, as well as other Jewish renewal organizations, are viewed by the majority of Israelis as a foreign implant—they do not seem local and native. This is changing though; Israeli society today is much more open to different forms of religiosity and to different expressions of our Jewishness. The Reform Movement, now in its second and third generation, has become more native and local. It is our task to provide valid and sustainable models of liberal religiosity and prayer that will overcome the initial suspicious attitude of Israelis toward anything that has a scent of religion. Therefore, the High Holy Days is an opportunity during the year when people seem to be more receptive to prayers and synagogue experience.
5. When thinking about prayer in Israel, one can detect a rather surprising phenomenon: The most serious treatment of the religious experience, questions of faith, and a true search for transcendence takes place in the last century in Israeli Hebrew "secular" literature, and especially in its poetry.[5] Israelis

encounter questions regarding God, peoplehood, and the search for holiness through poetry in a natural and direct (yet unthreatening) manner. This observation takes us back to Naomi Shemer's "Lu Yehi." Her popular song not only encapsulated the yearnings and hopes of the Israelis during one of their most painful trials but also became the genuine expression of an entire generation. Like the classical prayers that made their way into our prayer books, it, along with a growing list of similar songs-poems-prayers, transcends its concrete context. The Israeli Reform Movement was always aware of this: poems and songs by Leah Goldberg, Natan Zach, Yehudah Amichai, and many others, entered our siddur and *machzor*. The committee creating a new Israeli Reform Machzor for the Festivals has made a deliberate effort to incorporate as many of these texts as possible.

Due to increasing religious coercion and aggressive religious institutionalization, there are more and more Israelis who are committed to grappling with their Jewishness on their own terms. They are no longer willing to consume any kind of readymade Judaism. Prayer is an important part of these somewhat subterranean efforts; it emerges in some less expected places, such as Holon, where Galit and Amnon led the *T'filah* this year. I believe that in the near future we will see more and more fascinating and genuine forms of prayer emerging from Zion. *Lu yehi*!

Notes

1. For the lyrics of the "Lu Yehi" online, see http://shironet.mako.co.il/artist?type=lyrics&lang=1&prfid=4608&wrkid=1895.
2. Shemer told this story in an interview marking thirty years of the Yom Kippur War in 2003, shortly before her death. See http://www.ynet.co.il/articles/0,7340,L-2937862,00.html.
3. See Dalia Marx, "*Un'taneh Tokef* through Israeli Eyes," in *Who by Water, Who by Fire: Un'taneh Tokef*, ed. Lawrence Hoffman (Woodstock, VT: Jewish Lights, 2010), 117–21.
4. See Dalia Marx, "When *L'shon HaKodesh* Is Also the Vernacular: The Development of Israeli Reform Liturgy," *CCAR Journal* (Fall 2009): 31–62.
5. See A. Hirschfeld, "God's Place in Hebrew Poetry in the Contemporary Generation," in *The Full Wagon,* ed. Y. Bartal (Jerusalem: Magnes, 2002) [in Hebrew], 165–76.

Machzor: The Poetry of Truly Awe-Inspiring Days

Richard S. Sarason

I have always found the Yamim Noraim (the Awe-Inspiring Days) to be deeply meaningful at a personal level. Some of this clearly has to do with childhood memories of being surrounded by a sense of solemnity and of learning to take "I'm sorry" seriously on these days. (And now further memories of one generation down: how Yom Kippur, for one of our sons as a young child, was "My Sorry Day.") Much more of it has to do with the music of the High Holy Days, first learned in religious school and Intermediate Choir at Temple Emanuel in Oak Park, Michigan; then in Hillel Choir for Reform services at Brandeis University and in a traditional synagogue choir in Chicago with my college roommate; conducting the choir at Kehillat Kedem in Tel Aviv, learning High Holy Day *nusach* and trope for my first student pulpit in Newark, Ohio, forty years ago; and conducting services most years thereafter.

Still more has to do with the themes of the High Holy Days expressed in the liturgy, which, for me, are the great existential themes of life, death, and ultimate meaning: Yom HaDin as (in the rendering of Karen Armstrong) "the moment of truth," when each of us must acknowledge our finitude and mortality, our limits and vulnerability: that, in the end, we are not in charge, as much as that hurts our vanity, and that, so many times, we fall short and miss the mark, whether or not we choose to call that "sin." But the possibility of turning and returning, of repentance and renewal (of *t'shuvah*) is always there when we reach out or when we allow ourselves to be touched by the Hand that reaches out to us (*Atah notein yad*).

RABBI RICHARD S. SARASON (C74) is Professor of Rabbinic Literature and Thought, HUC-JIR/Cincinnati. He has taught Jewish liturgy at HUC-JIR annually for twenty years and sporadically for thirteen years before that.

As a musician and a wordsmith, I have always been attuned to the musicality of words, to the music *inside* the text. As a lover of theater, opera, film, and narrative, I have always viewed the *machzor* as the script for a profound sacred drama that we enact both together and separately in the synagogue. Liturgical texts are essentially poetic—they are meant to be declaimed, heard, and internalized. I find myself always responding to the music of the words and to their deeper meaning—the intense yearning (*hit-gaaga-ut*) that they both encapsulate and enact.[1]

Unlike some of my friends and colleagues, I don't have a huge theological problem with most of these texts. I relate to their imagery on the symbolic, rather than the literal, level—and am very much aware of the distance between my own stance in this regard and a more traditional one that gives them literal assent. The imagery of *Un'taneh Tokef*, for example, does not upset or offend me; instead it brings me up short and forces me to confront my own mortality ("Repent one day before your death" [*Mishnah Avot* 2:15]). I find that I have a capacity for deep empathy with these texts (an important trait, to be sure, for someone who has devoted his adult life to their study). I know these feelings and yearnings: they are my own—even if I am less certain that Someone is out there listening or that the Universe cares about me or anyone else. But the "human, all too human" feelings, the gut responses, the aspirations and yearnings are intensely genuine and honest. I know why my ancestors wept while chanting this poem, and I sometimes find myself tearing over as well.

I respond powerfully to the imagery and the emotions in these texts without getting tied up in knots by their literal meaning. Given that *all* God-talk is figurative—how can anyone talk literally about that which is, by definition, ineffable?—I am content not to get stuck on the analogies, but simply to respond to their affective roots.

I am aware, however, that much of what I have written above pertains to my appreciation of, and association with, the *Hebrew* text of the *machzor*. This derives, at base, from a personal, visceral identification as a Jew with the inherited rituals and liturgical texts of my people and with the religiosity that they embody—an identification that was nourished by two and a half years of formative study in Jerusalem (through Brandeis and HUC) and that motivated my decision to devote my professional and personal life (there is no dichotomy) to the interpretation of, and engagement with, Jewish religious texts and culture. There is certainly a strong Kaplanian undercurrent here.

As a Reform Jew by upbringing and choice, I choose not to enact the entire traditional liturgy of the *machzor*, but to abbreviate (since for me, at least, less indeed is more) and—more crucially—to reinterpret. To take the imagery of the *machzor* figuratively, in the manner that I have described above, is certainly, at one level, to reinterpret. At another level, however, it is to assert that the larger human processes of taking responsibility for our actions and their consequences, of struggling to make meaning and to transcend limit and mortality *in fact* underlie that imagery—so there is nothing forced or disingenuous about my stance. Even though it might be theologically conflicted, it is not (for me) affectively reductive.

Which brings me to the issue of prayer in the vernacular, of the English text in the *machzor*. Reading poetry (or the *Tanach*) in translation has famously been likened to kissing your bride through a veil: something—perhaps even the very essence—inevitably gets lost.[2] Since Jewish liturgical speech, too, is poetic, the same can be said about praying Hebrew prayers in English. Prayers and other religious speech in the English language inevitably carry connotations of Protestant Christianity (the King James Bible, the Book of Common Prayer—these books, after all, were landmarks in the development of the English language). English is also our language of secular communication; there is nothing "holy" or "other" about it. The danger of prose prayers in English is that we automatically construe such texts literally unless the content is conveyed in poetic form, in somewhat heightened and figurative speech, with words that lift us up rather than weighing us down or infelicitously calling attention to themselves by being too colloquial or prosaic or syntactically awkward.[3]

Most members of Reform congregations do not understand Hebrew (although Hebrew prayer, for that very reason, may hold for them a powerfully numinous, symbolic quality). Therefore, it is crucially important for me that our English renderings—translations and paraphrases (both, I believe, are necessary)—attempt to convey a comparable numinosity through their style and poetic quality that may help congregants to get past the "literal" meaning of the texts and to perceive their figurative and allusive qualities. Religious speech by its very nature is allusive, not denotative. It is a kind of verbal gesture, used to allude or point to something beyond itself. There is no need, on the one hand, to over-specify that something. (This is the main reason why I am inherently suspicious of too much God-talk: better to talk less and, with humility and reverence for the mystery of our lives in the world, do more. *L'chah dumiah t'hilah* [Ps. 65:2], in the rendering of Maimonides: "For You, silence is praise.") But our paraphrases must also be careful not to completely reduce or deflate the traditional metaphors and figures; then we become "literalists" again and move from poetry to prose. I do not wish to pray either to "humanity" or to a philosophical concept. And that is the unavoidable dilemma of praying in the vernacular. How do we navigate between the extremes of prosaic reductionism (like Horton the elephant's "I meant what I said and I said what I meant") and poetic figures that stick in many people's craws when they are taken literally? For me, an answer (since there is no "the" answer) lies with clearly poetic rhetoric that is both allusive and elevating, and that possesses its own aesthetic value. This is why it is so important, to my mind, that the new CCAR *machzor* include well-crafted translations and paraphrases as well as suggestive reinterpretations, all literary work of high quality, on both the right-hand and the left-hand pages. And, of course, the more texts are sung, or are accompanied by music, the more layers of affective meaning they acquire.

To return to the beginning: The themes, images, and figures of the *machzor*, when enacted and accompanied by plaintive and stirring musical renditions, by the sights, colors, sounds, gestures, and community of the High Holy Days that we have inherited as part of our personal and communal histories force me to confront my own limitations, failings, inadequacies, and mortality in a realistic but hopeful way. *T'shuvah* and renewal are possible. The *machzor* teaches us that we have some control over the course of our lives and, with intentionality and attentive hard work, can make amends and changes in the way we live. And as for those things over which we have no control—most powerfully, our own deaths—Jewish tradition and community, as embodied in the work we are enjoined to do through the rituals of the High Holy Days, give us rich resources to acknowledge them without succumbing to despair. Rather, we must face them with hope and with affirmation of the abiding worth of our lives, that something of us will not be lost.

Han'shamah lach . . .

Notes

1. Catherine Madsen has written eloquently—and forcefully—on this topic. See her book, *The Bones Reassemble: Reconstituting Liturgical Speech* (Aurora, CO: Davies Group, 2005), as well as her articles "Kitsch and Liturgy," *Tikkun* 16, no. 2 (March/April 2001):41-47; and "The Common Word: Recovering Liturgical Speech," *Cross-Currents* 54, no. 3 (2004), both available at http://catherine-madsen.com/Essays.html.
2. The saying has been attributed to Chaim Nachman Bialik in various forms: ללמד תרגום זה כמו לנשק את הכלה דרך **צעיף** ("To study a translation is like kissing the bride through a veil") or, in a literary Hebrew more akin to Bialik's own style, תרגום דומה לנשיקה מבעד לצעיף ("Translation is like a kiss through a veil"). Amos Oz has often repeated this dictum. I have not (yet?) seen the source in Bialik's writings. The Welsh poet R.S. Thomas also is reputed to have said that reading poetry in translation is like kissing through a handkerchief.
3. Once again, the writings of Catherine Madsen listed in note 1 are germane. While a principled supporter of gender-neutrality in English prayer, I am painfully aware that the avoidance of gendered pronouns creates a huge stylistic pressure on English syntax. Psalm translations are a particular challenge in this regard.

A Tale of Three *Machzorim*

Richard N. Levy

I grew up at Temple Israel of New Rochelle (NY) in the 1940s and 1950s, where of course the *machzor* (though we didn't use the Hebrew name) was the *Union Prayer Book*, Newly Revised Edition, Volume II, which I also used when I led services as a rabbinic student and a newly minted rabbi in the early to mid 1960s. When I came to teach at the Hebrew Union College in 1999, I helped students find their way through *Gates of Repentance*, and I have participated in several pilotings of the new Reform High Holy Day *machzor*. Though derived from the same basic traditional text, the books are very different, and so I thought as we work our way toward the publication of the new *machzor*, it might be instructive to reflect on the three of them.

It is significant that since the beginning of the discussion of the new volume, it has been referred to as a *machzor* and not as a High Holy Day prayer book. The word, from the root *ch-z-r*, meaning to repeat, conveys the important reminder that this is a book of prayers for a unique time of the year that will repeat itself, like the seasons themselves, every year. It thus sets itself apart from a siddur, a word meaning the order of prayers, used for daily and Shabbat worship. But it was understood that the traditional *machzor* followed the same *matbeah hat'filah* ("coinage" or outline of prayer) as the siddur, only enhanced by special prayers used only at festival or High Holy Day time. There is, therefore, in its very name a tension between the recurring and the unique, between the new and the old. In some ways this tension helps to illumine the significance of the changes we

---

RICHARD N. LEVY is the rabbi of the synagogue and director of spiritual growth at the Jack H. Skirball (Los Angeles) campus of HUC-JIR. He was the director of the School of Rabbinic Studies at the LA Campus for ten years and was president of the CCAR from 1997–1999, where he shepherded passage of the 1999 Statement of Principles for Reform Judaism (the Pittsburgh Principles). He is the author of *A Vision of Holiness: The Future of Reform Judaism* (URJ Press, 2005) and editor of *On Wings of Awe: A High Holyday Machzor* (Hillel and KTAV, 1985, 2011).

have seen since the *Union Prayer Book* was last put on the shelf (though there are a couple of congregations in the United States that still use it, or a revision of it) and as we await the publication of the new (as yet untitled) *machzor*.

Reviewing the *Union Prayer Book* for this essay, I was struck by how intimate a book it is. It's small, its leatherette cover has a wonderful tactile feel, and its text is very personal:

> Unto Thee, O Lord my God, I open my heart at this time in the turn of the year. As I review my conduct during months that are passed, I am deeply conscious of my shortcomings . . . Lead me and guide me, for my times are in Thy hand. Amen. (Silent prayer after *Amidah*, p. 27)

> O merciful Father! May I find tranquility for my troubled soul. Help me to look into mine own heart and thus come to know myself . . . May I seek to be reconciled, O Lord, with my fellowmen and with Thee . . . Hear my prayer, and in Thy mercy answer me. Amen. (Meditation before Yom Kippur Morning Service, p. 168)

But it also offered some majestic passages:

> . . . though we cherish and revere the place where stood the cradle of our people, the land where Israel grew up as a tender plant, and the knowledge of Thee rose like the morning-dawn, our longings and aspirations reach out toward a still higher goal. The morning-dawn shall yet brighten into a radiant noonday; the tender sprout shall yet become a heaven-aspiring tree beneath which all the families of the earth will find shelter. (Yom Kippur Afternoon Service, p. 273)

While the themes are the themes of the High Holy Days, the voice is the voice of the familiar book used every Shabbat. Indeed, one might argue that both the intimacy and the majesty were greatly aided by the Thee/Thou archaisms that provided a different word for addressing God from that used to address human beings. The prayers common to the High Holy Days and Shabbat were used mostly without revision, so the book was familiar to Shabbat worshipers at the same time as it invited people to start coming to Shabbat worship with the assurance that they would find a similar experience.

The passage quoted above from the Yom Kippur Afternoon Service represented another aspect of constancy: the recurrence of classic Reform beliefs, in this case the belief in the coming of the messianic age. The Rosh HaShanah Morning Service concluded with the stirring hymn "All the World Shall Come to Serve Thee," and the various Torah services are introduced with messianic passages from the Prophets, establishing the belief that our mission is to bring Torah to all the nations of the earth. Other passages evoke the classic Reform belief that Israel is to be a priest people, pure in spirit, dedicated to bringing the nations to God's service. The *Union Prayer Book* was clearly a Reform prayer book, reflecting the beliefs of the Columbus Platform of 1937, whose main author, Samuel Cohon, was also one of the major writers of the Newly Revised *UPB*.

This tight integration of Shabbat and High Holy Days, prayer book and theology, began to loosen as the 1960s dawned. Protestants eliminated archaic English in their new Bible translations and in their liturgy, and Reform Jews began to grow restless with language that seemed now to distance people from God rather than drawing them close. Many leaders in the Reform Movement wished to restore some of the traditional prayers that had been cast out of both the Shabbat and High Holy Day liturgy, to provide roadmaps of the structure of the service as it was being prayed, and to introduce more Hebrew as the authentic language of closeness to God. As the Movement grew, and grew more diverse, the prayer book was seen as a vehicle to celebrate this diversity. The *UPB* had laid the groundwork: there were five Shabbat Evening services and five introductions to the Shabbat Morning Service. *Gates of Prayer* offered a total of eleven evening services and a variety of other services as well, most of them geared to a particular theme, which reflected many aspects of Reform theology.

How could a companion High Holy Day prayer book echo these changes? It could—and did—restore some prayers that *UPB* II either omitted (a full version of the text of *Kol Nidrei*) or buried (*Un'taneh Tokef*, hidden in the Yom Kippur Afternoon Service without the final paragraph outlining the life and death decrees of Judgment Day), and it increased the amount of Hebrew in the book (though, like *Gates of Prayer*, because of an embarrassment at offering transliteration—lest it appear to others that Reform Jews did not know Hebrew—it buried the transliteration at the back of the book). Like *Gates of Prayer*, *Gates of Repentance* identified the names of prayers to help worshipers find their way. But the major innovation of *Gates of Prayer*, the multitude of services with their diverse themes, a *machzor*—used once a year—could not replicate. Evocations of the messianic age continue ("There will come a time when morning will bring no word of war or famine or anguish"—*Hashkiveinu*, p. 29), though the priest people had faded out of Reform liturgy.

But while the Gates series provided an integrated, authoritative liturgy for the Reform Movement, some elements were lost. Its publication made us realize belatedly how beautiful *UPB* English was, and since most of Reform worship is conducted in the vernacular, the new books made it hard for the service to soar. While Hebrew is properly the language of intimacy, because so many Reform Jews do not really know Hebrew, its sound often provokes nostalgia for one's own or one's ancestors' past rather than an immediate encounter with the God who created the world with it. And while transliteration enables one to pray with Hebrew sounds, it doesn't look like Hebrew, and so for some people transliteration only emphasizes the gap between language and the God to whom it is addressed. Because some rabbis felt that *UPB* language was too personal, many of its intimate prayers were not carried over into *Gates of Repentance*, and where there are prayers in the first person (e.g., the Silent Confession on Yom Kippur morning, p. 325) they often read more like a meditation than like a direct address to God. There are sections of *GOR* that contain what my wife Carol calls "a wall of words"—most notoriously in the Memorial Service (pp. 477–94). Yet where the traditional *Yizkor* Service offers individual *Yizkor* prayers for each category of person one is remembering, encouraging a person to spend time with specific memories of one's beloved, *GOR* has only one generic *Yizkor* prayer (p. 491). Even the *UPB* offered an English memorial for each category of family member or friend (pp. 319–21).

What are we to say about the pilot editions of the new *machzor*? Because we do not know what the *machzor* will look like in its final form, it may be most useful to express some hopes of what it will enable us to do on the High Holy Days. First of all, I would hope that the new *machzor* will provide significant continuity with *Mishkan T'filah*—not necessarily in appearance, but in language and theology. We have had an "authoritative" liturgy now for a decade; I would hope that the *machzor* reflects that fact. *Mishkan T'filah* made some important liturgical choices that have helped guide our prayer: restoring the third paragraph of the *Sh'ma* (tz-itzit) to the morning but not the evening service; continuing the elimination of the second paragraph of the *Sh'ma* but offering an English interpretation of it (p. 67); continuing the emphasis on a messianic age rather than a single Davidic messiah; restoring prayers from older traditions of the siddur (e.g., the prayer before offering the *Sh'ma* on p. 227—the equivalent in the *machzor* might be the restoration of some *piyutim*, not for the sake of restoring archaic prayers but for the sake of uplifting our prayer with invigorating themes). While the left hand pages in *Mishkan T'filah* have been faithful and creative extensions of the diverse services in *Gates of Prayer*, the need for variety is less in a *machzor* used only once a year. If the new *machzor* does include interpretive passages, I would hope that they would be in the service of reflecting diverse Reform understandings of specific High Holy Day themes, rather than introducing variety for its own sake.

I would also hope that the *machzor* is, as *Mishkan T'filah* proclaims itself, "a Reform *machzor*." I hope it includes uplifting English prayers, as well as evocations of the messianic age, of the prophets as inspirations for our actions, and of the vision of Israel bringing the nations closer to God. I would hope that it does not only restore traditional prayers like *Un'taneh Tokef*, but offers interpretations that speak to the diverse theologies of Reform Jews. I would hope that while it encourages rapprochement with and understanding of other streams of Judaism, it affirms the value of maintaining and strengthening the diverse streams and nurtures our determination to continue the remarkable creativity of Reform worship. Would that the coming of the messianic time and the realization of God's sovereignty be deepened by the diversity of all the movements' liturgical attempts to draw close to the Holy One. I hope that it will take on the challenge of responding to the theme of God's *malchut*—helping us understand what it means for a liberal movement to affirm and live by the principles of the sovereignty of God.

Intimacy and majesty: as these polar experiences of God have marked the best of our liturgical endeavors over a century and a half, so do they encompass our understanding of the God we Reform Jews seek every day, every Shabbat, and, in a unique fashion once a year, on the Days of Awe.

Doing It Right or Doing It Well?

Lawrence A. Hoffman

At the *chavurah* that I have attended over the years, liturgy is done well. A telling example is the Yom Kippur afternoon service, "From Creation to Redemption." In many congregations, it is treated as a throwaway, an afternoon opportunity to delegate several pages of reading to lay volunteers, while the officiating clergy rest up for the *N'ilah* finale. But "From Creation to Redemption" was composed as a liturgical highlight: a modern version of the traditional *Avodah*, updated with exquisite Reform sensitivity to the nature of sacred history for our time. The *chavurah* pays attention to this potential, outfitting the text with music and choosing readers well in advance, who then practice their parts and speak them from many foci in the room. The resulting liturgy becomes a multimedia dramatic script that engages the entire congregation in the experience of moving through Jewish history, encountering its voices of the past, and reliving the highs and lows that have brought us to where we are.

It is not, technically, a service, because it has no *Amidah*—no official status whatever, in fact, since it deviates so widely from the *Avodah* on which it is based. That is probably why most officiating clergy overlook it as secondary. It is also why it has such potential: it need not answer to halachic standards; it can be newly composed, imaginatively configured, and matched with music and with mood to carry the congregation to a climactic recognition of the eternities suggested by Jewish peoplehood through time.

I think, by analogy, of another free creation for which no adequate model existed, and which, therefore, depended entirely on the creative inspiration of its composers: the *Kabbalat Shabbat* Service that the kabbalists largely invented in the sixteenth century.

RABBI LAWRENCE A. HOFFMAN, Ph.D. (NY69), author or editor of some three dozen books and a two-time winner of the National Jewish Book Award, serves on the faculty of HUC-JIR and is cofounder of Synagogue 3000—Next *Dor*. He consults with synagogues and lectures widely across North America.

Descriptions of the way *Kabbalat Shabbat* was done—whole communities dressed in white while watching the setting sun and reciting psalms with symbolic double entendres, leading up to *L'chah Dodi* (itself a poetic work of genius)—suggest a liturgy brimming with the possibility of encountering a moment of transcendence, the certainty of God, and the surety that life could matter. Whether our ancestors attended worship with these specific goals in mind we cannot know. We do know of ourselves, however, that transcendence, God, and meaning are issues highly to be sought. The liturgy for the High Holy Days should provide them. "From Creation to Redemption" inevitably did, at my *chavurah* experience of Yom Kippur year after year.

By contrast I think back to my initial year as a rabbinic student, when, for the very first time, I was dispatched to lead High Holy Day services: traditional davening in a nursing home, from a hefty *machzor* that I had never seen before. There was no Israel program yet (so I knew almost no Hebrew), but back home in Canada, my local shul had been Orthodox, so the College figured I would manage somehow. Besides, the people were elderly, they explained; an hour and a half would do it.

Ten minutes into the service, it became clear that the gaggle of worshiping seniors knew more than I did. One man particularly—call him Schwartz—uttered audible sighs of discontent at each of my several errors, mumbling grotesquely at the prayers I skipped and the inauthentic tunes I invented. Like most of the worshipers in attendance, Schwartz had been deposited at the home against his will with no option to leave. He would have driven me out of town on a rail, but hadn't the power.

"How did it go?" the director of the home inquired as I left the next day.

"Not so well," I admitted, "One man especially was pretty upset."

"That would be Schwartz," she confirmed. "Don't worry, he'll get used to you by Yom Kippur."

Indeed, I arrived on Yom Kippur to find Schwartz waiting at the door to greet me. "How good to see you, Rabbi," he acknowledged. "Glad you are back." I can only imagine what dire threat the director must have leveled upon him in the interim.

Throughout services that night and the next day, Schwartz sat as he had for Rosh HaShanah, but in silence, despite the fact that my ignorance of the massive Yom Kippur liturgy knew no bounds. Despite copious notes drawn from a close reading of Max Arzt's classic *Justice and Mercy*, I forgot or botched one thing after another, culminating in my somehow skipping the afternoon haftarah. As I moved instead to the later parts of the service, there arose from the crowd a swelling wave of antagonism, culminating in the chant, "yoinah, YOINAH, *YOINAH !!*" I didn't get it right away, but just as it dawned on me what the unhappy congregants were saying, Schwartz raised himself up from his front-row seat to turn and face my detractors. "Shah!!" he bellowed, "*He* is the rabbi; not *you*. What *he* says goes."

I have thought frequently of that unlikely introduction to liturgy, once just a personal trauma, but now a symbol of what is problematic about the Jewish approach to prayer: the assumed question over which the battle was fought was whether I had done the service *right*—not *well*, but *right*. My *chavurah* experience, by contrast, is all about doing the liturgy *well*. *Rightness* is a function of following the rules; it responds to external standards of liturgical form and content and the technicalities associated with them. *Wellness* focuses on the worshipers; while rules remain relevant, they become secondary to the experience of worship that they either further or impede.

This obsession with doing things *right* is a consequence of living with a liturgical tradition, a tradition, that is, that treasures a canon of required readings, melodies, actions, and dress, all governed by strictures of order, style, and performance. All ritual is scripted, but rituals in liturgical traditions are closed-scripted—that is, they over-determine things to the point where performers of it are trained above all not to sing, say, or do something wrong. Non-liturgical traditions are relatively open-scripted; performers get largely to make them up. They have their own challenges: planning everything from scratch, for example. Our problem, however, is that we are constantly being judged (and judging ourselves) by criteria of rightness. Doing it right is what counts for success.

The "right doing" of liturgy has become a fetish. Rabbi Eliezer taught, "If your *Amidah* is *keva* it can hardly be *tachanunim*" (*Mishnah B'rachot* 4:4), advice grasped admirably by Bertinoro, whose accompanying commentary describes *keva* as those occasions when "the *Amidah* feels like a burden . . . a fixed duty to say the *Amidah* and be quit of responsibility." In tannaitic times, *keva* could hardly have been rote recitation of a siddur or *machzor*—not in an oral era when no written prayer books were possible and when *sh'lichei tzibbur* improvised wording around a fixed liturgical structure that determined just the order of topics (*seder avodah*, taken over into Christianity as the *ordo*, the same idea). But by Bertinoro's time (1455–1520), wording had been set, codes were established, *nusach* was fixed, and rules had multiplied. A student recently asked me (trembling as she did so) whether she might conceivable omit the *k'dushat hayom* from a Yom Kippur *Amidah*. We still, apparently, judge our liturgical labor by the extent to which we have done it all, and done it all *right*.

It took several centuries for this fixation on rule-centered rightness to set in. Originally, local *custom* determined much of liturgical practice—and custom, not being written down, is flexible over time. But the codes and the printing press changed all that. The first great gaon, Yehudai, initiated an attack on Palestinian custom, only to be told that "custom trumps halachah" (*minhag m'vatel halachah*). Amram was more successful, if not in his own time, then at least later, when scribes copied his prayer book as the model for all of Europe.[1] Local custom remained critical well into the Middle Ages, however, as we see from *rishonic* works like Abraham ben Nathan's *Sefer Hamanhig*, which surveys custom throughout France, Provence, Spain, and elsewhere, in the thirteenth century. The final victory of halachah came only with the codifiers, Maimonides, Asher ben Yechiel (the Rosh), Jacob ben Asher (his son), and Joseph Caro, because, says Ruth Langer:

> In the wake of persecutions, [they had] emigrated to countries where their wisdom and knowledge brought them recognition and leadership positions, but where the dominant *minhag* was quite different from that of their birthplaces . . . Unable to be fully invested in their original customs and unwilling to adapt fully to the *minhag hamakom,* they tended to devalue the halakhic weight of *minhag* as a category and enhance the status of the strict theoretical *halakhah* in their rulings . . . Their pronouncements were turning points in the history and development of Jewish liturgy.[2]

The rhetoric of authoritarian control thus became normative, as the following centuries fixed this wording rather than that, one custom rather than another, these additions but not those, and in this way but not that one.

Printing solidified these choices—with horrible consequences. Communities refused to pray together, over trivial differences. Worshipers watched and judged, while *sh'lichei tzibbur* quaked in fear of doing the wrong thing. It is noteworthy that *Kabbalat Shabbat*, the last great positive example of all-out creativity, came on the eve of the printing revolution. On the one hand, the printing press allowed kabbalistic teaching—and liturgy—to sweep through Europe in record time; on the other, it became captured in print and was treated canonically ever after. Further creativity on that scale died until Reform Judaism recaptured its momentum. Until then, and in traditionalist circles still today, getting it all done right became the be-all and the end-all. Langer's study of this halachic victory over free-floating *minhag* is aptly entitled, *To Worship God Properly* [!].

Robert Nisbet's classic account, *Conservatism*, demonstrates how absolutely conservative this is. Rightness implies an objective standard of judgment, and conservatives see that standard in models from the past; these alone lend our actions "legitimacy." The classic liberal tradition of the age of reason valued individuals—the inalienable rights of John Locke and Thomas Jefferson, for whom the present is "the beginning of the future," not just "the latest point reached by the past." Conservatives, by contrast, rejected a future rooted only in the vagaries of today's reason; they enshrined instead the steady accumulation of the past, in what was called *character*. "Nations have character," Disraeli proclaimed. From a nation's character, one inherits prejudice, a term of opprobrium for liberals, but for conservatives, the proper appreciation of reasoning that flows from feelings, emotion, and experience of the people, the social group, and history. Individual reason, said Burke, is "soulless [and] icy." As to change, therefore, thought Falkland, "When it is not necessary to change, it is necessary not to change." Not that change is necessarily bad, but when it comes, it tends (for conservatives) to be additive; one improves matters just by altering the accumulation of the past, and by doing so as little as possible.[3]

Critical for modern conservatives has been the twin concepts of authenticity and legitimacy. Authentic—and, therefore, legitimate—alternatives are rooted outside the individual self. Authenticity, in our time, has experienced a radical change in meaning: We value an autonomous and authentic self in search of self-realization[4]—exactly what the conservatives feared. It is precisely against this notion of rampant individualism that conservatives espoused the prejudice of tradition—the experienced wisdom of the centuries, which, alone, can balance individual whim. It takes little imagination to see that if any of the authorities whom Nisbet cites had been practicing Jews, they would have championed halachic rightness, purely out of conservative principle.

I do not mean to demonize these conservatives, who operated with admirable thoughtfulness and with laudable intentions. Falkland supported King Charles I because he feared the populist attack on the rule by bishops of the church. Burke lived in proper dread of the extremes taken by the French revolution. Disraeli is a particularly good example, because despite his conservative credentials as Tory Prime Minister, he initiated policies to support the urban poor and sought valiantly to make his conservative party responsive to the far-reaching social changes that accompanied the industrial revolution. He opposed Gladstone's liberals because he thought an enlightened aristocracy the best bet for ameliorating poverty while retaining the nobility of England's past.

The issue, then, is not good guys who change and bad guys who don't. The question is an elemental gut-level judgment on who and what to trust: the mantle of history, tradition, and the past (which is to say group prejudice, positively conceived) or the reasoned imagination of an uncharted future (meaning the self-determining individual). Which one threatens us more?

Whatever else they did, the Reformers made history by answering that question differently. The intensity of Jewish assimilation among Jews who found no way to harmonize Judaism with modernity convinced the Reformers that the devil most to be feared was tradition. By modern standards, these pioneer rabbis were not liberal, if by liberal, we mean laissez-faire, anything-goes, live-and-let-live. They knew tradition exceptionally well, and valued it; but they knew also how the printed liturgy and its codified regulations had spun out of control to become a liturgical tail wagging the would-be worshiping dog.

I said before that our obsession with propriety depended on twin felons, the printing press and the codes. Reformers transformed the printing press into an ally. Technological advances from 1814 (the steam-powered press) to the 1860s (the substitution of wood pulp for rags, making paper abundantly available) made new prayer books economically feasible. And they used the science of Judaism to free themselves of slavish adherence to the codes. Seeing Jewish law as evolutionary and mastering the art of historical reconstruction, they could reject the end of the codifying process while substituting the "healthier" (as they saw it) stages of liturgical history that they discovered in the early years of rabbinic conceptualization.

This citing of the past to justify a future is a tried and true strategy for reformers. In his short monograph on tradition, Jaroslov Pelikan recalls both Martin Luther and Thomas Jefferson "summoning their contemporaries to move beyond tradition or behind tradition to authenticity. Tradition was relative and had been conditioned by its history. Truth was absolute and had been preserved from historical corruption."[5] So too with these nineteenth-century Jewish Reformers, who, having scientific history at their disposal, could make truth claims in ways not available to Luther or Jefferson. Tradition was an evolutionary composite with layers that could be peeled back to arrive at a critical core. The core would be kept. Nothing important would be lost, even though the worship would finally be truncated rather than expanded.

There was still, therefore, an absolutely right way to go about doing things. Only the *standard* of rightness had changed: from halachic to historical fiat, what I have elsewhere called the triumph of truth over limits—in this case, the truth of history, which became probative. Reform standards depended also on two other sources of truth: theological acceptability and elitist aesthetics, a commitment to a standard of beauty that might build refined moral character (*Bildung*).[6] As much as Reform changed the rules of the game, therefore, it did not abandon the game altogether: it simply replaced the limits of halachah with the truths of history, theology, and aesthetics, which were no less constraining than law. To take but one instance (from America), Orthodox Jewish men were not allowed to pray without *kippot*; Reform Jews in the synagogue across the street were not allowed to pray with them.

Nonetheless, the Reformers got two things right. From the perspective of halachah, the liturgy is comprised of the regular statutory prayers altered and augmented to fit the Shabbat or holiday in question. From the perspective of worshipers, however, timely additions like *Kol Nidrei*, *Un'taneh Tokef*, and *Yizkor* stand out as infinitely more important; one attends High Holy Day services with special anticipation of hearing *them*, not the standard prayers into which they are inserted (and which are often, at best, just tolerated). The Reformers faced up to the fact that unlike their pre-Enlightenment forebears, nineteenth-century German Jews no longer had to attend services to remain comfortably Jewish, and, in fact, were hardly likely to continue doing so if the service was not changed to satisfy their newly acquired standards of aesthetics and spirituality. The Reformers therefore broke new ground by looking at liturgy from the perspective of the congregants in the pews.

That meant accenting special prayers at the expense of the regular ones, the best example being the memorial liturgy which (as they inherited it) comprised just three necessary compositions (*Yizkor Elohim*, *Av HaRachamim*, and *El Malei Rachamim*) inserted at the end of *Shacharit*. Knowing that people came specifically for them, the Reformers extracted them as their own liturgical unit, added prayers in the vernacular, and relabeled them the Memorial Service. They did the same thing regarding the shofar. While tradition divided the blowing of the shofar between the period following the reading of Torah (*t'kiyot m'yushav*) and *Musaf* (*t'kiyot m'umad*) the Reformers combined them into a single Shofar Service, thereby giving them prominence. Thus was born the strategy of liturgical *highlighting*, a practice we follow successfully to this very day. We are most successful when we decide what makes a day's liturgy unique and then highlight it as a separate unit that people can anticipate and appreciate as a liturgical moment that epitomizes the holiday ambience, ethos, or message.

Simultaneously, the Reformers' commitment to keeping the service small and manageable led them to reverse the age-old process of adding but never subtracting to the liturgical corpus. Even as they highlighted holiday staples, they pared away the usual prayers, excluding a whole service (*Musaf*) for example, and truncating the *Amidah*. Their criteria for keeping or rejecting any given paragraph are not as important as the fact that they adopted criteria and did the cutting in the first place. Here, then, was the second major contribution: liturgical *editing*.

These two principles, *highlighting* and *editing*, should guide us. "From Creation to Redemption" is a superb example of highlighting; but the highlighting stands out because the editors of *Gates of Repentance* also edited the liturgy down to make room for the highlighted segment without having to squeeze it into an already overcrowded day in which its uniqueness would be swallowed up by page after page of meaningless verbiage. Our own worship will depend on how successfully we too highlight, on one hand, and edit, on the other.

How well are we doing? We do quite well at highlighting. Not so well at editing. Our ancestors edited the liturgy dramatically, omitting or shortening standard prayers that the codes demanded but that people would find offensive or just plain boring. I worry that we lack their courage. We do not take seriously enough our own mandate to save a progressive form of Judaism for our time. Unlike our Reform forebears, we no longer have to worry about people seeking baptism—the great Christian era is over. But the threat of Jewish meaninglessness is ubiquitous. Doing it *well* (rather than just *right*) is what will matter, and we cannot do it *well* if we insist on including all the statutory prayers just because it is our habit to do so or because the codes say we should.

Whatever book we end up with as our next *machzor*, the worship that results will depend on how judiciously it is used. Editing is not just the prerogative of prayer book compilers; it is also the requirement of prayer book users. Presiding rabbis and cantors will need to cut the service to a manageable size by highlighting the prayers that are most meaningful and omitting some staples that are hugely redundant.

Let me be specific. I have been at *Kabbalat Shabbat* services where the congregation sings its heart out, builds to a crescendo at *L'chah Dodi*, and is ready to return home with the good Shabbat angel shouting a heartfelt *Amen* in their ears—only to be forced back into the usual soporific boredom for *Maariv*. Why don't we jump directly from *L'chah Dodi* to a few highlighted English readings so beautiful that the angel might have written them herself; include, perhaps, *Hashkiveinu*, for the sake of invoking *sukkat shalom aleinu*, and conclude with *Aleinu, Kaddish* and a final song?

By extension, our Rosh HaShanah and Yom Kippur worship should highlight the traditional prayers and selective modern material that express the deep themes of the High Holy Day season: human sinfulness and nobility, for example, and the promise of life affirmed and renewed. Simultaneously we should drop great gobs of the standard material that we now drone through. We should even do away with the *Amidah* on occasion (editing) while retaining some of its holiday insertions—*Uv'chein*, for example, duly enlarged with modern readings that emphasize its ultimate faith in universalism (highlighting). As things stand, *Uv'chein* is swallowed up by the usual *Amidah* verbiage that renders it practically invisible. No one even realizes it is there—let alone the reason why.

Another good example is *N'ilah*, a brilliantly conceived service whose theme is the discovery that when all is said and done, *atah notein yad laposhim*, God extends a hand, regardless of where sin has taken us, no matter how low we have fallen, irrespective of how our life has unraveled. What a concept! What if worshipers really went home convinced that they are not, after all, alone! That they can start again! Imagine a service shaped around that theological insight, fashioned, that is to say, not by the canons of halachah (doing it all right) but the impact of the message (doing it well).

We don't do that because we are afraid to—the failure of nerve I mentioned above. But equally important is the "elite factor"—the fact that seminary education and clergy culture together make rabbis and cantors into an educated elite. We study the subtleties of liturgical form and content and then want to perpetuate them. We may even like sitting endlessly throughout all of Yom Kippur in order to feel renewed when its final blast announces life after death. But we are not the norm. The worshipers around us don't yell "yoinah, YOINAH, *YOINAH* !!" anymore. They don't yell anything at all. They have no idea what to yell in the first place; and they care too little to find out. Already, they don't come in droves the way they used to; and they may soon stop coming altogether. We are becoming a two-class system: the elite who love the liturgy and the "plebeians" who some day may never hear it.

The predictable conservative response (against which we should be on guard) is to reaffirm the value of the inherited liturgy as it is; then to offer the "masses" educational opportunities to raise themselves up to "acceptable" standards; and finally, to blame the people who don't take advantage of the opportunity.

But this self-righteous outcry may be masking rabbinic self-interest. Our claim to our own authenticity lies in popular acceptance of the cultural heritage that we claim to guard. Unlike our congregants, the "culture users," we are the "culture creators" whom sociologist Herbert Gans studied all the way back in 1974:

> [Culture creators] make culture their work, whereas users do not, and can rarely have as much interest or ego involvement in a

cultural product as a person who created it. For creators, culture is often the organizing principle of their lives, whereas users are more likely to treat it as a tool for information or enjoyment.[7]

Producers of culture develop expertise; they revel in each other's company, sharing a technical competence and vocabulary that explains, appreciates, and celebrates the culture they produce. Their productivity derives from the historical past: from tradition, which has its own justification in their eyes. They charge the user culture of the masses with failing to understand tradition, wanting only untutored satisfaction and enjoyment.

Producers thus critique users, but interestingly enough, "the critique has appeared when intellectuals [that is, the producers] have lost power and the status that goes with it."[8] All of this should make us wary of our own evaluation of tradition, authenticity, and the high art (for that is what it is) of the High Holy Day liturgy that we so carefully guard. Are we not the intellectuals, the producers, the very elite that Gans describes, and are we not, at this very moment, losing power and the status that goes with it?

Whatever our new *machzor* becomes, it will have to be a script that elevates doing it well over doing it right, and doing it well is an aesthetic judgment: aesthetics as a general category of experience, however, not a particular aesthetic that yet another elite judges higher, and, therefore, "righter." I mean simply the consideration of how the worship affects the worshiper, as opposed to how the worshiper abides by (and sometimes just "abides") the worship. Let us establish the axiom that worship belongs to the people. The least we can do is deliver a liturgy that makes a difference in the people's lives without demanding that they first become experts in order to feel the difference.

Our age of spirituality is nothing, if not a manifesto of the masses demanding that religion point the way to what matters—or cease mattering itself, if it cannot do that. Religion is slowly losing its grasp on North Americans. To miss this obvious long-term trend, says sociologist Mark Chaves, is like missing the reality of global warming.[9] If religion cannot deliver worship that is spiritual to its core, it will die.

People once came anyway. Less and less are they doing that. No one willingly submits to boredom anymore. People with advanced degrees in everything but religion know enough to expect that religion should speak to their lives without their having to feel stupid because they took a Ph.D. in physics or a masters degree in economics, instead of a seminary degree in the way the liturgy works. If we insist on playing the role of defender of the faith, we will end up defending it as an historical curiosity, set in synagogues as museums, with the liturgy under glass.

Freed from the burden of defending tradition, we can ask such questions as: What are the real liturgical messages of the *machzor*? What gets in our way of delivering them? What must we sacrifice by editing and what must we create by highlighting in order to do that delivering? Zero-based budgeting insists on justifying expenditures every year, rather than automatically replicating them just because they have always been there. Zero-based programming urges synagogues to reevaluate programming that way: to drop programs that are barely limping along and to program intentionally, so as to achieve their visionary goals; zero-based liturgy requires looking anew at the prayers we do by habit and asking ourselves what would happen if we changed or got rid of them:

- It will be objected that the liturgy is rich; that sitting for hours has a positive cumulative effect; that we cannot get the impact we want if we take a scalpel to tradition. But that is a judgment of the elite; our own view that may be irrelevant to everyone except us.
- Others will ask, "Who are we to make such far-reaching reforms?" But whoever we are, we are all we have; and we are either up to the task or not.
- Some will say that doing it right is the properly Jewish way. But that is only partly true. Think of the *payetanim*, think of Musar, think of elemental Chasidism, think of Reform.
- Still others will fear that by radicalizing our critique, we will lose what we abandon forever. But classical Reform saved Judaism for the majority of moderns by being radical. When the time came to reclaim what had been temporarily set aside, we managed to do it.

Some Reformers acted in excess, we now may say, and some of us will too, but all great movements—science, art, politics, everything—depend on radical freedom whereby wrong turns and dead ends by some are eventually eclipsed by lasting innovations by others. *Et laasot l'adonai*. It is time to act boldly, bravely, and decisively. We must risk all lest we lose all. For if we do not risk enough, we will lose everything.

Notes

1. See Lawrence A. Hoffman, *The Canonization of the Synagogue Service* (South Bend, IN: University of Notre Dame Press, 1979).
2. Ruth Langer, *To Worship God Properly* (Cincinnati: HUC Press, 1998), 248.
3. Robert Nisbet, *Conservatism* (Minneapolis: University of Minnesota Press, 1986), 23–27. Quotations above are from Disraeli, Burke, and Falkland.
4. See Charles Taylor, *The Ethics of Authenticity* (Cambridge, MA: Harvard University Press, 1991).
5. Jaroslav Pelikan, *The Vindication of Tradition* (New Haven: Yale University Press, 1984), 44.
6. See Michael Meyer, "'How Awesome Is This Place!' The Reconceptualization of the Synagogue in Nineteenth-Century Germany," *Leo Baeck Yearbook* 41 (1996): 51–63.
7. Herbert J. Gans, *Popular Culture and High Culture* (New York: Basic Books, 1974), 25.
8. Ibid.
9. See Mark Chaves, *American Religion: Contemporary Trends* (Princeton: Princeton University Press, 2011). Reference to global warming is from Chandra Swanson, "Q and A With Mark Chaves," *The Chronicle: The Independent Daily at Duke University*, October 31, 2011.

Section Three: From Our Colleagues

When I Hear the Shofar I Taste Chocolate: Seeking the Synesthetic on the High Holy Days

Evan Kent

An Introduction to Synesthesia

It's a glorious night at the symphony. Michael is listening to the Los Angeles Philharmonic play a Mozart violin concerto. The opening movement in G major is a longtime favorite of his and as he listens his mouth is filled with an overwhelming taste of chocolate. Not just any chocolate, but a slightly bitter Belgian chocolate. Sitting a few rows away at the same concert, Rosalie is enjoying the opening phrases of the concerto and as she listens red bars and green circles float in front of her as the soloist begins to play. Robert, sitting toward the back of the orchestra, glances down at this evening's program. As he reads the program notes, all the letters and numbers have different colors. For Robert, the number seven appears red, three is green, nine is black, and each letter of the alphabet has a corresponding color as well.

Michael, Rosalie, and Robert are not only symphony subscribers; these concert goers are also synesthetes: persons with a neurological condition in which two senses are physiologically coupled. These sensory matchings are not the same for every synesthete and no two people experience the exact same form of synesthesia.

EVAN KENT is the cantor at Temple Isaiah in Los Angeles and is also the cantor for the synagogue on the Los Angeles campus of HUC-JIR. Evan is also a doctoral candidate at Boston University, where he is researching how music at Jewish summer camp helps to create Jewish identity.

For example, one individual with musical-taste synesthesia may taste chocolate when they hear a musical composition in the key of D major. Another might experience the taste of wild blueberries when a middle C on the piano is played. An individual with grapheme-color synesthesia associates certain numbers or letters with colors. Whatever form the synesthesia takes, it is an involuntary action and cannot be turned on or off at will.

Estimates vary on how many people are synesthetic. Oliver Sacks in *Musicophilia*[1] approximated that one in two thousand persons exhibit true synesthesia. But these numbers are a mere estimate as many synesthetes refuse to self-identify for fear of social ostracization. Many fear if they reveal their condition to others they might be labeled "strange" or "crazy" or will be accused of fabricating their observations. Other synesthetes move through life aware they perceive the world differently, but never identify it as synesthesia—only because they do not have a name for their condition. Synesthetes, according to Veronica Gross of Emmanuel College in Boston, often do not know that anything is "wrong." In fact, many synesthetes are often silent about their condition until they hear about it on a television program, a radio broadcast, or read an article in a newspaper and only then realize that they are neither mentally ill nor alone in their observations and perceptions.

Cultural Synesthesia

There is another variety of synesthetic experiences that are also intersensory experiences but without the medical or neurological basis of the synesthesia as described above. This cultural or social synesthesia is a fusing of the senses through events that deeply implant within individuals specific events, experiences, or rituals. According to Professor Steve Odin, these synesthetic moments are so profound "that the boundaries of the senses actually merge, and the multivariate sense qualities—colors, sounds, flavors, tactile and thermal sensations—all seem to melt into a continuum of feeling."[2]

Odin employs the Japanese tea ceremony to illustrate this form of synesthesia. The tea ceremony includes visual elements (the various vessels and pots used for making and holding the tea), aural stimulus (the sound of water boiling in the kettle), scent (incense burning), and even touch (the asymmetry of the *raku* tea cup). Events such as this tea ceremony are described as a synesthesia forged through the "simultaneity and harmony of multivariate sense-impulses" with the end result being a gathering "of diverse sense impulses within a physiological sensorium."[3] This synesthesia is one in which the senses are not joined together but rather the "multivariate sensations of color, sound, scent, and flavor interpenetrate in profound unity while simultaneously retaining their unique qualitative natures."[4]

The synesthetic is possible in even more everyday events. Theologian Don Saliers in *Music and Theology* presented the example of his young daughters and neighborhood friends learning jump rope songs. The fusion of words, music, and communal dancing produced a multisensory form of embodied ritual that also enhanced community. According to Saliers, these children participated in a form of synesthetic matrix as they sang and jumped to "Miss Mary Mack Mack Mack . . ." This union of activity produced "a simultaneous blending or convergence of two or more senses, hence a condition of heightened perception."[5] According to Saliers, this synesthesia not only heightens our awareness, but assists in encoding memory and creating long-lasting associations.

Ethnomusicologist Steven Feld expands this notion by stating, "As places are sensed, senses are placed, and as places make sense, senses make place."[6] Our senses provide us with an appreciation and awareness of not only the event itself but the event's location, participants, and emotions and feelings associated with the event.

Although many synesthetic occurrences take place in the secular realm, the environment of sacred ritual is an opportune setting for the synesthetic. Rituals and liturgies that invite the participation of all the senses not only serve to create deeper and richer memory and help to form cultural religious and ethnic identity, but also "have the capacity to give value and meaning to the life of those who perform them."[7]

The Synesthetic in Jewish Tradition:
Sinai, Seder, Summer Camp

One of the most famous synesthetic events occurs after the Israelites are presented with the Ten Commandments. In Exodus 20:15 we read:

> Now all of the people were seeing
> the thunder sounds
> the flashing torches
> the shofar sound
> and the mountain smoking;
> when the people saw,
> they faltered
> and stood far off. (Exod. 20:15)[8]

According to the Torah, a communal synesthetic experience was present at Sinai: The multitude *saw* the sound of thunder; the Israelites *saw* the sound of the shofar. So powerful was the moment of revelation that the boundaries between sight and sound momentarily vanished and the synesthetic occurred.

The Passover seder is another ritual experience offering opportunities for the synesthetic. Like the tea ceremony, the seder involves all the senses. We read the Haggadah; we sing blessings and songs; we smell the soup heating on the stove and the brisket roasting in the oven; we taste the symbolic foods around the seder; we touch the decorative and sacred objects on the table; we reach out and hug and kiss family and friends gathered for the evening's celebration. All of this total body engagement contributes to the synesthesia of the event. A variety of senses are employed as part of the seder and this creates a sense-rich layering that in turn triggers other sensual memories and awareness.

Seder is not recalled in sequence or as a series of atomistic moments, but rather in its totality. The Haggadah's brilliance is that it leads us through an ancient ceremony, shuttling us back and forth between the historic and the contemporary: One moment we are slaves in Egypt, the next moment we are twenty-first-century Jews tasting *charoset*. The didactic nature of the Haggadah is enhanced through the use of story, song, food, and ritual. We not only learn the story of the Exodus, but the experience of seder becomes physically embodied. Leach describes this type of synesthetic event as one of condensation and fusion.[9] By the end of the evening, all of the multiple and multi-channeled elements of the ritual are combined and condensed into a single, memorable experience we call "seder."

My own research and analysis of the Shabbat experience at residential Jewish summer camp revealed Shabbat to be a synesthetic experience as well. When campers spoke of Shabbat, it was presented as a swirl of memory with the senses intermingled. Campers spoke glowingly of a Shabbat filled with songs, swaying with arms wrapped around each other as they sang "Shalom Rav," the scent of sycamore trees, the sound of the ocean's waves, the gleam of hundreds of campers wearing white shirts, the dining room filled with the scent of freshly baked challah and roasted chicken, and a joyous song session filling the dining hall. Those interviewed vividly recalled Shabbat at camp and considered it to be one of the most salient and long-enduring memories of their total camp experience. The multisensory summer camp Shabbat celebration enables a synesthesia that permits this experience to remain within the body and mind and acts as a focus of profound, long-lasting, and rich memories. Vibrant recollections of Shabbat at camp remain with the camper for years after the camp experience has ended. Because the initial experience was so profound, even isolated elements from the camp experience (the scent of baking challah, a favorite melody from the after-dinner song session, for example) can serve as a mental trigger that kindles a remembering of the camp Shabbat experience even though it initially took place many years before.

Opportunities for Synesthesia in the High Holy Days

There is no doubt that Rosh HaShanah and Yom Kippur create significant memories for congregants. The remembrances are forged from the sheer emotion, sacred importance, and the liturgical depth of these Days of Awe. Music and communal song undoubtedly play a large role in the creation of memories, especially the stirring melodies of *Kol Nidrei* and *Avinu Malkeinu*. But, I wonder, can the High Holy Days become more sensorially integrated like the Jewish summer camp Shabbat and the Passover Seder and thus ultimately provide the congregation with an experience that is not only synesthetic in nature but is also more memorable and thus creating a deeper connection to community and to the sacred.

Synesthetic opportunities are possible through the development of those senses not normally part of the liturgical experience: taste, smell, and touch.

Taste and Smell

The High Holy Days are filled with speech, song, and written word, but they lack the elements of touch and taste. Sephardic and

Mizrahi Jews have a tradition of an Erev Rosh HaShanah seder-like ceremony with Talmudic roots (*Horayot* 12a) in which a variety of fruits and vegetables are used to represent aspirations for the New Year. Congregants should be made aware of this custom to share with guests around the Erev Rosh HaShanah dining table, but it is also possible to bring this Rosh HaShanah seder into the synagogue. Imagine how delighted the community would be to see tables laden not only with the requisite apples and honey but with festive fruits and vegetables accompanied by blessings and explanations available to be tasted as part of a prelude to Erev Rosh HaShanah.

The ubiquitous honey cake could also enable an enhanced Rosh HaShanah synesthesia. Honey cakes baking in the synagogue kitchen and then served at the end of services as part of an *oneg* could help to enhance the relationship of scent and taste to the holidays. Like Proust's *madeleine,* the aroma and taste of honey cake could become associated with myriad memories connected with the joy of Rosh HaShanah.

Touch

The sound of the shofar is one of the most ancient sounds present in the synagogue's musical repertory and when the *baal t'kiah* raises the shofar and the calls of *t'kiah-t'ruah-sh'varim* resound through the sanctuary, the ancient world meets modernity. The most ancient of musical instruments could be used to create a synesthetic matrix featuring not only sound, but sight and touch as well.

The new CCAR *machzor*'s repositioning of the three rubrics for the sounding of shofar (*Malchuyot, Zichronot, Shofarot*) throughout the service rather than having them appear sequentially as is common in traditional High Holy Day prayer books is a first step in highlighting the shofar as elemental in the ritual of the Yamim Noraim. However, more can be done to enhance the shofar's power. For example, in lieu of just one shofar blower on the synagogue's bimah, a more dramatic approach with potential for greater impact would the organization of a shofar "choir" comprised of multiple *baalei t'kiah* lining the aisles of the synagogue. This choir of shofarot would present greater visual impact, surround the congregation with the clarion call of the ram's horn, and present worshipers with a vibrational and tactile energy from the shofarot. A singular shofar provides incredible impact; a shofar ensemble would be an unforgettable addition to the Rosh HaShanah liturgy.

Other opportunities for enhancing touch exist within the liturgy. During the chanting or singing of *Mi Shebeirach* congregants could be asked to hold hands or put their arms on each other's shoulders. As the cantor recites the Priestly Blessing or a final benediction, all those wearing tallitot could be asked to share their tallit with those around them and feel enveloped not only by the tallit but by the community as well.

We should also encourage congregants to experience the power of full prostration during the Great *Aleinu*. The physical act of falling to one's knees in the presence of God is not only humbling but a physical representation of full emotional and spiritual supplication before the Almighty in which we physically declare, "We surrender. Please help us, God. Protect us. Guide us." There are no words in the liturgy that can fully express this moment of physical prayer; no text in the *machzor* can adequately describe the moment of the Great *Aleinu*.

Tasting Chocolate

When we are part of synesthetic events, these experiences become encoded and implanted within us. We hold onto these memories and reflect upon them as years pass. When ritual is deeply embodied and synesthetic (like the experiences of summer camp Shabbat and the Passover seder) not only are our feelings and beliefs enhanced, but the participation in these rituals joins us to a larger, broader, Jewish collective. The new *machzor* will surely enhance the experience of prayer for a new generation of Jews. But that experience can be greatly enhanced if we make a concerted effort to move beyond the pages of the prayer book. We need to present our congregants (and I dare say clergy as well) with ritual moving beyond music and spoken or read text that permits worshipers to experience prayer with all their senses and moves our worship—and indeed ourselves as worshipers—to a higher spiritual plane. Creating synesthetic worship may transform the High Holy Day liturgy from beautiful and emotional words to life-altering fully embodied ritual. Don Saliers reminds us, "If we only take in the literal surface of what we hear in words and song, the awakening of the deeper dimensions of reality and of the soul are prevented.

When the singing and the hearing allow us to 'taste and see,' we come to 'hear' more. The soul is awakened to a humanity stretched more deeply before the mystery and the glory of God."[10]

May our prayer be guided not only by words of our mouth and the meditations of our heart, but the tastes and scents of the seasons, the reverberation of the shofar, the healing touch of our neighbors, and the communal embrace of our fellow worshipers.

Notes

1. Oliver Sacks, *Musicophilia* (New York: Alfred A. Knopf, 2007).
2. Steve Odin, "Blossom Scents Take Up the Ringing: Synaesthesia in Japanese and Western Aesthetics," *Soundings* 69, no. 3 (Fall 1986): 256.
3. Ibid., 259.
4. Ibid., 270.
5. Don E. Saliers, *Music and Theology* (Kindle ed.) (Nashville: Abingdon Press, 2007), Kindle location 171.
6. Steven Feld, "Waterfalls of Song," in *Senses of Place*, ed. Steven Feld and Keith H. Basso (Santa Fe, NM: School of American Research Press, 1996), 91.
7. Paul Connerton, *How Societies Remember* (Cambridge: Cambridge University Press, 1989), 45.
8. Translation from Everett Fox, *The Five Books of Moses* (New York: Schocken Books, 1983).
9. Edmund Leach, *Culture and Communication* (Cambridge: Cambridge University Press, 1976).
10. Saliers, *Music and Theology*, Kindle location 301.

Love, Liturgy, Leadership

Elyse D. Frishman

Sh'ma koleinu, Adonai Eloheinu, chus v'racheim aleinu. Does God hear us? How would we know that we have been heard?

Hear our prayer: not just listen, but comprehend, understand us. If God truly understands, God will listen with compassion and mercy (*chus v'racheim*), because despite our failings, God knows that we are desperate to become more.

Hear *our* voice: The plural reveals the power and essentiality of communal prayer. The individual voice gains not only in volume but also in measurable importance when offered in community: man, woman, child, lay leader, cantor, rabbi.

Hear our *voice*: because our voices' voice is one, opened in anguish to the exigencies of life. Prayer emerges in humility, facing existential desperation, hoping for understanding and embrace. That desire for embrace cries out, *"Racheim, have mercy!"* Since *racheim* is linked to the womb (*rechem*), it is as though we are pleading, "As once we were protected, nourished, and grown, so embrace us now."

Does God hear? Our liturgy affirms this with the priestly blessing. Moments after *Sh'ma Koleinu* is offered, the *kohanim* or clergy raise their hands to bless the people, and the people are assured: God hears.

But the priestly figure is the agent of that blessing, and how that blessing is communicated says a great deal about who God is, and where God is in that moment.

The *machzor*, magnificent script for our deepest hopes and dreams, must communicate consistently that God is present and that our voices are heard. But Larry Hoffman has taught that a prayer book remains a tool, as effective as its wielder: "No new

---

ELYSE D. FRISHMAN (NY81) is the editor of *Mishkan T'filah: A Reform Siddur*. She is the senior rabbi at The Barnert Temple in Franklin Lakes, New Jersey. She is married to Rabbi Daniel Freelander, and they have three children, Adam, Jonah, and Devra.

book *alone* will solve the problem . . . The problem is . . . systemic."[1] We have learned that successful worship requires attention to many additional components: environment, music, sermon, clergy, lay leaders, the people. The responsibility of clergy is *to inspire* the system, and to manage the *machzor* in the context of the whole. The implications are huge, not just for our worship experience, but because that experience will communicate a great deal about God's identity and God's accessibility. *We* demonstrate the ethic of inclusivity. Most importantly, we demonstrate the presence of *love*.

A Community of Strangers

A reflection on Shabbat worship and its application to the Yamim Noraim: In many Shabbat morning Reform sanctuaries, the worshipers constitute a "community of strangers"—gathered for *b'nei mitzvah*, often from "elsewhere," often not knowing each other. Yet, for that period of prayer, study, and celebration, it is an opportunity to link them to each other, to open the gates of prayer to them. They haven't necessarily come to pray; often their attire and attitude speak of enduring the service. Yet, it doesn't take much to open their hearts by *taking note of who they are that day*. To trust them to be present. To welcome the teens warmly and sincerely. To know and respect what matters to each person, each soul present.

Before worship begins, these should be strangers no more. Then, we will know which prayers will resonate: English? Hebrew? The right or left side? *Mishkan T'filah* allows the opportunity to choose in the midst of the service. Worshipers may be insecure about prayer. They might not want others to hear them pray or sing. They might feel Jewishly illiterate or lost in unfamiliar music. Perhaps there are complicated family dynamics; is this a *sanctuary* for them? How do we help create that safe environment that can open every person, every age, to matters of the heart? These are the questions that guide the content of our prayer books, *and the way in which we use them*. Group worship relies on trust of each other as well as with God. Relationships are being shaped during worship.

On Rosh HaShanah and Yom Kippur, our worshiping community shifts yet again. Blended are Shabbat regulars, High Holy Day guests, and High Holy Day regulars. The latter are as much a community of regulars as on Shabbat. They enter and look to see whom they know. They often sit where they did last year, with the same people. They rely on comfort and familiarity; and then they may be open to spiritual growth, to character refinement, to God.

How people discern God varies by personality. Different personality types are drawn to different spiritual expressions.[2] Individuals are hard-wired spiritually. Some resonate to action (community service or social justice) while others are drawn to meditation and mysticism. This should inform the development of our *machzor*—and the prayer choices we clergy make during worship. All spiritual types could be present; do we recognize them? Is every worshiper certain that *we* are listening?

The *machzor* itself must include feelings *and* thoughts. Different poetic *styles* matter as much as the content. The two-page spread allows for this variety. As in *Mishkan T'filah*:

> Theologically, the liturgy needs to include many perceptions of God: the transcendent, the naturalist, the mysterious, the partner, the evolving God . . . An integrated theology communicates that the community is greater than the sum of its parts. While individuals matter deeply, particularly in the sense of our emotional and spiritual needs and in the certainty that we are not invisible, that security should be a stepping stone to the higher value of community, privilege and obligation. We join together in prayer because together, we are stronger and more apt to commit to the values of our heritage . . . Prayer must move us beyond ourselves. (*Mishkan T'filah*, ix)

The contents of the *machzor* inform and propel *us* as well as our congregants. We are reminded, too, of the diversity of our community. As in *Mishkan T'filah*, the *machzor* will uphold the ethic of inclusivity, and the "awareness of and obligation to others rather than mere self-fulfillment." To be personally included and to serve others should be possible simultaneously.

Leadership from Love

The worship experience of the clergy is different than the person-in-the-pew. We attend to the people. Yet that attention need not distract from personal prayer; it may deepen it. Serving others is a form of *avodah*, serving God. How might we serve most effectively during the High Holy Days?

Humility and Love:
Levi Yitzchak of Berditchev cautions, "There is a danger that the performance of God's *mitzvot* could cause a *sin*, that sin being one's smugness about having performed even a single *mitzvah*. Such smugness is spiritual arrogance. Any Jew who considers himself 'a somebody,' as a result of having performed *mitzvot* instead of having acquired a more profound sense of humility, has failed to absorb basic lessons of Judaism. That person forgets or forgot that even the strength, physical and moral, to perform these *mitzvot*, was something granted to us by the Creator; it is not something 'homegrown' . . . We should be careful lest we acquire any notion of superiority, because if we were to do this, what was meant to be a blessing could turn into a curse due to our arrogance."[3]

Offering *Hineini* at the outset of the High Holy Days reminds us that we are bound to one another, clergy and community. We pray that our congregation will not falter on our account, nor we on theirs. *Hineini* downsizes us so that we can remember before whom we stand. We clergy stand before God *and everyone* humbly, so that *we can see our people, we can hear them, we can take note of and be with them.*

If we utilize the *machzor* to see into our people's lives, to hear their voices, we will be serving them. Service deepens humility. Humility opens the door for us to pay attention and to serve. To serve with love furthers humility, which opens our own hearts to personal prayer—and again to service.

The Sages describe the importance of *love* during the offering of the Priestly Blessing. First, the priest must face the people. "R. Isaac said, 'Let respect for the community always be with you, for you will note that (while blessing the worshippers), the priests' faces were turned towards the people and their backs were towards the Presence'" (*Sotah* 40a). By looking into the eyes of the community, of the people, the individuals before us, we see into their eyes and hearts. We don't stand before the people; we stand *amidst* them.

The priestly blessing brought God into the people's midst. So the priest needed to bless the people through *chesed* (*Zohar Naso* 145b).[4] As agents of that blessing, *we* emanate *chesed*. We love our people. Especially during the Yamim Noraim, standing before the congregation, looking into the eyes of individuals, we radiate care for each and every one of them. No matter what has taken place between us, we reveal *chesed*; we love them.

The *Zohar* also teaches that while the priest must love the people, *they must love him*:

> On one occasion, when a priest went up and spread forth his hands, before he completed the blessing he turned into a heap of bones. This happened because there was no love between him and the people. Then another priest went up and pronounced the blessing, and so the day passed without harm. A priest who loves not the people, nor whom they love not, may not pronounce the blessing. (*Zohar Naso* 147b)[5]

It is dangerous to pretend love. The hidden wisdom here is that while the priest must learn how to love, the people must also learn to love. We are all in need. On the Yamim Noraim, we come together to be reassured that we are seen, we are heard, we are loved.

Certainly, though, as clergy, there may be an obstacle to our love for the people, and theirs for us. Will we work to overcome this before we join in this sacred endeavor?

We learn from Esau, in Genesis 33, about forgiveness. After years of separation, Jacob and Esau must face each other. Jacob is afraid; it is their first encounter since Jacob's primal thefts from Esau and Esau's threat to kill him. Esau, too, is worried; what might his brother wrest from him now? Yet as they draw close, Esau observes, physically and spiritually, that Jacob is no longer dangerous: He bears no weapon and he appears humble. Can Esau be sure? No. Yet, he takes a risk. As Jacob arrives, Esau runs to embrace him, perhaps showering him with kisses. (There are several diacritical marks above *va'yishakeihu* suggesting an image of multiple kisses.) Esau's offers *chesed*, and then Jacob offers gifts.

> Esau said: "I have plenty, my brother; let what is yours remain yours." Yaakov said: "No, I pray! Pray, if I have found favor in your eyes, then take this gift from my hand. For I have, after all, seen your face, as one sees the face of God, and you have been gracious to me."[6]

Esau had become secure in his own life, so he could forgive Jacob. What might we clergy learn about forgiveness from Esau—the so-called enemy? About looking into the eyes of the other and finding *chesed* (love)? How can our own encounter at the High Holy Days bring a reunion of brothers and sisters?

In the system that is worship, how worshipers position themselves physically can impact the sense of God's Presence and where God is found. A *baraita* in *B'rachot* 30a teaches:

> One who stands outside of Israel should direct his heart towards *Eretz Yisrael*, as it says, "And they will pray to you by way of their land," (I Kings 8:48). One who stands in *Eretz Yisrael* should direct his heart towards Jerusalem, as it says, "And they will pray to God by way of the city which You have chosen," (I Kings 8:44). One who stands in Jerusalem should direct his heart towards the Temple, as it says, "And they will pray towards this House," (II Chronicles 6:32). One who stands in the Temple should direct his heart towards the Holy of Holies, as it says, "And they will pray towards this place." (I Kings 8:35) . . . Thus, one who stands: in the east—turns his face towards the west; in the west—turns his face towards the east; in the south—turns his face towards the north; in the north—turns his face towards the south. Thus, all of Israel directs their hearts to one place.

If worshipers around the world all look towards the Temple, we face each other. Seeking God, and with no Temple blocking the way, we find one another.

A sanctuary is traditionally designed to face the Holy of Holies. Within our sanctuaries, worshipers face the ark—and clergy. We are elevated by the bimah. This architectural design creates a spiritual impression that we are "higher up." Rather, let it impress upon us the *opportunity* to see into the eyes and hearts of our people.

And when we join together vocally in prayer, rather than "leading" most of the liturgy, we may be more apt to listen to the voices of others. The experience of sharing the prayers aloud may bring a deeper awareness of the other. Then, what might we hear?

Let's return to the priestly blessing. *Zohar Naso* 146a explains that the offering of *Yivarech'cha* connects the upper and lower worlds; it leads to completion. To effect this, the priest must *understand* this. "R. Judah said, 'If a priest is ignorant of this inward significance of the blessing and does not know whom he blesses or what his blessing connotes, his blessing is naught.'"[7]

In 147b, R. Judah continues: "Indeed, we find that a real blessing is associated with the opening of the eye. Thus it is written, 'Open

Your eyes,' (Daniel 9:18), that is, in order to bless."[8] "Open"—not *p'tach*, but *pokeiach* (take note). The verse references God taking note, but R. Judah infers that the priest must open *his* eyes and *take note*. To take note of the people in blessing them mirrors the empathy of God taking note of Sarah, hearkening to not merely her prayer, but her deep need. When Sarah was acknowledged, she became fruit-full (fruitful). Often negative emotions and behavior are the weeds of an untended spirit. A barren spirit, even more so, is parched for attention. *Taking note* therefore leads to fruit-bearing, positive action. Our people, as do we, need recognition and acknowledgment in the deepest sense. Consider the fuller context of the Daniel verse:

> Now, our God, hear the prayers and petitions of your servant. For your sake, Eternal, look with favor on your desolate sanctuary. Give ear our God, and hear; open your eyes and see the desolation of the city that bears Your Name. We do not make requests of You because we are righteous, but because of Your great mercy.

Daniel beseeches God to act from mercy and not judgment. So, too, our people want to be seen and understood through eyes of mercy and not judgment. *Sh'ma koleinu, Adonai Eloheinu, chus v'racheim aleinu*. Our challenge, in both sermon and liturgy, is not to preach but *to teach to action*. Where is God? Where action is inspired by *chesed* and love.

We need each other. *We clergy* need our *community*:

> And let them make me a sanctuary, that I may dwell among them, (Exodus 25:8). That is, any sanctuary whatever, in that any synagogue, wherever situated, is called *sanctuary*, and the *Shechinah* hastens to the synagogue (even before the worshippers arrive). Happy is the one who is of the first ten to enter the synagogue, since they form something complete, and are the first to be sanctified by the *Shechinah*. (*Zohar Naso* 126a).[9]

Ten people are necessary for a group to worship. Rabbi Zalman Shachter-Shalomi[10] teaches that each kabbalistic *s'firah* is an attribute of God. Each of the ten *s'firot* is emphasized in a different person. That is, each individual is a vessel for one *s'firah* in particular: wisdom, intuition, judgment, endurance, etc. We need each other, and we need community, because we bring different aspects of God together. When all ten of the attributes are present through ten different people, God is fully present. Technically, a minyan could accomplish this. Yet, likely it will take many more than ten people, since the distribution of these *s'firot* is so spread out. *Who knows which final person entering the sanctuary will complete us all?*

Continuing the discussion about a minyan, the *Zohar* teaches:

> For inasmuch as the single members are not together there is no complete body . . . Observe that the moment the body is made complete here below a supernal holiness comes and enters that body, and so the lower world is in truth transformed after the pattern of the upper world. *Thus it is incumbent on all not to open their mouths to talk of worldly matters*, seeing that Israel then are at their most complete and holiest. (*Zohar Naso* 126a)[11]

As people enter the synagogue environment, what would be considered "worldly matters"? Is ordinary schmoozing and greeting people out of place? No, for this renews relationships, and good relationships deepen spirituality. What matters would be deemed ordinary? Transaction of business, phone calls, texting—any action that distracts us from the *makom hakodesh*.

What might we do to encourage spiritual engagement before High Holy Day worship arrives? What training will our leaders need? What preparation might we provide our congregants? Considering again the reunion of Esau and Jacob: What will be the arena for wrestling before we greet one another? Preparing each and every person, congregant and guest, will deepen the experience of the entire community, and us. Skill and insight acquired by one impact all.

Our guidance of the community begins well before the commencement of worship. What occurs on the entire property matters, outside in the parking lot, into the building, in the lobby. The transition from profane to sacred is in the details. Imagine: patient, smiling parking attendants; warm greeters from all cohorts of the community, so one is likely to recognize and welcome each congregant; *and clergy who are ready to receive*.

Where are the clergy as people enter? If we are readying ourselves—rehearsing Torah readers, choir members, lay leaders, one another—then we do not model readiness to others. We must be fully present, all-ready for our people in the *makom hakodesh*.

And truly, *where are we?* What is our frame of mind? *The frame of our soul?* As we facilitate worship, no matter what, we must model the offering of *chesed* (of forgiveness and love).

How will we guide the ordinary to blend gently into the holy? Until suddenly each person will realize, "*Achein, yesh Adonai bamakom hazeh, vaanochi lo yadati?*" (Surely God is in this Place, yet I, I did not know?) (Gen. 28:16).

The experience of worship on the High Holy Days is unique to the season. The *machzor* varies from the siddur not only in traditional liturgy, but also in the choices of contemporary poetry. Will the *machzor* preach, or will it inspire? Will *we* preach or inspire?

Worship opens us to transformation of the self and of the community. If we don't transform ourselves, we won't be able to guide our congregants—or the world around us.

On the Yamim Noraim, we join together to be heard and loved and inspired to serve anew. Clergy and laity alike are uncertain, insecure, afraid, still searching for the Promised Land. Even Moses was unsure at times; he, too, needed the people as they needed him. The vision is extraordinary. The journey must be shared.

For we, too, must cry out, "I, I did not know." Weeping for the pride that has distracted us, praying for the humility that might save us, and listening to the hearts that surround us, we will offer: *Sh'ma koleinu*. And God will be there.

Notes

1. Lawrence A. Hoffman, *The Art of Public Prayer* (Washington, DC: The Pastoral Press, 1988), 44.
2. Consider four areas of distinct application:
    1) Concrete engagement through reciting Hebrew, chanting, singing, touching Torah, imagining the stories of our tradition;
    2) Meaningful symbolic language, and music that is deep, prayer-centering;
    3) Study and reflection, theological inquiry, existential thoughtfulness; and
    4) Socializing, being surrounded with friends, talking, sharing amidst worship.

    Cf. Timothy Noxon, "Myers-Briggs Type Indicator (MBTI) and Christian Spirituality," http://thenoxfactor.com/files/Noxon-Myers-Briggs.pdf; Charles J. Keating, *Who We Are Is How We Pray* (Mystic, CT: Twenty-Third Publications, 1987); Roberta Louis

Goodman and Sherry H. Blumberg, eds., *Teaching about God and Spirituality: A Resource for Jewish Settings*, Denver: A.R.E. Publishing, 2002).
3. Eliyahu Munk, *Kedushat Levi*, vol. 3 (New York: Lambda Publishers, 2009), 756–57; Levi Yitzchak, *Sefer Kedushat Levi Hashalem, Parshat Re'eh* (Jerusalem: Mishur Publishing), 89.
4. Harry Sperling and Maurice Simon, trans., *The Zohar*, vol. 5 (London: The Soncino Press, 1984), *Naso*, 192b.
5. Ibid., 198.
6. Translation from Everett Fox, *The Five Books of Moses* (New York: Schocken Books, 1983), 159.
7. Sperling and Simon, *Zohar*, 194.
8. Ibid., 198.
9. Ibid., 184.
10. Zalman Meshullam Schachter-Shalomi, *Spiritual Intimacy: A Study of Counseling in Hasidism* (Rowman & Littlefield, 1990).
11. Sperling and Simon, *Zohar*, 184–85

The Yamin Nora'im: Concentric Circles of Liturgy and Relation

Lawrence A. Englander

I do not understand
the book in my hand.

Who will teach me to return?
Loss of custom, ruin of will,
a memory of a memory
thinner than a vein.
Who will teach us to return?

To whom nothing speaks
Not shofar, not song, not homily. . . .

Suppose even God
turned out to be a god?

We do not want to come back.
We do not know where we are.
Not knowing where we are, how can we know
      where we should go?

This poem by Cynthia Ozick may capture the mood of many congregants who come to synagogue over the High Holy Days. Especially for those who attend only at this time, it is ironic that they confront the most complex liturgy of the entire year. As they attempt to reaquaint themselves with the prayers, they find that the *machzor* is replete with medieval *piytim*, originally composed by and for scholars, whose meanings can often be obscure. As they seek dialogue with a God who can make sense to them, these congregants find that the hierarchical images of Ruler and Judge

---

Lawrence A. Englander is rabbi of Solel Congregation of Mississauga, Ontario, Canada, and is a former editor of the *CCAR Journal*.

dominate the text. And as they struggle to reconcile the ancient stories of the Bible with contemporary values, the first Torah portion they encounter is the tale of a father attempting to slaughter a son—at God's command, no less!

On the other hand, there are aspects of the liturgy that are more majestic than at any other time of year. The stark content of *Kol Nidre* and *Un'taneh Tokef* is mitigated by their awe-inspiring musical settings. The blast of the shofar touches us in a spot that even the greatest symphonies cannot reach. The prevalence of white—from Torah mantles to floral arrangements to clergy attire—radiates a sense of purity and innocence.

In the midst of all these phenomena, rabbis, cantors and service leaders face a challenge: how can we manage to perform a "makeover" on parts of the liturgy that have become unintelligible to many—even obstacles to prayer—while at the same time maintaining the richness of the traditions we encounter at this time of Year? This challenge will be especially acute for any group—such as the CCAR at present—who plans to produce a new *machzor layamim nora'im*. Although there is no single solution, I shall concentrate on one approach. Rather than a wholesale deletion of material currently found in *Gates of Repentance*,[1] my recommendation is to add liturgy that will provide a balance of perspective for the contemporary Reform Jew. I see this process operating within three concentric circles of Jewish life, each of which we shall consider in turn.

The Inner Circle: The Self

If we were to ask the average thoughtful Jew, "What are you thinking about during services on the High Holy Days?" I believe we would often receive the following reply: "I'm thinking about my life: my behaviour during the past year, my relationships and how I can improve them." The liturgy of Yom Kippur inspires us—and ideally helps us—to perform the difficult task of *cheshbon hanefesh*. The *vidui* takes us through a range of attitudes and actions in which we have fallen short of the ideal, from conduct in business

על חטא שחטאנו לפניך בנשך ובמרבית
For the sin we have committed against You by financial exploitation.[2]

to intimate interpersonal relationships

עַל חֵטְא שֶׁחָטָאנוּ לְפָנֶיךָ בְּגִלּוּי עֲרָיוֹת
For the sin we committed against You by sexual immorality.[3]

to social justice.

For keeping the poor in chains of poverty.[4]

While the traditional *vidui* is phrased in the first person plural, a moving passage in GOR (pp. 325–6) provides an opportunity for silent, individual introspection as well.

These confessions certainly provoke us toward *teshuvah*; yet they also suffer a common drawback. They all deal with the negative side of our behviour. One the one hand, we acknowledge that the Rabbis, in their wisdom, instruct us to beat our breasts during the *vidui* in order to give us a sense of humility before the Holy Blessed One—all the more necessary in our current culture of self-entitlement. On the other hand, should there not also be an opportunity to celebrate our accomplishments during the past year, to identify those moments when we came closer to realizing our better selves? Is there a way to engage in a balanced self-evaluation without replacing the fist on the chest with a pat on the back?

To help achieve this balance, I recommended, in another publication,[5] the following addition to our liturgy. Along with the traditional recitaiton of the *Al Chet*, we might insert another list that begins with the phrase:

עַל תִּקּוּן שֶׁתִּקַּנּוּ לְפָנֶיךָ.

The word *tikkun* is difficult to translate, but in this context it would have the following sense: "For all our efforts, in Your presence, to work toward completion."[6] The intent of this language is to portray *tikkun* as a process rather than an accomplished feat. Then, as a counterpoint to *V'al Kulam*, this section might end as follows: "May all these efforts, O God of mercy, be recorded for belssing in our Book of Life for the coming year."[7]

The Middle Circle: Jewish Community

Another motivation for Jews to attend High Holy Day services—in fact, the overriding motivation for many—is to reconnect with their Jewish community. Electronic media and social networking have added new dimensions to our sense of self; and yet, as our identities become more diffuse, we run the risk of becoming fragmented into pieces of a pie without a uniform filling. It is therefore comforting to "return to the well" once in a while and draw from our Jewish source. For example, I especially enjoy watching the young adults of our congregation during the Yamim Nora'im. Returning from school or work that has taken them around the world, they mingle in the aisles of the sanctuary to catch up with each other and exchange contact information.

There are many congregations that excel in bringing this sense of community to their people. For example, special groups (Board and committee members, teachers, etc.) are called up for collective *aliyot*. Some congregations hold up a *tallit* or *chuppah* on the *bimah* for people to gather during the prayer for healing.[8] It is interesting to note that these are choreographical strategies that go *beyond the liturgy*. How do we capture this feeling of communal closeness within the pages of the Machzor itself?

I wish to suggest a couple of texts that may enable us to do so. In BT *Berakhot* 58a we find this statement: "The Rabbis teach: Whenever one sees a large gathering of Jews, one should say, 'Praised is the One wise in discerning secrets.' For no one is like another, either in mind or appearance." At the very beginning of the service for Rosh HaShanah, the following blessing could be recited:

ברוך אתה יי אלהינו מלך העולם, חכם הרזים.

Although many non-Jews will be present in our congregations, I believe that they will understand the import of this blessing and may also feel embraced by the community. For those uncomfortable with its ethnocentricity, there is the blessing found in the morning liturgy:

ברוך אתה יי מקדש את שמו ברבים
We praise You, Eternal One, whose Name is sanctified within assemblies.

Without doubt, creative *shlichei tzibur* will develop the choreography to accompany these liturgical words, in order to give expression to the reaching out that we all do at this holy time of year.

The Outer Circle: Relating to God

The dominant image of God on the *Yamim Nora'im* is that of a ruler, modelled after an ancient potentate, who sits in judgment of our deeds. This image is perhaps the most difficult of all for many congregants (and, I dare say, for many Jewish professionals). Although the English tries to soften the metaphor, many are still troubled by its hierarchical nature.

This matter has been addressed in a previous issue of this *Journal*.[9] Yoel Kahn refers to High Holy Day liturgy as reflecting "the theological assertion of God's absolute power and our human smallness and powerlessness,"[10] and yearns for "a prayer life that is authentic and honest, a prayer language whose metaphors and images are both comfortable and provocative, a prayer experience that reaches deep within and deep beyond the self."[11] Margaret Wenig analyzes the content of *Un'taneh Tokef* and suggests alternative ways of understanding this prayer that invoke human initiative and partnership with God.[12] Nevertheless, she acknowledges that these renderings bring no consolation to people who find the prayer hurtful and offensive. How, then, are we to bridge the growing gap between those worshippers who resonate to the ancient imagery of the Machzor and those who seek other metaphors in relating to God? Especially within Reform and Progressive congregations, the wide spectrum of theologies may necessitate an equally vast array of liturgy.

To address this question, it might be helpful to understand that this is not a new problem. The scholar Joseph Weiss noted that, even within Hasidic communities that we assume to have been homogeneous, we witness some serious theological differences.[13] Taking only two schools, the mystical contemplation of the Mezeritchers and the pietistic faith of the Bratzlavers, Weiss depitcts two very divergent relationships with God. By understanding these two approaches, we may find some means of addressing the variety of divine-human relationships among our own congregants.

The Bratzlaver school is closer to what we may consider to be classical Jewish theology. God is perceived to be "personal and voluntaristic."[14] Ruling from beyond the world, God intervenes in history to bring humanity toward redemption. For the Mezeritchers, however, God is not personal but is rather a "'divine essence' (*chiyyu*t), that 'divine spark' (*nitzotz elohi*) which dwell[s] in all worlds and in all beings."[15] Today we might describe this view as

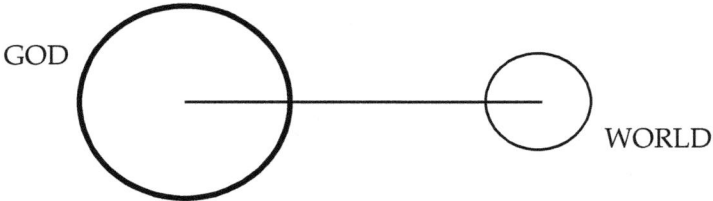

Figure 1

panentheistic: God embraces the entirety of the universe but is also greater than it—in other words, the universe is a subset of God.[16]

These two views result in two distinct attitudes toward prayer. For the Bratzlav school, since God is separate from the universe, there must be some bridge to connect the two (see Figure 1). When the direction goes from God to the world, we call it revelation. When it goes in the opposite direction, we call this prayer. Thus for the followers of Rabbi Nachman of Bratzlav, prayer is dialogue with a Being who transcends them and who is reached through faith (*emunah*).

The process is entirely different for the school of Dov Baer of Mezeritch. Since God's presence permeates the world, God is immanent rather than transcendent. The bridge thus performs a different function (see Figure 2). The direction from God to the world is not a bridge across a gap but rather an *acknowledgment* of our inhering within God. We attain this state through the mystical exercise of *devekut* (clinging to God), which results in *bitul ha-yesh* (an extinction of the ego) so that we apprehend the divine organism of which we are a part.

It seems clear how the traditional High Holy Day liturgy would work for the Bratzlavers, since the images of ruler and judge stress

Figure 2

God's transcendence. But how did the Mezeritchers deal with these metaphors? We know that they *davened* the same liturgy as the Bratzlavers, since no Hasidic school would arrogate to themselves the power of changing it. In order to reconcile the liturgy with his theology, Dov Baer taught the following approach to prayer:

> When one needs to request anything from the Creator, one should imagine that one's soul is a limb of the Shekhinah, as it were, like a drop of water in the sea. If one makes the request on behalf of the Shekhinah, in that a particular thing is lacking in her, then one will certainly possess the spiritual power to act beyond the Shekhinah. Only if one clings properly to the Shekhinah will the overflow spread upon one.
>
> (*Magid Devarav LeYa'akov*, #32)

The disciples of Dov Baer would pray with this *kavanah* in mind in order to receive the *shefa* of God who is both within and beyond.

We can therefore understand how the challenge of multiple theologies within any congregation is not a new one. However, there is also a significant difference between the Hasidic communities and our own. If a Hasid in the eighteenth or nineteenth century did not subscribe to the theology of the Tzaddik, that individual could migrate to another Hasidic court. Yet in our Progressive congregations today, we welcome individual differences and seek to cast a net wide enough to accommodate everyone who comes to us. In order to make the liturgy meaningful to such a broad variety of people, we have two options—neither of which excludes the other. First, as previous prayer books have done, we can add commentaries that explain how a prayer might be understood within a different theological context. Second, unlike the Hasidim, we do have the option of adding new prayers or of amending the old liturgy to yield new meanings. It is this second option, practised by generations of Reform liturgists, that I now wish to explore in more detail.

Fusing the Circles: a Recommendation for High Holy Day Liturgy

If we examine the liturgical additions that we currently find in many progressive machzorim, I believe that we can identify the following major categories of style:

1. Commentaries in the margins or at the bottom of the page, often designed to reinterpret the liturgy to appeal to contemporary outlooks. These selections are normally meant to be studied rather than prayed.
2. Readings that mention neither prayer nor God directly. These often deal with ethical matters and sometimes quote from Tanakh.[17]
3. Selections that "read" as prayer but do not mention God.[18]
4. Readings that mention God in the third person.[19]
5. Selections that address God indirectly.[20]
6. Direct address to God. Most of the traditional liturgy belongs to this category, along with many English readings.

Within each of these style rubrics, it is possible to reflect a range of theologies. Here are but a few examples[21]:

1. The "classical" view of an omnipotent, omniscient God who acts in the world to bring justice and goodness. Emil Fackenheim and Abraham Joshua Hechel are two examples of this view.
2. The "naturalist" view of a God who is a force within nature. The theologies of Mordecai Kaplan and Marcia Falk would fall into this broad category.
3. The "mystical" God, who is made manifest through nature and Torah. Contemporary advocates of this view are Lawrence Kushner and Arthur Green.
4. The "humanist" view in which God is perceived as an inner voice of conscience. Erich Fromm is one example.
5. The "non-absolute" or "evolving" god who leads the world toward perfection by influencing human action. Proponents of this view include Milton Steinberg, Henry Slonimsky and Harold Kushner.

Now here's the rub: it seems clear that the traditional liturgy reflects view #1 most accurately. As we go further along the list, holders of these views are faced with reinterpreting metaphors to such a degree that they may no longer hold up. What is to be done, then? With all the different styles of liturgy (first list), and all the theologies (second list) that they need to reflect, how do we construct a meaningful prayer experience for an entire congregation? How can all these permutations be contained between two covers of a book? Moreover, if the *machzor* provides so many choices for the worshipper to pray, how do we preserve the dynamic between individual and community that is so important for *tefilah b'tzibur*?

This brings me to my final recommendation, which is not original with me but rather has been under discussion for some time. Thanks to the computer and word processing programmes, the *written* word today has become as fluid as the *oral* word was to our Rabbinic ancestors. We know that it took many generations for the Oral Torah to be canonized into written form; and even now, we often wish that some of those principles and laws had been left to develop beyond the printed page.

In order to prevent a premature canonization of the liturgical word, we can use this technology to our advantage. In addition to publishing a printed Machzor, the CCAR could instead compile a vast digital array of prayers and readings, in Hebrew and English, reflecting the liturgical styles and the theologies outlined above, along with explanatory notes to guide *sh'lichei tzibur*. This content could be combined with the attractive layouts that have been produced through Visual Tefilah. There is also a bolder alternative to consider: rather than purchasing a *machzor*, communities would purchase the rights to use a compilation of electronic material long with whatever *machzor* they currently use. As well as keeping the liturgical content fluid, this approach has the added advantage of lifting people's eyes off the printed page to look up at a screen, at the *bimah* and, most importantly, at each other.

Once this project is launched, a reportage system could be set up to determine how the materials are being used in various communities, what successes and failures are encountered along the way and what new suggestions people may have to fine-tune the project. In this way, more and more professionals and congregants can become drawn into the process and feel that they have a stake in its outcome.

I wish to stress that I do not view this approach as a compromise to publishing a printed *machzor*. On the contrary, I see it as a way to open more doors to our exploration of liturgical content and method. After all, if our words to God are among the most important we can say, is it not worth the time and effort to examine them carefully?

Notes

1. Published by CCAR, 1978, hereinafter referred to as GOR.
2. GOR, p. 334, my translation.
3. GOR, p. 330.
4. GOP 328, among other selections under the title "Failures of Justice."
5. "We Can't Really be That Evil!" in Lawrence A. Hoffman, ed., *We Have Sinned: Sin and Confession in Judaism* (Woodstock VT: Jewish Lights, 2012). Se, in particular, p. 159.
6. Below are a few examples of how we might complete this sentence:
   - by dedicating ourselves to lifelong Jewish study (Torah)
   - by taking time to give thanks for our many blessings (Avodah)
   - by treating the elderly with dignity (Gemilut Chasadim)

   The liturgy might even provide an opportunity for worshippers to add their own achievements to the list.
7. I understand the the Machzor Editorial Committeee of CCAR is planning to insert such a prayer and I applaud their efforts.
8. Some congregations have introduced the practice of calling up those who are facing a new challenge during the coming year, such as moving to a new home, beginning a new job or sending a child to university.
9. CCAR Journal, Spring 2009.
10. Y. Kahn, "Wrestling with God's Image in the High Holy Day Liturgy," Ibid., p. 28.
11. Ibid., p. 36.
12. M. Wenig, "The Poetry and Power of Paradox," Ibid., pp. 52–74.
13. Joseph Weiss, "Contemplative Mysticism and 'Faith' in Hasidic Piety," *Studies in East European Jewish Mysticism and Hasidism* (London and Portland: Littman Library of Jewish Civilization, 1997), pp. 43–55.
14. Ibid., p. 45.
15. Ibid., p. 46.
16. This is reminiscent of the midrash (*Bereshit Rabbah* 65:9 and elsewhere) that comments on the divine name *HaMakom* by remarking: "God is the place of the world, but the world is not God's place."
17. One of many examples can be found in GOR, p. 27.
18. E.g. GOR, pp. 51–2 and 283–4.
19. E.g. GOR, pp. 102, 103 and 118.
20. Here I have in mind the original formula of Marcia Falk:
    נברך את עין החיים וכה נתנברך. See *The Book of Blessings* (San Francisco: Harper, 1996). This formula is Falk's means of connecting

with a God immanent in the world. A rough equivalent can be found in GOR, pp. 363–5.
21. Readers of this Journal can easily think of several more theological outlooks. In this list, I have chosen those which, in my opinion, would have significant representation among our congregants.

The Calves of Our Lips: The Inescapable Connections between Prayer and Sacrifice

Leon A. Morris

The notion of sacrificial offerings was an anathema in the shaping of a modern Jewish life. Since the earliest days of Reform Judaism, those most ancient forms of divine service were understood as primitive and outmoded.[1] Although the classic, traditional liturgy continued to reference the ancient sacrificial service that predated it, the very first nineteenth-century liturgical reforms removed most of the references to the Temple, and to the sacrifices that had been offered there.

There are many examples of this in both Reform liturgy and ritual. The wording for *Birkat Avodah* (*r'tzei Adonai Eloheinu*), the seventeenth blessing of the *Amidah* on weekdays, and the fifth blessing of the Shabbat and festival *Amidah*, was altered to remove the references to sacrificial offerings.[2] *Musaf*, a service specifically recalling the additional sacrifice on Shabbat and festivals, was either altered or eliminated altogether.[3] The *maftir* reading for special Sabbaths, particularly those that recalled the specific offerings of that festival day, were eliminated.[4] The Torah reading for Yom Kippur morning from Leviticus 16, describing the sacrificial service to be performed by Aaron and his sons—the original observance of Yom Kippur—was also eliminated and a different selection was chosen.[5] Likewise, the most distinctive liturgical rubric of the classic Yom Kippur liturgy, *Sefer HaAvodah* was either radically altered or excised altogether. Even the piyut *Ein Keloheinu* had the final line excised in order to avoid referencing that "our ancestors offered fragrant incense."

This deliberate distancing from the sacrificial service, and from memories of the ancient Temple, extended well beyond the prayer

---

LEON A. MORRIS is the rabbi at Temple Adas Israel in Sag Harbor, New York.

book into daily ritual life. The washing of the hands prior to eating bread with its accompanying blessing recalls the priests who washed prior to eating from the sacrifices. This practice was by and large eliminated. Similarly, the salting of bread recalling the salting of the sacrifices was no longer encouraged.[6] These reforms extended to the Hebrew calendar itself. Tishah B'Av, the anniversary of the Temples' destructions, has generally not been marked in the majority of Reform congregations, and even the newest American Reform prayer book has no liturgy to mark the day.[7]

To the sensibilities of modern Jews attempting to shape a nineteenth- and twentieth-century Judaism, the primitive nature of animal and grain sacrifices seemed to offer little by way of inspiration or critical ideas. The burning of animals in service to God seemed cruel. The idea that God was to be found in one central place, and the land of Israel in particular, was highly objectionable to Jews eager to demonstrate their loyalty to the countries in which they lived.

What was to be gained by this elimination of references to the sacrificial service? The most prevalent justification is rooted in a rejection of the hope for the rebuilding of the Temple and the reestablishment of sacrifice. In fact, many of the early Reformers seemed to assume a necessary and inseparable connection between referencing the centrality of sacrifices in our past and the undying hope for the Temple to be rebuilt and for sacrifices to be restored in our future.

The linking of those two ideas has continued to our time. For example, in an article almost a decade ago in this journal about the centrality of the *Avodah* service, Herbert Bronstein writes:

> The elimination of the Musaf service from Reform Jewish worship as early as the late nineteenth century is, of course, understandable in the light of Reform's constant and consistent opposition, from its beginnings, to prayers for the future restoration of the priestly sacrificial cult of the Jerusalem Temple.[8]

Does such a link have to be made at all? Certainly, there could be a recollection of the central role that sacrifices played in the past without any hope for their future restoration.

Indeed, even if deemed desirable, it would be impossible to entirely eliminate the memory of sacrifice from contemporary Jewish life. References to the Temple and to sacrifice are unavoidable in classical Jewish sources. Indeed, they are ubiquitous as a reference point, as metaphor, and as symbol. Specifically with regard to prayer, references to sacrifices are indispensible. The sacrificial offerings are the very basis for our having morning and afternoon services. The names of the services themselves bear the name of those daily sacrifices.

The early Reformers assumed that what was most needed for a meaningful and relevant Jewish life was a severing of the connection between prayer and sacrifice. However, severing the link between prayer and the sacrificial system may have subverted that goal. More was lost from dropping the connection between them than was gained. There is much to be learned from the sacrificial system that has the potential of deepening our experience of prayer. These ancient practices present notions of relationship, closeness and distance, gift giving, and mystery.[9] Our age opens us up to new possibilities of meaning that such connections can provide for us. Texts about the ancient sacrifices call upon us to develop approaches and methods of interpretation that can treat such texts seriously. To do so, we need to more clearly understand the relationship between sacrifice and prayer.

Sacrifice, Study, and Prayer: Replacement or Substitution?

Once the Temple was destroyed, and sacrifice was no longer being performed, an expanded notion of the sacred space and sacred service was required. Upon resolving to build the Temple, Solomon sent a message to King Huram of Tyre requesting wood and additional craftsmen. He writes:

> See, I intend to build a House for the name of the Eternal my God; I will dedicate it to God for making incense offering of sweet spices in God's honor, for the regular rows of bread, and for the morning and evening burnt offerings on Sabbaths, new moons, and festivals, *as is Israel's duty forever*. (II Chron. 2:3)

הִנֵּה אֲנִי בוֹנֶה־בַּיִת לְשֵׁם ה' אֱלֹהָי לְהַקְדִּישׁ לוֹ לְהַקְטִיר לְפָנָיו
קְטֹרֶת־סַמִּים וּמַעֲרֶכֶת תָּמִיד וְעֹלוֹת לַבֹּקֶר וְלָעֶרֶב לַשַּׁבָּתוֹת וְלֶחֳדָשִׁים
וּלְמוֹעֲדֵי ה' אֱלֹהֵינוּ לְעוֹלָם זֹאת עַל־יִשְׂרָאֵל:

Nothing lasts forever; not the Temple, nor its offerings. The Rabbis, living in the aftermath of the Temple's destruction, are faced with the challenge of explaining what is meant by "Israel's duty forever." This interpretive and symbolic challenge is expressed in BT *M'nachot* 110a:

> Rav Gidel said in the name of Rav: This refers to the altar built [in heaven], and Michael, the great ministering angel stands and offers a sacrifice upon it. Rabbi Yochanan said: These are the students who engage in studying the laws of sacrifice. The verse regards them *as though* the Temple were built in their days.

> א״ר גידל אמר רב: זה מזבח בנוי ומיכאל שר הגדול עומד ומקריב עליו קרבן; ורבי יוחנן אמר: אלו תלמידי חכמים העסוקין בהלכות עבודה, מעלה עליהם הכתוב כאילו נבנה מקדש בימיהם.

In many ways, the disagreement between Rav Gidel and Rabbi Yochanan is about what constitutes *avodah* (the sacrificial service) in their day, and by extension, in ours.

Rav Gidel posits a "virtual" temple in heaven in which the ancient rites of the Temple continue unabated. In contrast, Rabbi Yochanan claims that the very meaning of *avodah* has changed in the aftermath of the Temple's destruction. The place of *avodah* has shifted from the *Beit HaMikdash* (Temple) to the *beit hamidrash* (study hall). All post-exilic Jewish communities, both Orthodox and Reform, are in many ways an extension of Rabbi Yochanan's reasoning. The form of divine service has changed.

Rabbi Yochanan's boldly adaptive interpretation is representative of the Rabbinic project in which the human-God encounter shifts from the Temple to the study hall. Sacrifice lived on, not as performance but rather in memory, language, and imagination. Study is redefined as a religious act, not simply learning in order to do, but as a performance itself.

Following the debate between Rav Gidel and Rabbi Yochanan, on the very same Talmudic page we read the opinions of Rava, Resh Lakish, and Rabbi Yitzchak. Their voices cover a spectrum of opinions regarding the relationship between study and sacrifice.

> Resh Lakish said: What is meant by the verse, "This is the teaching [*Torat*] of the burnt offering, the meal offering, the sin offering, the

guilt offering . . ."? (Leviticus 7:37) Anyone who engages in [the study of] Torah, it is as though they sacrificed a burnt offering, a meal offering, a sin offering and a guilt offering. Rava [objected] saying: This [verse] says *for* the burnt offering, *for* the meal offering. [According to Resh Lakish's opinion] it should have said the burnt offering *and* the meal offering . . . Rava said: Anyone who engages in [the study of] Torah does not need a burnt offering, nor a meal offering, nor a sin offering, nor a guilt offering. [The repetitive use of the prefix *lamed* here is interpreted as meaning *lo*, "no."]

Rabbi Yitzchak said: Why is it written, "This is the teaching [*Torat*] of the burnt offering, the meal offering, the sin offering, the guilt offering . . ."? [In order to teach that] anyone who engages in the study of the sin offering is regarded as though he sacrificed a sin offering; anyone who engages in the study of the guilt offering is regarded as though he sacrificed a guilt offering. (*M'nachot* 110a)

אמר ריש לקיש, מאי דכתיב: (ויקרא ז') זאת התורה לעולה למנחה ולחטאת ולאשם? כל העוסק בתורה, כאילו הקריב עולה מנחה חטאת ואשם. אמר רבא: האי לעולה למנחה, עולה ומנחה מיבעי ליה אלא אמר רבא: כל העוסק בתורה, אינו צריך לא עולה (ולא חטאת) ולא מנחה ולא אשם. אמר רבי יצחק, מאי דכתיב: (ויקרא ו') זאת תורת החטאת וזאת תורת האשם? כל העוסק בתורת חטאת כאילו הקריב חטאת, וכל העוסק בתורת אשם כאילו הקריב אשם.

On one end of the spectrum, Rabbi Yitzchak suggests that study of a particular type of sacrifice is the equivalent of offering that specific sacrifice. For him, study and sacrifice are most closely linked when study parallels the sacrifices for which it serves as a substitute. On the other end of the spectrum, Rava suggests that there is no need to measure study against sacrifice—ours is a whole new world, and the study of Torah, regardless of its subject, replaces sacrifices and precludes a need for engaging with the memory of the sacrificial system at all.

While this particular *sugya* deals with the relationship between sacrifice and study, it nonetheless presents us with two conceptual frameworks that are equally helpful to us as we consider the relationship between sacrifice and prayer: prayer as replacement for sacrifice and prayer as substitution for sacrifice.

By replacement, I mean to suggest that prayer or study obviates the need for sacrifice and takes on the same value sacrifice once had. This replacement model completely severs the connection between sacrifice and prayer. Like Rava's position above, prayer in itself replaces sacrifices and is not reliant upon liturgical recollections of the sacrificial system.

One Talmudic example of this approach might be found in the rhetorical question posed in *Taanit* 2a, "What is the *avodah* of the heart?" דתניא לאהבה את ה' אלהיכם ולעבדו בכל לבבכם, איזו היא עבודה שהיא בלב-הוי אומר זו תפלה.
Drawing upon the words of the *Sh'ma*'s second paragraph, "If, then, you obey the commandments that I enjoin upon you this day, loving the Lord your God and serving Him with all your heart . . ." (Deut. 11:13) the Talmud states that it is prayer that is now the service of heart.

In contrast, by substitution I mean to suggest that prayer or study evokes the sacrifices themselves and reminds us that these words recall and represent the sacrificial service that can no longer be performed. These prayers or study texts serve as substitutes for the sacrifices themselves. This approach is demonstrated in BT *B'rachot* 26b:

> It has been taught also in accordance with R. Joshua b. Levi: Why did they say that the morning Tefillah could be said till midday? Because the regular morning sacrifice could be brought up to midday. R. Judah, however, says that it may be said up to the fourth hour because the regular morning sacrifice may be brought up to the fourth hour. And why did they say that the afternoon Tefillah can be said up to the evening? Because the regular afternoon offering can be brought up to the evening.

ותניא כוותיה דרבי יהושע בן לוי: מפני מה אמרו תפלת השחר עד חצות – שהרי תמיד של שחר קרב והולך עד חצות ורבי יהודה אומר: עד ארבע שעות, שהרי תמיד של שחר קרב והולך עד ארבע שעות. ומפני מה אמרו תפלת המנחה עד הערב – שהרי תמיד של בין הערבים קרב והולך עד הערב

When trying to delineate Rabbinic sources about prayer and sacrifice along this conceptual framework of replacement and substitution there is a great deal of ambiguity. Indeed, this is the case with the Rabbinic interpretations of one of the most widely cited texts about the relationship between sacrifice and prayer, Hosea 14:3:

> Take words with you and return to the Eternal. Say to God: Forgive all guilt and accept what is good; *we will pay the calves of our lips.*

קְחוּ עִמָּכֶם דְּבָרִים וְשׁוּבוּ אֶל־ה' אִמְרוּ אֵלָיו כָּל־תִּשָּׂא עָוֺן וְקַח־טוֹב וּנְשַׁלְּמָה פָרִים שְׂפָתֵינוּ׃

The end of this verse, *un'shalmah farim sefateinu*, which JPS translates as "instead of bulls, we will pay [the offering of] our lips," notes that the meaning of Hebrew is uncertain. There are subtle differences in interpretation found in various midrashim that could be understood to be reflective of our conceptual framework—prayer as substitution or as replacement. In *P'sikta D'Rav Kahana, Shuva* 24, Rabbi Akiba asks, "Who pays for those calves that were offered before You? Our lips in the prayers that we pray before You." (א"ר אבהו מי משלם אותם הפרים שהיינו מקריבים לפניך, שפתינו, בתפילה שאנו מתפללים לפניך.) The midrash asserts that our words and prayers are the equivalent of our offerings of old. They are now the equivalent of the calves that had been offered. Alternatively, in *Shir HaShirim Rabbah* 4:9, the midrash states, "What shall we pay *in place of* the calves and *in place of* the scapegoat? Our lips." (מה נשלם תחת פרים ותחת שעיר המשתלח שפתינו) Our words will serve as substitutions in place of the calves and other sacrifices that were once offered. They will be our offerings. In *P'sikta D'Rav Kahana*, our words *are* our offerings. They are a replacement. In *Shir HaShirim Rabbah*, our words are offered *in place of* those offerings. They are a substitution.

The *Musaf* Model

Our early Reform heritage already presents us with some models of how this "substitution model" might take hold in a postmodern context. Jakob Petuchowski demonstrated the complex relationship that has existed with regard to the *Musaf* Service and Reform liturgies.[10] While most of the European rituals retained some form of the *Musaf* Service, the liturgy needed to be adjusted to make it theologically in line with Reform sensibilities. Part of

THE CALVES OF OUR LIPS

the compelling reasons to maintain it had to do with the fact that, as with many traditional congregations, a critical mass of the congregation does not attend the earlier part of the service.

As religious reform in Europe began to take on the forms of a movement, the discussion of how to treat *Musaf* arises. In the 1884 Frankfort conference, an appointed Commission on Liturgy found themselves unable to decide decisively on whether or not to retain the *Musaf* Service.

One of the supporters of retaining the *Musaf* Service with references to the sacrifices was Abraham Adler, whom Petuchowski notes was regarded as a "radical reformer." Responding to the notion that the idea of sacrifice had become obsolete, Adler responds (as cited by Petuchowski),

> The idea of sacrifice must be an eternally true one, since we cannot and must not assume that, throughout the millennia, Judaism has retained a lie. There is a confusion between the idea itself and the form in which that idea was outwardly expressed. The idea of sacrifice is one of devotion, of the union of the finite individual with the Infinite, the submersion of the transitory in the eternal Source. As long as man himself still stood on the level of externality, he was in need of the external act, through which alone he achieved self-consciousness . . . Only when Judaism transcended the level of externality, did sacrifice become something abstractly external, and only then did the Prophets begin to fulminate against it. The idea then created for itself a new and more appropriate form, that of prayer. In that sense we must understand the Talmudic passage, *tephilloth keneged temidin tiqqenu* (the sacrifices found their counterpart in the prayers). [11]

Adler concludes with a statement that could serve as a basis for a twenty-first-century "substitution model" of prayers about sacrifice.

> *We cannot, therefore, become indifferent to the sacrificial cult, since, in it, we possess the original form of devotion. I, therefore, demand the retention of those liturgical passages which refer to the sacrificial cult—as a reminiscence.* On the other hand, the prayers for its restoration, about which we cannot be serious, are to be omitted.[12] (emphasis mine)

Petuchowski notes that Adler's recommendations for liturgical practice were adopted.

Petuchowski shows how these various Reform *Musaf* liturgies shift from preserving a memory of the sacrifices to those that deliberately sever such connections. Early nineteenth-century Reform liturgies include a *Musaf* Service that is contextualized as a *substitution* for the sacrifices they recalled. This is reflected in Adler's perspective above and became the prevalent approach to *Musaf* prayers. However, Geiger's prayer book of 1870 includes *Musaf* but shapes the liturgy in ways that see it as a *replacement*. The *Musaf* Service continued to be included, but once the theoretical basis had been eliminated from the prayer itself, it was only a matter of time before *Musaf* itself would be eliminated.

Apart from *Musaf*, one can find in earlier Reform prayer books other examples of the "substitution model" at play. In Einhorn's *Olat Tamid*, as in *Gates of Repentance*, a reference to the sacrificial element of Yom Kippur is unavoidable. Here we see ways in which the ancient rites can be unapologetically referenced and used as a metaphorical application to our own lives:

> Like this priest of old, we, too are called to this duty; our priestly service demandeth that we, to the fullest extent of our ability and opportunity, bring the tidings of peace and reconciliation unto all. We, too, must lead back upon the right path those that have gone astray, and honor Thee by keeping alive and deepening the consciousness that all the children of Abraham are bound together by the ties of the common responsibility to sanctify Thy name in the eyes of the world.[13]

Preserving the Power of the Sacrifice

In Reform liturgy, barring the exceptions noted above, we have almost entirely approached prayer as *replacement* for sacrifice rather than *substitution*. In doing so, the centrality of sacrifice has been muted and its memory deemed insignificant. In contrast, by embracing a model of substitution rather than replacement we open up a symbolic universe that greatly increases the significance of prayer.

The "post-modern turn" has renewed an interest in symbols and ritual. There is a greater openness toward the very experiences that were dismissed by previous generations as "primitive." There is a recognition that reason is the not the sole criteria for determining what can have religious meaning for us:

Obviously modern Jews can do as they please with the prayerbook without fear of sanction, but it is important that, if they make any changes, they do so for reasons which are very good indeed. Simply to remove the sacrificial readings because of a conception of "higher" and "lower" religion, which will not stand the test of scrutiny, is an injustice not only to one generation but to the generations which are heir to the fruits of this misconception.[14]

Approaching liturgy as a *substitution* for sacrifice, rather than a *replacement*, keeps the memory and symbolism of sacrifice alive. That memory and symbolism, in turn, expands the meaning and significance of our prayer life. The notion that prayer is *avodah sh'balev* (the sacrificial service of the heart) is only meaningful so far as one continues to understand what *avodah* itself once was. Once that connection is severed, the effect is a diminishment of the significance of prayer, a narrowing of the wide spectrum of meaning that prayer can have.

If a connection between sacrifice and prayer is maintained or reestablished, it offers vital ideas that can revive our spiritual lives. Prayer becomes an offering, a gift, something we deeply long to be received. The language of sacrifice in the context of prayer also reminds us that ours is a communal relationship with God, and that prayer too is not just about the individual, but about the collective. Furthermore, a connection between prayer and the ancient *korbanot* underscores the enormous gap that exists between ourselves and God, a needed counterpoint for us in a spiritual climate in which God is increasingly presented exclusively as "our friend" or "our conscience." When we see our prayers as a substitution for sacrifice—on the *Yamim Noraim* and throughout the year—we assert that every home and every synagogue is a Temple, and that each Jew is a priest.

Once we construct prayer as a *replacement*, rather than as a *substitution* for sacrifice, we diminish our spiritual vocabulary, lose central frames of reference, and allow a locus of Jewish memory throughout the ages to disappear. Restoring this connection allows such words and memories to contribute a myriad of ideas we need in our prayer life now more than ever before.

Notes

1. Paragraph 5 of the Pittsburgh Platform states: "We consider ourselves no longer a nation, but a religious community, and therefore

expect neither a return to Palestine, nor a sacrificial worship under the sons of Aaron, nor the restoration of any of the laws concerning the Jewish state."

2. The traditional wording includes the words, "Restore the service to Your most holy House, and accept in love and favor the fire-offerings of Israel and their prayer." Jonathan Sacks, *The Koren Siddur* (Jerusalem: Koren Publishing, 2009). Compare with *Mishkan T'filah* (and previous Reform prayer books), where the words *v'hashev et haavodah lid'vir beitecha v'ishei Yisrael* are omitted, but creatively, the words remaining are joined to make one coherent statement.
3. The diverse approaches to *Musaf* in Reform liturgies are explored below.
4. For example, Num. 28:9–15 for Shabbat Rosh Chodesh; Num. 29:1–6 for Rosh HaShanah morning; Num. 29:7–11 for Yom Kippur morning; Num. 29, selected verses for each day of Sukkot; Num. 28, selected verses for each day of Passover, and for Shavuot.
5. *Union Prayer Book II* and *Gates of Repentance* substitute selected verses from *Parashat Nitzavim*, Deut. 29:9–30:20.
6. For the absence of ritual hand-washing and salting of bread, see *On the Doorposts of Your House* (New York: CCAR, 2010), 62. In *Gates of Shabbat* (New York: CCAR, 1991), 28–29, although the ritual blessings are not included in the liturgy itself, both the mitzvah of hand-washing and the custom of salting bread are explained and presented as an option.
7. The only official American Reform liturgy exclusively for Tishah B'Av is the work of Herbert Bronstein, in *The Five Scrolls* (New York: CCAR, 1984). *Gates of Prayer: The New Union Prayer Book* (New York: CCAR, 1975) includes a liturgy that can be used interchangeably for Yom HaShoah or Tishah B'Av.
8. Herbert Bronstein, "Yom Kippur Worship: A Missing Center?" *CCAR Journal* (Summer 2004): 7–15.
9. See Moshe Halbertal, *On Sacrifice* (Princeton: Princeton University Press, 2012).
10. Jakob Petuchowski, *Prayerbook Reform in Europe: The Liturgy of European Liberal and Reform Judaism* (New York: World Union for Progressive Judaism, 1968). See chapter 9, "Reform of the Musaph Service."
11. Ibid., page 243-244. Petuchowski cites *Protokolle und Aktenstrücke der zweiten Rabbiner-Versammlung,* p. 382.
12. Ibid.
13. David Einhorn, *Olat Tamid: Book of Prayers for Jewish Congregations* (1913). "Services for the New Year's Day and The Day of Atonement," p. 185..
14. Richard Rubenstein, *After Auschwitz: Radical Theology and Contemporary Judaism* (New York: Macmillan, 1966), 108.

"Baavur Sheani Noder Tzedakah Baado"

Margaret Moers Wenig

Thoughts about *Yizkor* and mourning, *Yizkor* and memory, *Yizkor* and mortality, *Yizkor* and the living, *Yizkor* and Yom Kippur, and *Yizkor* and God.

Mourning

Mournful music is common during *Yizkor* services, at least in Reform synagogues, where *Yizkor* also often ends with or includes the recitation of Mourners' *Kaddish*.

A mournful tone to *Yizkor* rings true for many for whom mourning does not end, even years after a loved one has died. As attested by these mourners, the pain from some losses never fully heals: I have learned one has "to honor the part of oneself that's irreparable. Not to apologize for it, disguise it, not to try to mend it in any seamless way."[1] "The break from now on is an inescapable part of who I am, perhaps the inescapable part. Hasn't it become my essential definition, my central fact: I loved a man who died?"[2] "If you ask me whether this . . . [feels] like closure, I'll tell you what I've come to believe: Closure is bullshit."[3]

A mournful tone to *Yizkor* rings true to be sure. But do those who still mourn *need Yizkor* to afford them an opportunity to express their grief? I think not. I think for most who are still grieving it is a fairly private process for which no ritual prompting is needed.

Memory

We call *Yizkor* the "Memorial Service." What does it mean to remember those who have died? What does it mean to remember?

MARGARET MOERS WENIG (NY84) is instructor in Liturgy and Homiletics at HUC-JIC/New York since 1985 and rabbi emerita of Beth Am, The People's Temple, New York. She thanks Helen Blumenthal, Daniel Fleshler, Rabbi Lawrence A. Hoffman, Ph.D., Marion Marx, Elizabeth Lorris Ritter, Steven Rosenberg, Liba Rubenstein, Monica Saez, Ph.D., and Rabbi Elaine Zecher for feedback to, and in some cases, trenchant criticism of, an earlier draft.

Neurologists, who study the effects of trauma or neglect on the development of children, argue that "early influences can literally leave imprints on the brain that last a lifetime."[4] "Memories make us. . . . What we experience first filters what comes afterwards."[5] Even people whom we have known later in life, even people whose effect was wholly positive, may leave indelible impressions on us. Some people we'll never forget.

> My friends are dying [wrote Grace Paley z"l]
> well we're old   it's natural
> . . . but this is not what I meant to
> tell you   I wanted to say that
> my friends were dying but have now
> become absent   the word dead is correct
> but inappropriate
> I have not taken their names out of
> conversation gossip   political argument
> my telephone book or card index in
> whatever alphabetical or contextual
> organizer I can stop any evening of
> the lonesome week at Claiborne   Bercovici
> Vernarelli   Deming and rest a moment
> on their seriousness as artists   workers
> their excitement as political actors in the
> streets of our cities or in their workplaces
> the vigiling   fasting   praying in or out
> of jail   their lightheartedness which floated
> above the year's despair
> their courageous sometime hilarious
> disobedience before the state's official
> servants   their fidelity to the idea that
> it is possible with only a little extra anguish
> to live in this world   at an absolute minimum
> loving brainy sexual energetic redeemed[6]

I, for one, light two *Yizkor* candles for my parents, but those two candles already stand for, and will one day stand for, even more of the dozen who have helped to shape me, including teachers and members of the congregation I served,[7] some dead and some, thank God, still living. I think of the older synagogue member, who never had children of her own, quietly cradling and soothing every baby wheeled in through the doors. I think of the young man, whose parents were long dead, who visited every hospitalized or homebound elderly member. I think of the mentoring I received from the first president with whom I worked. They continue to affect me to this day. I think of the social studies teacher who, in 1967, suspended her curriculum to explain to us the war in the Middle East and melt the ice that had frozen relationships between the Syrian, Lebanese, and Jewish members of our class.[8] I think of the high school math teacher[9] who testified to me about the love of Jesus, impelling me to search for God's love in Judaism that was always there but never discussed. I think of the college history professor who taught us to ask of every secondary source: "How do you know?"[10] I think of the rabbinical school sage who taught his students to test every theological proposition against "the toughest case."[11] I think of my spouse who regularly interrupted my intense concentration on whatever I was cooking to take me in her arms and, singing, dance with me around the kitchen floor. In addition to my parents, these people have also left their imprints on my brain. They, too, have shaped the person I've become and will remain. If they have died, their legacy did not die with them and when the others die, their legacies will not die when their bodies give out.

And yet remembering those who have affected us is not simply a process of opening a window and looking through it back in time. For memory doesn't simply "equal events plus time.... Time doesn't act as a fixative, rather as a solvent."[12] "Narrative memory is not simply a videotape of experiences that can be replayed with accuracy."[13] We "cut and splice the magnetic tape on which our lives are recorded."[14] Yes "memories make us" but "we make memories."[15] "What we feel now can influence what we recall from the past. When we retrieve a memory from where it is stored in the brain, just as when we open a Word file, we automatically open it to 'edit' and when we 'save' the memory again and place it back into storage, we may well have modified it."[16]

Yizkor, then, cannot be about simply remembering people who have died. For the act of remembering is more complicated than that.

The Living

Memories come to us. We may be unconsciously driven by them as we are driven by a *yetzer hatov* or a *yetzer hara*. And yet, we are held accountable as if we had free will. *T'shuvah* is, in part, a process of gaining, little by little, greater mastery over our inclinations, including those present inclinations driven by memories of the ways in which people have treated us in the past.

How can we even begin to gain such mastery? It took me six months to clean out my parents' house after my mother died: many trips to the library to donate books, many trips to Goodwill to donate clothes, many trips to the town dump to unload recyclables, an auctioneer to buy furniture, a moving company to put things in storage, and eight dumpsters to fill with things that simply crumbled in my hands. And boxes of things to save: personal papers from seventy years of life and even from previous generations—many I'd never seen—with great emotional and/or historical significance; and a large envelope with the words "For Maggie only" written in my mother's hand.

Cleaning the house, painting it, and readying it for rental and eventual sale was a monumental task, a part-time job for six months. When the job was finished and I'd handed over the keys to the tenants, I came home and fell, satisfied, into a deep sleep. That very night my mother appeared in my dream, irate. "Now that you have rented my house," she complained, "where am I supposed to live?" In a moment, my pride in a difficult job well done was deflated.

In life, I don't recall ever arguing with my mother's relentless criticisms of me. But in the dream I talked back, saying: "But, Mom, you've been dead for six months. How was I supposed to know that you would come back and need a place to live?"

My mother was not warm or affectionate, at least not after tragedy had hardened her. When I was very young, however, she used to read to me at bedtime. And I remember well the books she read. Among them: *Winnie the Pooh*. Last year, missing her terribly, I looked for recordings of Pooh. I found one in which Judy Dench plays the narrator! Now, I sometimes listen to the recording in bed at night as if the loving part of my mother is once again reading me to sleep.

During *Yizkor*, we do not have time to compose long eulogies in our heads. If we give ourselves over to memories, they are by necessity brief: sound bites, excerpts, fragments. Not dissimilar to the ways in which we must memorialize our loved ones when we choose what to inscribe on their tombstones. With what final words do we choose to remember a loved one whose body has been returned to dust?

In Eastern Europe there was a custom of engraving a symbol of the deceased's trade on his tombstone, or, if the deceased had been a *kohein*, two hands in the position of priestly blessing might have been engraved. Hundreds of years following a person's death, those symbols may be the only way he or she is remembered.

My father was many things, a labor lawyer, an arbitrator, a teacher of labor law, a less than admirable husband, a father whose parenting was hampered by depression, but who, when well, made us laugh. Sailing was his greatest pleasure and source of peace. On his tombstone we chose to engrave his own drawing of a sailboat. My grandmother was a tyrant as a mother, a bitter wife, a doting grandmother, and a serious painter. Before we gave up her apartment, we found all of her paint brushes, many of them decades old and well used, as clean as the day she purchased them, and dozens of rolled-up tubes of paint carefully organized in her art closet. On her headstone we engraved my daughter's drawing of three of my grandmother's own paint brushes and a half-used tube of her oil paint. My mother was a pioneer in her field of law. And we mentioned that on her stone. But she cared a great deal about her home and, while she never fulfilled her dream of creating a loving and safe home for her family, she always filled her home with fresh flowers that she arranged herself. When my daughter was young, she made a sketch of a cut glass vase my mother had just filled with flowers. And for over ten years my mother kept that sketch taped to her bathroom mirror. It was that sketch that we engraved on my mother's stone.

Memories make us. And we make memories. *Yizkor*, I believe, is about making memories.

Mortality

For some, burying a loved one, erecting a tombstone, reciting *Yizkor*, focuses their attention on their own mortality, a feared or even a welcomed fate, as suggested by this widow's engraving on her husband's stone:

> Mrs. Beranek . . . had engraved on the monument not only Mr. Beranek's name and dates but her own name and birth date, followed by an eloquent hyphen waiting in the stone like a held breath.[17]

Is *Yizkor* on Yom Kippur a time for the living to focus our attention on our own mortality? Some *machzorim* have chosen to fill their Yom Kippur *Yizkor* liturgies with words such as these from the *Gates of Repentance*:

> We are feeble. We live always on the brink of death. Scarcely ushered into life, we begin our journey to the grave . . . our fondest hopes are buried with us.[18]

> The number of our days may be many or few; yet vain toil fills their span, for it is soon ended, and we fly away.[19]

Even Lewandowski's musical setting of *Enosh*, which opens many a Reform *Yizkor* service, concludes *not* with "*Chesed Adonai mei olam v'ad olam*," that text's final promise of God's everlasting love, but rather with a reprise of the text's *opening* words: "Our days are like grass. We shoot up like flowers that fade and die as the chill wind passes over them. And they are no more. *V'lo yakirenu od*. [Not to be remembered ever again.]"[20] sounded with notes of doom. The music is sublime, but is "*Lo yakirenu od*" the right note to sound for *Yizkor*?[21]

There is a time and a place for our expressions of humility, for acknowledgments of our minuteness in the grand scheme of things, our relative powerlessness, the futility of some of our schemes. But is *Yizkor* on Yom Kippur that time? Isn't *Yizkor* precisely the time in which we consider the *lasting impact* people have had on us, the significance of their lives, the legacy they have left behind? Should *Yizkor* liturgies express the notion that our lives are futile because they end in death? I think not.

On many a Jewish gravestone you'll see carved an open book. It's *Sefer HaChayim*. On Rosh HaShanah and Yom Kippur we pray to be inscribed "*b'sefer chayim b'rachah v'shalom, ufarnasah tovah*."[22] That's clearly a reference to an earthly life in which we have to earn *parnasah*. But some use the term *Sefer Chayim* to refer to the Book of Eternal Life, a book from which no one's name is omitted; a book we don't have to plead to be inscribed in because we ourselves inscribe our own names on its pages. "*V'tiftach et sefer hazichronot umei eilav yikarei v'chotam yad kol adam bo*." [God will open the Book of Memories and from its pages will be read the signature of every human being.][23] We inscribe our legacy in *Sefer HaZichronot* with our own words and our own deeds *as others have inscribed their words and deeds, on our very brains.*

Is *Yizkor* about the futility of human endeavors, all of which evaporate with death? I think not. I think *Yizkor* is, rather, about what remains.

Yom Kippur

Yizkor is about what remains. But what remains of the dead is not fixed and unchanging, as what is embodied by the living is, hopefully, not fixed and unchanging.

Yizkor is original to Yom Kippur. Some say we call this day Yom Hakkipurim, in the plural, because both the living and the dead are in need of *kapara*, not infrequently from each other.

Maimonides is clear that the living may need absolution, even if those we have wronged have since died:

> If you sin against another and he dies before you have had a chance to repay him and ask his forgiveness, you bring ten Israelites to the dead person's grave as witnesses and say before them: I have sinned in such and such a way against so and so. If the deceased has heirs, you pay your debt to the heirs. If the deceased has no heirs, you pay your debt to the *bet din* and confess.[24]

A Chasidic tale imagines the other side of the dynamic in which a dead husband seeks forgiveness from his surviving spouse (or his widow *needs* to forgive her deceased husband):

> In the night after the seven day mourning for Reb Abraham the Angel, his wife had a dream. She saw a vast hall and in it thrones, set in a semicircle. On each throne sat one of the great. A door opened, and . . . Abraham, her husband, entered. "Friends, my wife is angry with me because in my earthly life I lived apart from her. She is right and therefor I must obtain her forgiveness." His wife cried out: "With all my heart, I forgive you." And [she] awoke comforted.[25]

Note, in both cases, these acts of confession or pleas for forgiveness are made in public before a minyan, a *beit din*, or an angelic court. That I believe is, or should be, the purpose of a reciting *Yizkor*, in a *kahal,* on Yom Kippur: to make a public pledge to do *tzedakah* on behalf of the deceased, for the *kapara* of the deceased or for our own *kapara.*

Thus many *Yizkor* formulas begin: "*Yizkor Elohim et nishmat* ____ *baavur sheani noder/noderet tzedakah baado/baadah . . .*"[26] Why was this phrase omitted from some *Yizkor* liturgies? Out of discomfort with the notion that a person may face judgment following death and that the verdict could possibly be improved by deeds the living perform on the deceased's behalf. I am not uncomfortable with those notions. But even if you are, consider this: Did not our relationship with those who raised us, and with partners who loved and/or deserted us, not shape, to a large extent, the ways in which we can, do, or cannot relate to others to this day? Do not even deceased parents or spouses, or the loss of children continue to influence us for good and for bad, in complicated and often unconscious ways?

Yom Kippur is the cathartic climax to (though not the final end of) a long period of repentance, during which we examine our words, our thoughts, and our deeds and endeavor to change them for the better, if only incrementally. We work to improve our relationships with our peers, with those who depend on us and with those upon whom we depend, including, I believe, the dead. For, isn't it often difficult to separate our relationships with the living from our relationships with the dead?

Earlier American *Yizkor* liturgies were more affirmative about the continued presence of the dead even in their absence, the ongoing connection between the dead and the living. Perhaps this is what Moses meant when he said to the Israelites, "*Atem nitzavim hayom kulchem*" [You are all standing here this day], even "*et asher einenu po imanu hayom*" [those who are not present with us this day].[27] People can be physically absent but still very much present. These earlier liturgies, some in German, included prayers *addressed directly to the deceased,*[28] prayers of gratitude, prayers asking for the deceased to continue to look out and care—even intercede—for the living,[29] prayers looking forward to being reunited with the deceased,[30] petitions for forgiveness from the deceased,[31] prayers hoping to live a life worthy of the values imparted or examples set by the deceased.

If today we recite, "*Yizkor Elohim et nishmat* _____ *baavur sheani noderet tzedakah baadah,*" we might mean:

May God take note of _____ for whom I pledge _____ so that her sins may be diminished and her merits magnified.
Or . . . for whom I pledge ____ so that *my* sins may be diminished and my merits magnified.
Or . . . for whom I pledge _____ as an expression of gratitude for all that she has taught me.
Or . . . for whom I pledge _____ so that their deaths not be entirely in vain.
Or . . . for whom I pledge ____ so that I may be worthy of the gift they have bequeathed to me.

And if we are able, we might add:

I hereby forgive _____ for the sin he/she committed against me.
I hereby ask _____ to forgive me for the sin I committed against him/her.

I think that reciting *Yizkor* on Yom Kippur is less about mourning, mortality, or memory and more about connection, continuity, and change.

God

Is *Yizkor* addressed to God, or, as some liturgies render it, are we, in effect, saying: "I remember . . ."? It is, I believe, an intersection of the two.

When we recite "*Yizkor Elohim et nishmat* _____" are we uttering a petition? "*May* God remember (or notice) the soul of_____"? Does the God we imagine ever *forget* what's written in *Sefer HaZichronot*? Archival photo prints last "forever." But "forever," in this case, means for two hundred years. Two hundred years is not a long time compared with the durability of other works of art and artifacts, manuscripts, engravings, and inscriptions in pottery or stone. And two hundred years is but a moment in God's sight. What's written by a person in *Sefer HaZichronot* is not written in ink that fades or on paper that deteriorates with time. *Yizkor Elohim* can't be a petition, *May* God remember, may God take note,[32] *unless* we are asking God to take note of something that hasn't happened yet: namely, a *change* in our relationship with the deceased, a change in the deceased, a change in ourselves that we are about to attempt to bring about; for example, "By pledging and then doing this act of *tzedakah*, I hope to extend the reach of my mother's legacy. By pledging and doing this act of *tzedakah*, I hope to open my grandmother's heart a little more in forgiveness. By pledging and doing this act of *tzedakah*, I hope to add to my father's merit to tip the scales a bit from his bad deeds to his good deeds. By pledging and doing this act of *tzedakah*, I hope to resurrect in my life a person from whom I have been estranged. By pledging and doing this act of *tzedakah*, I hope, little by little, to externalize and thus internalize my lost one's love and, perhaps, feel her presence more and more and grieve her absence less and less."

"*Yizkor Elohim et nishmat* _____*baavur sheani noderet tzedakah baadah* . . ." May God notice how the soul or the legacy *of the deceased* will change, if ever so slightly, through this act of *tzedakah*; and may God notice how *my* own soul, my inner life, and my outer life will change, if ever so slightly, through this act of *tzedakah*. For with this pledge and act of *tzedakah*, I open the files inscribed and stored in my brain and *edit* them before resaving them."

Yizkor on Yom Kippur is, I believe, not about human frailty or the futility of human endeavors. *Yizkor* on Yom Kippur is about the power of others to affect us, about our power to affect others, about the power of the dead and the living to continue to affect each other. *Yizkor* on Yom Kippur is, I believe, not simply about remembering the dead, but about attempting to affect *change* in our relationships with the dead and thus to affect change in ourselves and in our relationships with those who are still among the living.

Notes

1. Mark Doty, *Heaven's Coast: A Memoir* (New York: Harper Perennial, 1996), 287. (Note: Thank you to my spouse, Rabbi Sharon Kleinbaum, for giving me this book while we were staying in Provincetown.)
2. Ibid., 286.
3. Elizabeth McCracken, *An Exact Replica of a Figment of My Imagination: A Memoir* (New York: Little Brown and Company, 2008), 103.
4. Bruce D. Perry and Maia Szalavitz, *The Boy Who Was Raised as a Dog: And Other Stories from a Child Psychiatrist's Notebook: What Traumatized Children Can Teach Us About Loss, Love and Healing* (New York: Basic Books, 2006),19, citing the work of Dr. Seymour Levine, neuroendocrinologist, who "conducted pioneering work on the impact of stress during early life on the development of the brain."
5. Ibid., 156.

6. Grace Paley, from the poem "Sisters" in the collection of poems entitled *Fidelity* (New York: Farrar, Straus and Giroux, 2008), 78–79.
7. Beth Am, The People's Temple in New York, New York, where I served as rabbi from 1984–2000 and where, since 2002, I have returned as rabbi for the High Holy Days and now for a few Shabbatot a year.
8. Mrs. Sylvia Gordon at the United Nations International School.
9. Mr. Alan Jolly at Staples High School in Westport, Connecticut
10. Professor Jacob Neusner, Brown University.
11. Professor Eugene Borowitz, HUC-JIR/New York.
12. Julian Barnes, *The Sense of an Ending* (New York: Knopf, 2001), 69.
13. Perry and Szalavitz, *Boy Who Was Raised as a Dog*, 156.
14. Barnes, *Sense of an Ending*, 143.
15. Perry and Szalavitz, *Boy Who Was Raised as a Dog*, 156.
16. This quotation has been excerpted from a longer passage in ibid.
17. Patricia Hampl, *I Could Tell You Stories: Sojourns in the Land of Memory* (New York: WW Norton and Co.,1999), 69. (Note: Thank you to Rabbi Stacy Offner for recommending this book to me.)
18. *The Gates of Repentance*, 479–80.
19. Ibid., 482
20. Text in ibid., 477.
21. Interestingly, *Gates of Repentance* does not translate these Hebrew words into English. But worshipers who understand the Hebrew know what they mean. Other examples of this expression of futility and emphasis on mortality abound: Look at what *Gates of Repentance* has included and what it has omitted from Psalm 8: Included:"When I behold Your heavens, the work of Your fingers, the moon and stars that You have established, what are we that You are mindful of us, what are we mortals that You consider us?" (p. 479) Omitted: "But You have made . . . [mortal man] *m'at mei-Elohim* [little less than divine] and adorned him with *kavod v'hadar* [glory and majesty]." *Yizkor* in *Gates of Repentance* includes these words that appear elsewhere in the *machzor*: "All the heroes are as nothing in Your sight. The men of renown as though they never existed. The wise as though without knowledge. The intelligent as though they lacked insight. Most of their actions are worthless in Thy sight. Their entire life is a fleeting breath. Man is not far above beast, for all is vanity. But when those same words appear in *N'ilah*, they are immediately followed by: "*Ata hivdalta enosh meirosh* . . ." [But, from the first you singled out mortal man and considered him worthy to stand in Your presence . . .]. Philip Birnbaum, trans., *High Holiday Prayer Book* (New York: Hebrew Publishing Company, 1951), 1005; *Gates of Repentance*, 520–21.

22. This petition is inserted in the final blessing of every *Amidah* for all of Rosh HaShanah and Yom Kippur.
23. From the *piyut Un'taneh Tokef*, recited, in the Reform tradition, during the morning *Amidah* and in other Ashkenazi traditions, during the Reader's Repetition of the *Musaf Amidah*.
24. Maimonides, *Mishneh Torah, The Laws of Repentance*, 2:11.
25. Buber, *Tales of the Hasidim*, vol. 1, 117, quoted in Simcha Paull Raphael, *Jewish Views of the Afterlife* (Northvale, NJ: Jason Aronson Inc., 1994), 353.
26. Birnbaum, *High Holiday Prayer Book*, 731. "*Baavur* . . ." is also included in the *Yizkor* formula that's recited at the end of each of the three Festivals. There the pledge is understood to echo the offerings Ancient Israelites brought to the Temple on each of those Festivals.
27. From the Torah reading for Yom Kippur morning according to Reform *minhag*.
28. "What is perhaps most surprising of all is that the climactic private prayers in the vernacular, German, or English, were as a rule addressed to the departed themselves." Eric L. Friedland, *Were Our Mouths Filled With Song: Studies in Liberal Jewish Liturgy* (Cincinnati: Hebrew Union College Press, 1997),147; e.g., in the High Holy Day prayer books edited by Leo Merzbacher (ibid., 148), David Einhorn (ibid., 151), Isaac Meyer Wise (ibid., 156), Adolph Huebsch (ibid., 159), J. Leonard Levy (ibid., 170).
29. Ibid., 160, 161, 163.
30. Ibid., 151, 158, 160.
31. Ibid., 161.
32. *ZCHR* [remember] and *PKD* [take note of] are sometimes used interchangeably. See Lawrence A. Hoffman, "Does God Remember? A Liturgical Theology of Memory" (unpublished manuscript).

Visions for a New/Old Reform Yizkor Service

Donald B. Rossoff

If there are any holidays that bring Jews to synagogue more than any others, they are Rosh HaShanah and Yom Kippur. And if there is any one element during these Awesome Days that engages more Jews during this sacred season, it is the *Yizkor*/Memorial Service for Yom Kippur. The question that our temple office is asked the most in the days before Yom Kippur is: "What time does *Yizkor* begin?" From the beginning of the Yom Kippur Afternoon Service to its end, the number of filled seats in our synagogue nearly doubles. And in the minutes following *Yizkor*, the number of occupied seats more than halves. For reasons known perhaps only to theologians, sociologists, psychiatrists, and thanatologists, the *Yizkor* Service is a Jewish/spiritual/psychological magnet of the highest order.

 Having lost both of my parents as a young child, I have attended more than my share of *Yizkor* services. It is no surprise, then, that this service as historically and currently observed within Reform Judaism would be of heightened interest to this particular orphan. I wanted to have a better sense of where this service came from, how it has developed within the tradition and within our own movement, and what its theological, spiritual, and emotional underpinnings were. Were there elements of the service as they have been or might be that might inform and deepen our experience of remembering, honoring, and sanctifying the memories of our dear departed, regardless of the particular liturgy we used?

 My initial sense of *Yizkor* was based on my experiences with the *Yizkor* services in the *Union Prayerbook II*, *Gates of Prayer*, *Gates of Repentance*, and, to a smaller degree in *Mishkan T'filah*. That understanding was expanded through study of the *Yizkor/Hazkarat*

DONALD B. ROSSOFF has been a rabbi at Temple B'nai Or in Morristown, New Jersey, since 1990. He is the author of *The Perfect Prayer* (URJ) and composer (with Cantor Bruce Benson) of "Adonai Li" (Transcontinental Music).

HaN'shamot Service in both its traditional expression[1] as well as in earlier Reform iterations. And, of course, my appreciation of *Yizkor* has been illumined by years of being with and learning from family, friends, and congregants who have faced the most profound of losses.

More and more, I saw the power the *Yizkor* Memorial Service has to be deeply meaningful, comforting, consoling, cathartic, healing, and perhaps even transformative. Trying to think creatively, I began to explore a flow of a service and modalities of worship that, regardless of whatever liturgies we use, might provide for the worshiping community a coherent and meaningful "journey." These ideas are rooted in practices and concepts from our tradition, which includes our rich Reform tradition, which, more than any other Jewish expression, has taken the *Yizkor* moment and the opportunities it offers most seriously and creatively.

I. Background on Reform *Yizkor* Services

Although special memorial prayers, such as *Yizkor, Av Harachamim,* and *Hazkarat HaN'shamot,* have long been part of the traditional liturgy for the Festivals and Yom Kippur, the expanded *Yizkor* service as experienced by most North American Jews (Reform, Conservative, modern Orthodox) is, in large part, a creation of Reform Judaism. As Prof. Larry Hoffman points out:

> The Memorial Service is distinctively ours . . . Though rooted in memorial prayers that reach back a few centuries, "*Yizkor*" (as it was known) was at best a tiny interlude at the end of the Morning Service, by the time the Reform Movement was born. But Reform Jews were convinced of the merit of a deeper experience of memorializing the dead on Yom Kippur. So they granted the Memorial Service its own structural autonomy, an idea that has since been adopted by Conservative and Orthodox Jews as well.[2]

The first such liturgy was found in the first *Gebetbuch* of the first Reform Temple in Hamburg in 1819.[3] While the historic trend in our movement has been to shorten the traditional liturgy to fit our needs and proclivities, this trend was reversed when it came to the Memorial Service for Yom Kippur. When compared with the "bare-bone" traditional *Yizkor/Hazkarat HaN'shamot* Service following the Torah reading on Yom Kippur morning, Reform

Yizkor services (known by various names), in their European and especially American expressions, have incorporated many more prayers, traditional and original, as well as medieval *piyutim*, and an expanded cantorial/choral repertoire.[4] By and large, each of these services built on those that proceeded, while addressing the historical experience and perceived needs of their particular generation.[5]

What this said to me was that the Reform *Yizkor* Service, both in content, and to a large degree, structure, presents a wide open field in which we have the opportunity to reenvision a meaningful and beautiful worship experience that will speak to our own historical and personal experience and needs.

II. Possible Elements

As we have received it, there are certain elements typically found in Reform *Yizkor* services for Yom Kippur. These include:

- Readings on the universality and inevitability of death
- Presentation, either through the spoken word or through musical renditions, of particular psalms, including Psalms 23, 121, and 90
- Remembrance of Jewish martyrs
- Individual remembrance of one's family members who have passed on, minimally using the actual *Yizkor* prayer
- Public reading of the names of those who have died during the past year
- Recitation or chanting of the *El Malei* (although this has varied from community to community)
- Recitation of *Kaddish* (not a part of the traditional *Yizkor* liturgy)

There are, however, other concepts and thematic elements undergirding or embedded within *Yizkor* that could be explored more deeply and perhaps reimagined in a way that might speak to our own generation and those that follow. These include:

1. Belief in immortality
2. The dead need *kaparah*
3. Pledging צדקה\גמילות חסדים in memory of the dead
4. Readings addressed to the departed
5. *Yizkor* as catharsis

6. Learning history through the martyrs
7. Jewish transcendence

1. Belief in Immortality

The cornerstone of the traditional memorial prayers, *Yizkor*, *Hazkarat HaN'shamot*, *Av HaRachamim*, and *El Malei*, is the presumption of the "soul's" continued existence after the death of the body. While it is possible to read any of these prayers in a less literal, more metaphoric way, it would be like swimming upstream in the face of a powerful opposing current, generated both by the words themselves as well as by the desire by many of our worshipers in that moment to believe that there is something still existent that God can remember and bind up in the bonds of (eternal) life.

Luckily, Reform Judaism enables us to swim with, not against, the current, and affirm the "eternality" or immortality of the soul. Irrespective of any individual rabbi's personal beliefs, CCAR platforms, from Pittsburgh to Pittsburgh, have consistently affirmed, in differing ways, that "the spirit within us is eternal" (1999) (i.e., that there is some sort of continued existence beyond death). Yet as consistently as our platforms have affirmed the concept of immortality, this affirmation has inconsistently, hesitantly, and only sporadically been given expression in our liturgical publications, the literature in which our theology is most effectively embodied and promulgated.

I think this approach needs to be rethought, especially as we contemplate creating the one worship moment when memory and hope most naturally converge. In the *Yizkor* moment, we have an opportunity to express what we say we believe in ways that will bring a modicum of understanding, comfort, and hope. Inquiring minds and hurting souls want to know. It may be enough to say that we believe that there is something, not nothing; and perhaps that, in its simplest form, is all we can say. Even though we already affirm in our liturgies that "the world to come ... is our sure inheritance and our everlasting portion,"[6] we admit that "beyond the gate ... all is darkness to our mortal sight,"[7] "hidden ... by an impenetrable veil."[8] But there are poems and readings—a small number of which are scattered in our various liturgies—that express this understanding in ways that are affirmative, beautiful, and comforting. Some of these writings are learned and lofty (as those just quoted), while others use concrete image and metaphor to give the concept a warm overcoat.[9]

And since there is no unanimity as to what "immortality of the soul" means, and since worshipers think, feel, conceptualize, and believe in so many different ways, the use of a *Mishkan T'filah*–like, multi-option format could be very effective in presenting alternative ways through which we can affirm something, not nothing.

2. The Dead Need *Kaparah*

The belief that the dead are in need of *kaparah* (atonement/forgiveness/absolution), while largely foreign to our sensibility, is in fact the major linchpin that connects the recitation of the *Yizkor/Hazkarat HaN'shamot* prayers with *Yom HaKippurim*. One of the traditional interpretations of the plural form of *Yom HaKippurim* (lit. Day of Atonements) is that the Holy Day atones for both the living and for the dead.[10]

כַּפֵּר לְעַמְּךָ יִשְׂרָאֵל אֲשֶׁר־פָּדִיתָ — דברים כא:ח
כפר לעמך: אלו החיים.
אשר פדית: אלו המתים מלמד שהמתים צריכי׳ כפרה
— ספרי פרשת שופטים פיסקא סז

Absolve Your people Israel whom You have redeemed.
(Deut. 21:8)

Absolve Your people Israel: these are the living . . .
Whom You have redeemed: these are the dead, which teaches that the dead need atonement.
(*Sifrei, Shoftim* 67)

I doubt that any of us would advocate belief in an after-life system in which the souls of the departed are being punished or simply not enjoying the heavenly bliss they otherwise might have and are thus in need of postmortem forgiveness via vicarious atonement. However, I believe that there are ways in which these concepts could be fruitfully utilized. First, there is the tradition of making ongoing commitments in memory of the dead, as discussed below in section 3. Second, and addressing the concept of *kaparah* more directly, we recognize that there are many among us for whom the forgiving of and reconciling with departed dear ones—not by God but by us—might be desirable and even possible. But this requires providing for moments of intimate connection between the mourner and the mourned, as discussed in section 4.

3. Pledging צדקה\גמילות חסדים in Memory of the Dead

From a traditional point of view, one of the ways in which the dead can earn *kaparah* and better their portion in the next world is by having the living perform *mitzvot* on their behalf, specifically *tzedakah* and *g'milut chasadim*. This is why some of the traditional prayers include a pledge (בלי נדר) made in memory of the deceased to advance the cause of their soul in עולם הבא.

> נהגו לידור צדקות ביוה"כ בעד המתים
> ומזכירין נשמותיהם דהמתי ג"כ יש להם כפרה ביה"כ (מרדכי):
> —שלחן ערוך אורח חיים סימן תרכא:ו

"It was customary to contribute charity on Yom Kippur on behalf of the departed" [Isserles, quoting the Mordechai, adds the comment,] "And we make mention of the names of the departed souls, since they also obtain atonement [absolution?] on the Day of Atonement."

(*Shulchan Aruch, Orech Chaim*, 621:6)

Making—and then fulfilling—a pledge to do a *mitzvah* in memory of the departed is but one way that our dear ones live on in the immortality of their influence in our lives and, through us, in the world. We do have elements of this in our liturgy already (e.g., how we aspire to live "as, in their higher moments, they themselves wished to live").[11] But beyond whatever wishes they might have had in those precious higher moments, we could take a cue from the tradition and, creatively and prayerfully, point our people in a more concrete direction (e.g., giving *tzedakah* in memory of their dear one).[12] Acts of *tzedakah* and *g'milut chasadim*, while perhaps not atoning for the dead, keep their memory and their influence alive. We may have a different understanding than our traditionally believing coreligionists of how צדקה תציל ממות, but I think we believe it with equal conviction.

4. Readings Addressed to the Departed

In 1855, Rabbi Leo Merzbacher introduced a new concept into the Memorial Service in his *Order of Prayer*: private readings in which the worshiper "spoke," not *about* their dear departed but *to* them. Prayers addressed "To my beloved father," "to my beloved mother" or "spouse" or "child," gave voice to feelings of loss, longing, and gratitude and provided moments when, for many, worshipers felt that they were in the presence of, perhaps even in dialogue with, deceased loved ones. Such readings were also part of subsequent American Reform *Yizkor* services, including the *Todtenfeier* in Rabbi David Einhorn's *Olath Tamid* (1858), the *Seelenfeier* in Rabbi Isaac M. Wise's *Minhag Amerika* (1866), and in the Memorial services of the various editions of the *Union Prayerbook II*.[13]

Such readings were not included in *Gates of Repentance*. Perhaps sensing that something important was missing, many congregations such as ours brought back this personalized element through supplemental readings.

Reintroducing such personalized readings in which departed relations are addressed in the second person presents certain challenges, but offers unique opportunities as well. One of the challenges is to offer readings that are meaningful and respectful, understanding that, while most people had a fairly good (though not perfect) relationship with, let's say, parents, many did not. Often there is pain, anger, brokenness, and unfinished business between the worshiper and the deceased upon who she or he is focusing.

But within the challenge such hurt and brokenness present lie opportunities to heal broken hearts and bind open wounds. While we cannot account for every family constellation, I believe we can find and/or compose any number of personalized readings through which our people would reconnect with their loved ones in honesty, sincerity, and love. Done skillfully and sensitively, such prayers would lead the worshiper through a spiritual process by which understanding, forgiveness, and emotional reconciliation might be experienced, granting, in a sense, *kaparah* for the dead. *Yizkor* can provide the opportunity for worshipers to mourn the loss, not only of that which was and can never be again, but of that which might have been and should have been, but was not and, perhaps, could not have been. And this just might set the stage for reconciliation with, perhaps even forgiveness of, those from whose memories we might have hitherto been estranged. Such opportunities might enable and empower us to מחיה מתים (resurrect our relationships) ברחמים רבים (by means of our increased compassion, understanding, and love).

5. *Yizkor* as Catharsis

But can a *Yizkor* Service serve in this way, as a therapeutic cathartic, a means through which unresolved feelings vis-à-vis past relationships can find resolution and guilt can be addressed and perhaps cleansed? Historically, the answer may very well have been yes, suggesting that it can again. In his examination of the development of American Memorial Service liturgies, Eric L. Friedland suggests that some of these liturgies were meant to do just that, to provide a cathartic relief of guilt, the mixed feelings experienced by more than one generation of immigrants who left behind (abandoned) the older generation and their graves.

> A swift comparison between the nineteenth-century American prayerbooks and their European correlates shows the former by and large to be on a somewhat grander scale, and more involved and imposing. The suggestion might be ventured that the elaborateness of the American *Yizkor* Service stems from an implicit wish to ward off or cleanse oneself of guilt, [satisfying] a felt need for a *kippur* or *kapparah* between the generations . . . The role of the Yom Kippur *Yizkor* Service as an occasion for catharsis was to last a fairly long time, if not at least an entire century, chiefly because of the two major waves of immigration and their overlap.[14]

While the guilt presumed to be felt by the immigrant generations has long since passed, worshipers of subsequent generations often feel their own specific guilt, also stemming from trans-generational relationships. Through the use of well-crafted "second-person" readings, a Reform *Yizkor* Service has the potential to address these issues and on some level move the worshiper closer to resolution and reconciliation.

6. Learning History through the Martyrs

From its inception, the theme of martyrdom has been a seminal focus within Jewish Memorial services. Through the centuries, Jews have felt a sacred obligation to pay due homage to those who died *al kiddush Hashem,* and in doing so, we have maintained a relationship with the martyrs and their convictions. By and large, today's Jew in the pew has little or no grasp of the historic experience of the Jewish people and sparse knowledge of the martyrs of the past, save for those souls lost during the Shoah, as victims of terrorism, and in defense of the State of Israel. While we cannot teach the entirety of Jewish history on one foot, nor should we perpetuate the lachrymose theory of Jewish history, the *Yizkor* moment offers an opportunity to help our people become more aware of those of every age who have found something in Judaism worth dying for.

7. Jewish Transcendence

The *Yizkor* Service provides a unique opportunity to build upon the sense of obligation and/or connectedness that brought the worshiper to the service in the first place, by fostering a feeling of greater connectedness with or obligation to his or her extended meta-family (i.e., the Jewish People). Moments of transformative spirituality are often born when one experiences on a deep level the sense that he or she is part of something that transcends the self and connects with something greater and of ultimate meaning. For both the "regular" and the "*Yizkor*-only" Jew, this service has the potential to help one feel that one is a part of and a needed conduit of the legacy, both of his or her own family as well as that of the Jewish People. The hope would be, of course, that a *Yizkor* service would motivate a higher level of Jewish engagement, especially those for whom the *Yizkor* service is their primarily, perhaps sole, engagement with synagogue life.

III. Suggestion on Putting It Together

Were the concepts and thematic elements presented above to be included in a new *Yizkor*/Memorial liturgy, a thematic flow might look something like this:[15]

1. Human frailty and finitude
2. Reference to *Yizkor* as rooted in martyrdom as a transition to
3. Readings regarding martyrs of the past
4. Transition to present day "history," leading into
5. Reading names of the year's deceased
6. Extended time of private reading/prayer, perhaps with directed musical background:
   a. Readings/poems/psalms relating to immortality
   b. Readings/poems/personalized prayers—in the second or third person—relating to specific relatives (e.g., parent, spouse, child). These might also consist of guided meditations.[16]

c. Readings/poems/psalms relating to perpetuating the "immortality of influence," through *tzedakah* and acts of kindness in memory of . . .
   d. Recitation of personalized *"Yizkor Elohim . . .,"* as well as *Yizkor* prayers relating to martyrs and the fallen soldiers of our particular countries and the IDF
7. Communal *"El Malei"*
8. Reading(s) on Jewish transcendence, referring to the history of the martyrs and the connection with one's own families, and helping the worshipers see themselves as those who are privileged and tasked to carry on the Jewish legacy of their individual families as well as that of the meta-*mishpachah* of the Jewish People[17]
9. Communal recitation of *Kaddish*
10. A final moment of comfort and continued closeness with God, such as the reading and/or singing of *Shiviti*

When contemplating a new Reform *Yizkor* Service, my hope is that we will be able to create liturgical moments that will most effectively, most personally, most spiritually, and most beautifully enable individuals and communities to look into the mirror of the past, link memory and hope, and connect deeply and personally with those who are no more with us in *haolam hazeh*—those to whom we owe so much. I pray that this article will add to and enrich that sacred enterprise.

Notes

1. A fine source is Daniel Goldschmidt, *Machzor l'Yamim HaNora-im* (Jerusalem: Koren, 1970).
2. Lawrence A. Hoffman, *Gates of Understanding 2: Appreciating the Days of Awe* (New York: CCAR, 1984), 147.
3. Ibid., 149.
4. The *Yizkor* Service found in MARAM's *Avodah Shebalev* also continues this tradition with poems and readings from modern Israeli poets and authors.
5. Eric L. Friedland, "The Atonement Memorial Service in the American Mahzor," *Hebrew Union College Annual* 55 (1984): 243–82.
6. *Rabbi's Manual* (New York: CCAR, 1988), 159.
7. *Gates of Repentance*, 483.
8. *Gates of Prayer*, 548.

9. For example, Henry Van Dyke's "Parable of Immortality (A ship leaves . . .)."
10. Jeffrey M. Cohen, *Understanding the High Holyday Services* (London: Routledge & Kegan Paul, 1983), 155.
11. *Gates of Prayer for Weekdays and at a House of Mourning*, 43.
12. This is actually embodied in the *Yizkor* booklets that congregations prepare that lists names of family members in whose memory a donation has been made to the synagogue.
13. Friedland, "The Atonement," 245.
14. Ibid., 277.
15. My thanks to Gail Lalk, grief therapist, for her help in this.
16. I am grateful to Rabbi Mary Zamore for the suggestion of guided meditations within the quiet, personalized readings. Perhaps this might be in the form of open paragraphs or paragraphs with brief guided readings, directing the worshiper then to "fill in the blank"; for example:
    I remember . . .
    I am grateful . . .
    I regret . . .
    I mourn . . .
    I forgive . . .
    I resolve . . .
17. In this context, inclusive consideration should be given to persons of other faith backgrounds in our congregations, those who are not Jewish and/or those whose honored departed were of other faiths.

We, the *Avaryanim*, Chant *Kol Nidrei*

Donald P. Cashman

A powerful mystique surrounds *Kol Nidrei*, derived from the combined elements of the drama of the ceremony: the seasonal white of the *parochet*, the Torahs' mantles, and on the officiants themselves; the removal of many, if not all, of the scrolls from the ark, to be held by congregational leaders or elders; the proclamation of the unique formula *"biyshivah shel malah . . ."* before the chanting; and the larger than usual crowd for the service, garbed uniquely for the evening service in tallitot, all contribute to the drama of the moment.

Then there is *Kol Nidrei* itself, with its unique words, unlike anything else in our usual liturgy. And, of course, we have the Ashkenazic melody, which is many hundreds of years old. Made up of melodic fragments strung together, it is unlike either the patterns of *nusach* or biblical cantillation on one hand, nor like the chorus and verses style of later song on the other. By virtue of its words and music, not to mention the great solemnity of the occasion, *Kol Nidrei* is a piece for the well-trained, or at least the well-practiced. Aramaic legalese coupled with runs and leaps join to make the chanting of *Kol Nidrei* one of the most advanced synagogue skills—one customarily reserved for a professional.

As with virtually every other Jewish ceremony, the *Kol Nidrei* ritual has evolved over time and place. Every epoch in Jewish history has contributed to the evolution of the *Kol Nidrei* ceremony as we have it today. The story begins with the Torah's statements about obligation to fulfill one's vows (e.g., Deut. 23:22–24, Num. 30:3). Other biblical literature gives examples of the length to which people went to keep their vows, perhaps most dramatically the story of Jephthah (Judges 11:30-40). Yet while the Bible does

---

RABBI DONALD P. CASHMAN (NY83) is the spiritual leader of B'nai Sholom Reform Congregation in Albany, New York.

not allow for the nullification of vows and oaths,[1] the desirability of being able to extricate oneself from them if necessary was readily apparent. By the Second Temple period, Josephus stated that "some were of the opinion that they should disregard those oaths as having been sworn under the sway of passion, without reflexion or judgement . . . and that perjuries were not grave or hazardous when they were prompted by necessity, but only when rashly committed with malicious intent."[2] Philo took a different tack, expressing in *Hypothetica* 7:5 that priests were empowered by God to accept or reject dedicated property and thus can release someone from a vow to dedicate property.

While the Mishnah, *Tosefta*, and Gemara contain tractates on vows and on oaths, the issue of nullification is ascertained in *Mishnah Chagigah* 1:8 to have no biblical basis. The *Tosefta* on that passage adds that "a sage may nullify by means of his wisdom" (*Tosefta Chagigah* 1:9), which may mean that he has the skill to determine how the vow was in fact not valid to start with. It has also been suggested that dissolution of vows may in fact be "a power vested in the Rabbis" that is "an outgrowth of the role of priest and sage as Temple functionary."[3] The Rabbinic literature therefore includes the particulars required for dissolving or nullifying vows.[4]

Eventually, a formula for the dissolution of vows appears in the liturgy for Yom Kippur in *Seder Rav Amram*.[5] Various *geonim*[6] and *rishonim*[7] are linked to the text, changes in the text, establishing the ritual around the text, and discussions of its limits. But the established fact is that *Kol Nidrei*, whether referring to vows of the recently concluded year, or of the newly begun year, became part of the Yom Kippur liturgy.

The old paradigm behind *Kol Nidrei*, indeed, behind much of Rabbinic Judaism, is of halachic responsibility: How do we deal with unfulfilled vows, which are supposedly inviolable? Our newer paradigm is one of meaning: How do we derive meaning from our performance of the *Kol Nidrei* ceremony?

As we are poised on the threshold of creating a new *machzor* for North American Reform Judaism, we are wondering what to do with some pieces of the liturgy for the Days of Awe. We ponder retention, rejection, modification, addition; we equivocate, we gloss over, or we leave untranslated. We want a *machzor* that has integrity as both a Jewish prayer book for the Days of Awe as well as having integrity as a Reform Jewish prayer book.

To be sure, Reform Judaism has struggled with *Kol Nidrei* for two hundred years. Our *machzorim* have changed the words, substituted Psalms, and left it out. We have omitted the words and played instrumental versions instead.[8] In 1978, the words appeared in *Shaarei T'shuvah/Gates of Repentance* after an accidental appearance in the first edition of the *Union Prayer Book II, Newly Revised* (1945).[9]

In the twenty-seven years I have served my congregation, we have tried a variety of approaches to bring meaning to *Kol Nidrei*. Still emerging out of classical Reform in the late 1980s, an organ accompanied our vocal soloist. When the organist retired, we moved to harp accompaniment for the Days of Awe, a dignified and formal sound, with biblical antecedent. Those who heard the organ and thought "church" as well as those who heard no accompaniment and thought "Orthodox" were pacified, as were those who felt guitar too colloquial. Twice we began the service with the Bruch cello composition using the piano reduction, not an orchestra, with musicians from the outside. The first time was a disaster because no one thought to make sure that the beautiful Steinway in the sanctuary was tuned. Several years later we tried again, but I did not find the ten or twelve minutes particularly moving, even with a tuned piano and a better cellist. Perhaps a decade ago a past president serving on the regional URJ board brought to the ritual committee the idea of calling up all the past presidents for *Kol Nidrei*. This certainly adds a measure of formality and uniqueness to the service.

In 2010, it was brought to my attention that one of these past presidents, a fiddler in a klezmer band, wanted to play *Kol Nidrei*. There's a tradition, first cited in *Machzor Vitry*,[10] about *Kol Nidrei* being done three times; the instrumental could be the first, the soloist and harp would be another. What could a third, *different* version be?

In 2010, the *avaryanim* (all the sinners) sang *Kol Nidrei*: We had a congregational sing-along. It provided a sense of ownership and opened up a text for people in a way like never before. We began with the instrumental version of the tune on violin, followed it up with the sing-along, and concluded with our soloist and harp.

Fortunately, the congregation loves to sing, and is willing to learn new pieces, even in the midst of the solemnity of services during the Days of Awe. Within the last few years we've introduced the responsive chanting of *Ashamnu, Bagadnu*, with them repeating each word after me—no transliteration involved! The following year, they were receptive to the congregational responses during the "Chasidic" Full *Kaddish* written by Jacob "Yankl der Heizeriker" Gottlieb (1852–1900) during *N'ilah*, a piece often associated with the great *chazan* Yossele Rosenblatt (1882–1933). A year later, following a moving few days learning and performing an arrangement of Israel Goldfarb's "B'sefer Chayyim" at the North American Jewish Choral Festival, I crafted a sermon around this text, noting that it may be the essence of our prayers, and taught it during Rosh HaShanah; we've continued with it ever since.

The sing-along was carefully planned and rehearsed. There were two elements to the single-page handout the ushers distributed with the *machzorim*: sheet music and the words. I took a simple version of the Lewandowski arrangement,[11] and using Finale Notepad (musical notation software)[12] input it, making a few changes, including transliteration into Sephardic Hebrew. This software, available as a free download, permits key changes with a mouse click. The arrangement has a vocal range of an octave + a fifth, identical to the notoriously difficult to sing American national anthem, "The Star Spangled Banner." Thus, finding a key that would be good for me as well as conducive to group singing was paramount. I decided on E minor, with a range from G2 to D4 (the women, of course, sang in their register an octave higher), which gave me the slightest clearance on the highs just above middle C and wasn't too low for most congregants. The lowest and highest notes are only touched upon twice.

The handout also included four columns in tabular form. From left to right they were the measure number corresponding to the sheet music; the transliterated word or words that would be sung at one time; a translation of the word or phrase; and the actual Aramaic or Hebrew text. For example:

| 23 | l'tovah | for good | לטובה |
| | kulhon | all of them | כלהון |

The two elements on the handout allowed the music readers to have pitches, rhythms, and words, while the nonreaders would simply go down the column of words and repeat each phrase after me.

I began with brief introductory remarks about the source of the power of *Kol Nidrei*. Is it the day? The ritual? The text? The melody? *The Jazz Singer* complex, where the day is saved because the hero can sing *Kol Nidrei*?[13] Probably, I mused, it is a combination of all of these. After a tiny bit of historical information, I explained what we would be doing.

First, we listened to the melody on violin. Then, with our sheets in hand, I had them repeat after me each word, or a short phrase such as *"mi Yom Kippurim zeh."* We then drilled four especially challenging musical phrases (measures 9–11, 34–37, 45–48, and 52–54). With the words and the most difficult passages already experienced, we began from the top.

Phrase by phrase I sang, and the congregation repeated: full-voiced, a full sound from a full sanctuary. I could sense the excitement as we worked our way through this significant piece, and I could see the joy on their faces as we accomplished what we had set out to do: everyone sang *Kol Nidrei*.

Then we invited up the past presidents as a group, not by name as in the past so as not to interrupt too much the power of the moment. The congregation rose, the Ark was opened, the scrolls removed, and our vocalist chanted *Kol Nidrei* with the harp accompaniment. The scrolls were returned, and only then, as has been our practice, did we turn back a few pages to light the candles to establish the start of Yom Kippur proper.

I debriefed our experiment with a short sermon about the empowerment of Jewish competency. If they could chant *Kol Nidrei*, an advanced skill, how simple should it be to accomplish a wide variety of other Jewish behaviors.

Programmatically, the sing-along was a huge success. Congregants were genuinely pleased not only with what they had done, but with the entire scripting and drama of the evening: descriptive introduction, melodic prelude, working through of the words and melody, the communal singing, the rendering of it by soloist and harp, and the follow-up sermon. We all felt empowered to do the serious work of atonement that lay ahead of us in the rest of the day.

Could this be replicated? Should it be? Should we make it congregational *minhag*? Might we suggest to others to try this? Was it even a good idea to begin with?

Who should sing *Kol Nidrei*? The extent of possibilities of any piece of the traditional liturgy is limited: a particular prayer may be recited either by the prayer leader (*sh'liach tzibur*), by the congregation, by all, or by one then the other. *Kol Nidrei* is a *sh'liach tzibur* prayer, recited by the prayer leader. Or, are there other possibilities?

The *Shulchan Aruch* (*Orach Chaim* 619) tells us the *sh'liach tzibur* recites this. The Rema uses the verb in the plural: "afterwards we pray the evening prayer, and we customarily say *Kol Nidrei* on that day, and [the *sh'liach tzibur*] continues with tunes (*nigunim*) until night, and says it three times, each time the voice raised more loudly than the first." One could try to make a case from the plural verb that this signifies that it is the congregation reciting *Kol Nidrei*, but the return to the singular "the [*sh'liach tzibur*] continues" and "the voice," would very much seem to negate that.

Before the *Shulchan Aruch*, however, Yaakov ben Moshe haLevi Moellin, the Maharil (1365–1427), stated that "it is meritorious that everyone recite *Kol Nidrei* with the prayer leader quietly [דניחא *d'nicha*]."[14] The notion that everyone should actively recite along with the *sh'liach tzibur*, rather than passively listen or even just follow along, is a nugget that surfaces through later traditions, although is practically invisible in the Ashkenazic liturgy. Perhaps the development of the Ashkenazic melody, along with the rise of the virtuoso cantorate, held back the Ashkenazic masses.

In the Sephardic world, however, it seems as if communal recitation, albeit quietly, is the norm in many communities. Ya'akov Chaim ben Yitzhak Baruch Sofer (b. Baghdad 1870, d. Jerusalem 1939), in *Kaf HaChaim*, a 1905 commentary to the *Shulchan Aruch*, states that "all the congregation will recite it quietly [בנחת *b'nachat*] with the *sh'liach tzibur*."[15] Shem Tov Gaguine (b. 1884 Jerusalem, d. Manchester, England 1953), scion of a Moroccan rabbinic dynasty and who served as a *dayan* in Egypt, authored *Keter Shem Tov* (published 1934–1953) where he similarly stated that *Kol Nidrei* is recited quietly (בנחת *b'nachat*) with the *sh'liach tzibur*.[16]

Sephardic *machzorim* give similar instructions. *Machzor Rinat Yisrael* has the *sh'liach tzibur* say *Kol Nidrei* three times "and the congregation says it with him silently [בלחש *b'lachash*]."[17] *The Complete ArtScroll Machzor, Yom Kippur, Nusach Sefard* informs us in an introduction that "it is customary, therefore, for everyone to recite it quietly with the chazzan."[18] Above *Kol Nidrei*, itself, the instruction is "the congregation recites along with him in an undertone."[19]

Other sources reveal even more active congregational participation. In the *machzor* of Congregation Shearith Israel in New York, edited by David de Sola Pool, "the Rabbi intones the formula of Kal[20] Nidre" from the opening words until "from the preceding Day of Atonement unto this Day of Atonement (may it come upon us in peace)." At this point the congregation answers with the remainder of the passage; about 40 percent of the text is recited by the congregation and not by the prayer leader.[21]

The Syrian Jews chant the *Kal Nidrei* prayer twice in unison, and only the third time is it sung by the rabbi or *chazan*.[22] The Moroccan Jews have three *chazanim*, each taking a turn chanting *Kal Nidrei*.[23]

While the well-circulated American Ashkenazic Orthodox *machzorim* (i.e., those edited by A. Philips [1931], P. Birnbaum [1951], and H. Adler, [1959]) do not have any such instruction, at least one did. In this volume[24] above *Kol Nidrei* the English instructs that "the Congregation join in prayer softly." Above that, in Rashi script, the instructions say that "each person says it silently and with great concentration יאמרנו בלחש ובכוונה גדולה (*yomruno b'lachash uv'chavanah g'dolah*) with the *sh'liach tzibur*."

Who recites *Kol Nidrei*? In most of our earliest records since *Seder Rav Amram*, it has been the *sh'liach tzibur*. The *ArtScroll Machzor* refers to the *chazan*, while De Sola Pool places it in the mouth of the rabbi (החכם *hechacham*). In De Sola Pool's historic synagogue, Congregation Shearith Israel, the rabbi was considered the *chazan* (the prayer leader), while someone like the Amsterdam-born Rev. Abraham Lopes Cardozo (1914–2006), who served as its *chazan* from 1946–1984, was titularly the "assistant hazzan." Cardozo himself wrote: "In many Sephardic congregations the *hakham* or the rabbi also not infrequently acts as reader."[25]

In Orthodox and Conservative synagogues, where the liturgy is chanted, the chanter may or may not be the rabbi. In Reform congregations, however, we have a more pronounced bifurcation of the roles of rabbi and cantor: the rabbi reads, and the cantor sings. In the Spanish-Portuguese synagogue, "apparently . . . the rabbi can feel free to take the juicier liturgical items for himself, including the main plum of the year, *Kol Nidre*."[26] Do we diminish the impact of *Kol Nidrei* by transforming a solo rendering into a triptych such as I have suggested of instrumental/congregational/solo? Do we diminish the honor and prestige of the cantorate with this?

To both of these questions I must not only say "no," but I must say that we are perhaps doing just the opposite.

By highlighting *Kol Nidrei* in three different ways, we call added attention to it. It is not just another piece of music in an un-understood language to which the congregation will listen. Rather, by putting their mouths around every single geonic and Rabbenu Tam-ic word, worshipers will have a greater appreciation of the text, and of the musical phrases that make up this unique work. Also, our cantors and other musical professionals, indeed all those synagogue functionaries who practice before they get up in public—*baalei k'riyah, baalei t'kiah*, soloists, instrumentalists, and yes, rabbis—make their tasks look easy. They have spent weeks, months, and years practicing their lines, learning their skills, honing their crafts. If the Jew in the pew is given an opportunity to try something, he or she will realize that it is not as simple as the person on the bimah makes it seem.

Moreover, in the suggested scenario, we build up to the solo recitation of *Kol Nidrei* by the congregation's chosen *sh'liach tzibur*. "In matters of holiness, we only increase, we do not decrease."[27] From this point at the beginning of Yom Kippur, we increase our repentance, hoping to reach a personal pinnacle before the gates close.

Notes

1. Except for a woman's vows in Numbers 30, which can be nullified by her father or husband.
2. *Antiquities of the Jews*, 5:2:12 (=5:169) .
3. Moshe Benovitz, *Kol Nidre: Studies in the Development of Rabbinic Votive Institutions* (Atlanta: Scholars Press, 1998), 152, 164.
4. For full discussions of the texts and history of *hatarat n'darim* and *Kol Nidrei*, see Stuart Weinberg Gershon, *Kol Nidrei: Its Origin, Development, and Significance* (Northvale, NJ: Jason Aronson, 1994), and the Benovitz study cited in note 3 above. See also Eliezer Diamond, "*Kol Nidre*: A Halakhic History and Analysis" and Daniel Landes, "Choice, Commitment, Cancellation: Vows and Oaths in Jewish Law," in *All These Vows: Kol Nidre*, ed. Lawrence A. Hoffman (Woodstock, VT: Jewish Lights, 2011).
5. *Seder Rav Amram* (Warsaw, 1865), 47, www.hebrewbooks.org/pdfpager.aspx?req=42696&st=&pgnum=101.
6. Lawrence A. Hoffman, "Morality, Meaning, and the Ritual Search for the Sacred," in Hoffman, *All These Vows*, especially 7–19, a summary of the early history.
7. See Gershon, *Kol Nidrei*, chap. 9.

8. A thorough presentation of the treatment of *Kol Nidrei* in Reform Judaism is Annette M. Boeckler, "The Magic of the Moment: *Kol Nidre* in Progressive Judaism," in Hoffman, *All These Vows*, 39.
9. Lawrence A. Hoffman, "*Kol Nidre* from the *Union Prayer Book* to *Gates of Repentance*," in Hoffman, *All These Vows*, 99. I am pleased to own one of these 1945 first editions with the full text of *Kol Nidrei*.
10. S. Hurwitz, ed., *Machzor Vitry* (Nurnburg, 1923), 388.
11. See, e.g., Gershon, *Kol Nidrei*, 155; Nathan Ausabel, *A Treasury of Jewish Folklore* (New York: Crown, 1948), 710; A.Z. Idelsohn, *Jewish Music* (NY: Schocken, 1967), 155; *Shirei T'shuvah/Songs of Repentance* (New York: Transcontinental, 2000), 263.
12. http://www.finalemusic.com/notepad.
13. *The Jazz Singer* versions include 1927 (Al Jolson), 1940 (Moyshe Oysher, "Overture to Glory"), 1952 (Danny Thomas), 1959 (a live television version with Jerry Lewis), and 1980 (Neil Diamond).
14. *Sefer Maharil* (Warsaw, 1875); *Hilchot Leil Yom Kippur*, 45, http://hebrewbooks.org/pdfpager.aspx?req=14721&st=&pgnum=89.
15. *Kaf HaChaim*, vol. 8 (Jerusalem, 1965), *Orach Chaim* 619:18, p. 120, http://hebrewbooks.org/14425.
16. *Keter Shem Tov*, vol. 6 (London, 1955), 323, http://hebrewbooks.org/14391.
17. S. Tal, ed., *Machzor Rinat Yisrael L'Yom Kippur, Nusach S'fard* (Elon Sh'vut: Yad Shapira, 1979), 40.
18. *The Complete ArtScroll Machzor, Yom Kippur, Nusach Sefard* (New York: Mesorah Publications, 1986), 63.
19. Ibid., 66.
20. "*Kal*" is the pronunciation within the Sephardic community. See S. Morag, "Pronunciations of Hebrew," in *Encyclopedia Judaica* (1972), 13:1136.
21. David de Sola Pool, ed., *Prayers for the Day of Atonement according to the Custom of the Spanish and Portuguese Jews*, 2nd ed. (New York: Union of Sephardic Congregations, 1939), 26.
22. Herbert C. Dobrinsky, *A Treasury of Sephardic Laws and Customs* (New York: Ktav/Yeshiva Univ. Press, 1986), 334.
23. Ibid., 340.
24. *The Form of Prayers for the Day of Atonement according to the Custom of the German and Polish Jews*, with an English translation, carefully revised by Samuel Summer (New York: I. M. Alter, 1934). Printed on both the Hebrew and English Title pages is "Made in Austria," which is overstamped with "Made in Germany."
25. Mark Slobin, *Chosen Voices: The Story of the American Cantorate* (Urbana and Chicago: University of Illinois, 2002), 207.
26. Ibid.
27. E.g., BT *B'rachot* 28a, BT *Yoma* 20b.

The *Un'taneh Tokef* Prayer—Sealing Our Faith, Not Our Fate

Y. Lindsey bat Joseph

וּנְתַנֶּה תֹּקֶף קְדוּשַׁת הַיּוֹם . . .

Let us proclaim the sacred power of this day; it is awesome and full of dread . . .
On Rosh HaShanah it is written, on Yom Kippur it is sealed;
How many shall pass on, how many shall come to be;
Who shall live and who shall die;
Who shall see ripe age and who shall not;
Who shall perish by fire and who by water;
Who by sword and who by beast;
Who by hunger and who by thirst;
Who by earthquake and who by plague;
Who by strangling and who by stoning;
Who shall be secure and who shall be driven;
Who shall be tranquil and who shall be troubled;
Who shall be poor and who shall be rich;
Who shall be humbled and who exalted.
But repentance, prayer and charity temper judgment's decree.[1]

In the *Un'taneh Tokef* prayer we are confronted with the classic Yamim Noraim theme of the Holy One sitting in judgment and sealing the fate of every soul for the coming year, which seems at odds with our contemporary worldview. We often tell our congregants to read the prayer metaphorically, but without providing a metaphorical framework, that advice seems to be little more than code for "don't read it literally." And if we are not going to read and

---

RABBI Y. LINDSEY BAT JOSEPH (C96) is the director of the Sol Mark Centre for Jewish Excellence, an outreach program to unaffiliated Jews in Western Canada. She has been involved with small Jewish communities in various locations throughout British Columbia as well as teaching and studying in the Greater Vancouver Region. She has been awarded the Alberta Centennial Medal for community service and was a contributing writer to the Jewish Lights' *Women's Haftarah Commentary*

understand it literally, then how do we understand it? Can this prayer speak to our contemporary circumstances and sensibilities?

The God of the "Big Bang" and of particle physics is an impersonal God; the God of the *machzor* and the Torah is not. We seldom think of God as being intimately involved with our day-to-day lives the way our ancestors did, and many doubt whether the God of our science-based worldview is the author of human history either. In this article I examine the *Un'taneh Tokef* prayer within its historical context and that of the Yamim Noraim prayer services and consider the question of whether or not this prayer belongs in a modern *machzor*. In recasting the poem within the context of contemporary philosophical debate and emerging physical science, I argue that the seeming discordance between the text and our contemporary worldview is not as pronounced as it first appears. Lastly, I offer a new approach to interpreting this text that can, perhaps, speak more appropriately to our experience and our lives.

Un'taneh Tokef in its Historical and Liturgical Context

According to tradition, the *Un'taneh Tokef* prayer was written by Rabbi Amnon of Mainz, Germany, in the eleventh century. Documentary evidence, however, establishes that this poem was most likely composed in Israel at least five hundred years prior to the time of R. Amnon.[2] Moreover there are Italian liturgical traditions that allude to this poem well before the time of R. Amnon. Nevertheless, for us the prayer is tied to the story of his martyrdom, which is known primarily from the account preserved in the *Or Zarua* (thirteenth century) by Rabbi Isaac of Vienna.[3] R. Isaac's account cites an earlier chronicle by Rabbi Ephraim of Bonn.[4]

The standard versions of this tale, which are often found in the commentary of traditional *machzorim*, describe R. Amnon of Mainz as an affluent and respected Jew who was being pressured by the local bishop to convert to Christianity. At one point, the rabbi tries to forestall the badgering by requesting three days to meditate upon the question. Subsequently the rabbi feels terribly grieved for even hinting that he might seriously consider abandoning Judaism and he fails to show up for his appointment with the bishop. His failure to appear before the bishop was punished by having his hands and legs amputated, joint by joint. At various stages during this torture, he is again asked if he would be willing to convert, but the rabbi declines. Then the bishop orders that he and his amputated body parts be carried home.[5]

Rosh HaShanah arrived a few days later and R. Amnon asked to be placed on the bimah of the synagogue, along with his dismembered limbs, prior to the chanting of the *K'dushah* of the *Musaf* Service. As the story goes, R. Amnon recited the *Un'taneh Tokef* and then died. The legend continues three days after his death when he reportedly appeared in a dream to Rabbi Kalonymos ben Meshullam, to whom he taught the text of the *Un'taneh Tokef* and asked him to send it throughout the Jewish world.

The harsh and complex realities of Jewish medieval life are the backdrop of this story of suffering and sacrifice. Its portrayal of the strained relations between Jews and the non-Jewish dominant culture (in this case medieval Christianity) that culminates in martyrdom is a story that was often repeated in Jewish history, from the days of Babylonian and Roman emperors to Christian and Muslim medieval Europe, to the brutality of the Shoah. It is hardly surprising that it resonated so strongly with our ancestors or with the generation that survived the concentration camps. These were the generations who lived firsthand the horrors of oppression. In addition to recalling R. Amnon within the context of the *Un'taneh Tokef* recitation, their stories, along with those of martyrs from the Rabbinic Era, are woven into the Yom Kippur *Minchah* liturgy as part of a remembrance of Jewish martyrs throughout our history.[6]

Within the context of his own personal tragedy, R. Amnon's actions constituted a supreme statement of surrender to divine justice—a justice that is as enigmatic as it is unpredictable. By reciting the poem as a prelude to the *K'dushah*, the central theme of which is God's holiness, R. Amnon transformed the meaning of the *K'dushah* from a prophetic vision of an angelic declaration of God's holiness to a meditation on the human sanctification of God's Name that is measured by our willingness to suffer martyrdom for the sake of our faith.[7]

However, these are the contexts that seem to resonate poorly with many contemporary Jews. Sixty years plus after the establishment of the modern State of Israel, we are hesitant to see ourselves as victims. We are *victors* who have survived the vicissitudes of Jewish history and continue to struggle for Judaism and for Israel. Even though today that struggle still sometimes results in death, we resist seeing ourselves as victims and martyrs—we are much more comfortable with that being part of our past.

Free Will, Determinism, and Contemporary Physics

The *Un'taneh Tokef* reminds us that our ultimate destiny does not lie entirely in our own hands. The future is not something we can contemplate with absolute certainty, but as I noted at the beginning of this discussion, this is not out of step with our contemporary science-based understanding of the world. For centuries philosophers and theologians alike have debated the notions of free will, determinism, and human fate. In the determinist worldview, whatever we do depends on our choices, decisions, and wants, and that whatever those choices may be they were determined by the circumstances that preceded them. Determinism does not claim that we can predict what will happen in the future—there are too many unknown factors involved and, unlike God, we can never have perfect knowledge of all the conditions that lead up to a given decision—but there are laws of nature and everything that happens in the world is governed by those laws, in accordance with which the circumstances before any action will determine its outcome and rule out any other possibility. In other words, all our choices are inevitable and free will is a myth.[8]

Critics of determinism question how it is possible to be held morally accountable for our actions if we are not ultimately responsible for our choices. If everything is determined, then morality doesn't seem to be possible and yet we do want to hold one another accountable for our actions. Those who argue in favor of free will often cite the unpredictable nature of particles at the quantum level as proof that the world is not quite as determined as some might suppose. However, our rapidly evolving understanding of physics only adds more complexity to the debate about the nature of human existence and the possibility or impossibility of free will. On the one hand, much of what goes on at the quantum level is indeterminate. It is largely unpredictable, which would suggest a certain amount of freedom in the universe. On the other hand, our empirical observations of the physical world is that it is filled with objects and systems that seem, for all practical purposes, to be quite deterministic, which suggests a certain lack of freedom. Compatibilists argue that it is possible to have free will in a largely deterministic universe, which would make moral accountability still possible.[9] Philosophically, this claim is not without its difficulties and yet, as our emerging new physics clearly demonstrates, despite the randomness of quantum particles and the predictability of the macro (physical) world, the two levels manage to coexist. So perhaps the entire universe is "compatibilist."

Free Will, Jewish Tradition, and Human Suffering

The intersection between free will and determinism occurs early in Jewish tradition. In the story of the expulsion from Eden, the chain of events that leads to humanity's exile from paradise begins with the Tree of Knowledge being placed in the middle of the Garden and the divine admonition to Adam and Eve that they should not eat from it. In some ways, it seems a foregone conclusion that that is precisely what they are "destined" to do. In a state of innocence where we do not know the difference between good and bad, good and bad technically do not exist. It is not until we acquire the capacity for moral discrimination that humanity becomes capable of committing sin. Without the capacity to commit sin, there would be no need for the mitzvot. So, while on the "quantum level" Adam and Eve choose to disobey and eat the fruit, on the "macro level" of the physical world this all seems to be part of a grander plan that God has set into place.[10]

In *Parashat Nitzavim*, a portion of which is read in Reform synagogues on Yom Kippur, the notion of choice is affirmed for Israel: "I have set before you life or death, blessing or curse; choose life, therefore, that you and your descendants may live" (Deut. 30:19).[11] There is always the possibility that one could reject entirely the inheritance from our ancestors, indeed the medieval commentator Isaac Abarbanel considered this very question but asserted that Israel would not and could not ever do such a thing. Our history has demonstrated that we continue to choose to cling to the covenant.[12] And it is to the future that this revelation is also directed. When God addresses the entire nation of Israel, the covenant is made "not with you alone, but with those who are standing here with us this day before the Eternal our God and with those who are not with us here this day" (Deut. 30:13–14).[13] The covenant is extended to future generations, which makes sense in terms of guaranteeing the continuity of Torah, but there is a philosophical/

theological component in this unfolding drama. As Rabbi Plaut explains: "That the present can and does commit the future to some extent is unquestionable. We are who we are because of our ancestors and their achievements and failures."[14] On the personal or quantum level, each of us, individually, decides how we connect with the covenant and our obligation to follow the mitzvot, but at the macro level, we, as a people, are bound by the decisions and actions of our ancestors; so in some sense our choices are also already determined.

Returning to the legend of R. Amnon, we can see more than a meditation on human suffering through the lens of martyrdom and the seemingly capricious nature of divine judgment. The *Un'taneh Tokef* is the nexus where the notions of free will and determinism and the personal versus the impersonal God come together. Like R. Amnon and our ancestors, many of us crave the intimacy of a relationship with a personal God, but at times we feel that the separation between us and God is a chasm that cannot be bridged. God and divine judgment remain inscrutable, our future remains hidden, yet it remains within our power to choose. Recall that R. Amnon's spiritual crisis was of his own making. He is wracked by guilt for having given the impression that he would even consider abandoning his faith—that is the sin for which he seeks to make *t'shuvah* at Rosh HaShanah. His treatment at the hands of the bishop is the result of his actions. Recast in this light, his recitation of the *Un'taneh Tokef* can be understood as an acknowledgment of his moral failings, his acceptance of responsibility for them, and a reaffirmation of the faith to which he was bound by the choices of our ancestors. His death may be understood as inevitable given the nature of his injuries, or it may be interpreted as an act of divine mercy that relieves him from both his spiritual suffering and his physical pain, but the rabbi's anguished spiritual struggle for redemption and forgiveness mirrors our own.

The *Un'taneh Tokef* in the Twenty-First Century and Beyond

I noted above that reading a text metaphorically without understanding or knowing the metaphorical framework is ultimately self-defeating. It leaves the text devoid of meaning. Similarly to simply advise worshipers to not take it literally doesn't offer much theologically or spiritually unless we also provide another way of understanding the text. I believe it is possible to employ the traditional imagery of the Yamim Noraim—that of God taking an account of every soul within God's dominion, passing judgment, and sealing that judgment in the Book of Life—and reinterpret it in such a way that the original beauty of the text need not be sacrificed to bring it into accord with our contemporary sensibilities.

First, an anecdote that provides the background for my rethinking of this prayer: The day after Yom Kippur, 1998, my eldest daughter was hit by a car on her way to school.[15] In the immediate aftermath of the accident, the *Un'taneh Tokef* prayer came back to me in a most haunting way, not because I took it literally, but because it was clearly troubling so many of those around me. As congregants poured into the hospital to offer support, I repeatedly heard the refrain, "the day after Yom Kippur, the day after Yom Kippur!" I couldn't think much about it then, but I knew that ultimately I would have to find a way to reconcile "on Rosh HaShanah it is written, on Yom Kippur it is sealed" and the fact that this accident happened *the day after Yom Kippur*! I had a full year to reflect on the words of this prayer and on the following Yom Kippur I was finally able to articulate how I understand it in light of my life's experiences and my theology.

The *Un'taneh Tokef* poem enumerates various tragedies that can befall us, none of which are strictly limited to bygone days. There are a myriad of reasons why people live and die and why some seem to lead charmed lives while others struggle daily just to survive. To lay the blame for all of this squarely at God's feet is a very simplistic, counterintuitive theology that is ultimately devoid of meaning for most of us. While some things are clearly beyond our control, the fact of our lives is that we make choices every day and those choices affect others as well as ourselves. It behooves us, then, to be diligent in our decisions. Whether we choose to provide funding for education, health care, and other social services, or cut it back; whether we choose to protect the environment or only exploit it; whether we choose to drive too fast or too recklessly or choose to obey the rules of the road; whether we drink too much or indulge in illicit drug use or choose a life of sobriety; whether we choose to respond quickly to natural disasters or not; whether we choose to wage war or not—with all these choices we affect our lives and the lives of potentially many others. That is the intersection of both the micro and macro worlds—individual choices affect the larger, overall picture for everyone. This is the case whether we envision a personal God or not.

This raises the question of whether or not there is a role for God in all of this. I believe so. Returning to the traditional imagery of God and the Book of Life, the liturgy describes God as writing and sealing the events of our lives, but if we are the ones making the choices, then what is it that God "writes and seals"? The only rational answer, for me, is that God seals the outcomes of our choices. If we approach Rosh HaShanah with the notion of the Book of Life being opened up and turned to a new page for the new year, then God is placing the pen *in our hands*. We write on the pages and God seals the outcomes—some immediate, some long term; some good, some bad, and some neutral—of *our* decisions. That is the blessing and curse of having the right to choose. The question to ask as we look forward is: What will we write? Will we write pages of kindness, of love, of reconciliation with each other and with God? Or, will we write pages of cruelty, neglect, hatred, and ignorance?

The *Un'taneh Tokef* is a stark reminder that we cannot control everything that happens to us and sometimes the choices we make lead to completely unanticipated consequences. The legend of R. Amnon and the other martyrs recalled on Yom Kippur remind us that what we can control is how we handle the challenges and tragedies that befall us. We should, therefore, strive to make the best choices we can in thos situations where we do have a measure of freedom and control over the outcome so that when Yom Kippur concludes, we will hand the pen back to God to close the book, and seal ourselves for blessing rather than sorrow.

לשנה טובה וגמר חתימה טובה

Notes

1. Chaim Stern, ed., *Gates of Repentance*, rev. ed. (New York: CCAR, 1996), 107–9.
2. Eliezer Segal, "Legend and Liturgy: the Elusive Tale of the Unatanneh Tokef," *The Jewish Free Press* (Calgary), September 29, 2005, 26, http://people.ucalgary.ca/~elsegal/Shokel/050929_RabbiAmnon.html.
3. According to Segal there is also some scholarly debate as to whether or not R. Amnon actually existed.

4. A reference to this story appears in the prelude to the recitation of *Un'taneh Tokef* in the Rosh HaShanah *Shacharit* Service in *Gates of Repentance*, 106.
5. Noson Scherman, *The Complete Artscroll Machzor for Yom Kippur, Nusach Sefard*, ed. Meir Zlotowitz and Avie Gold (New York: Mesorah Publications, 1986), 560.
6. See the "*Eleh Ezkerah*" section of the Yom Kippur *Minchah* Service in *Gates of Repentance*, 429–449; especially the section beginning on page 432, which recalls the Ten Martyrs from the time of Emperor Hadrian.
7. Segal, "Legend and Liturgy."
8. See John Hospers, "What Means This Freedom," in *Determinism and Freedom in the Age of Modern Science,* ed. Sidney Hook (New York: Collier, 1961); Thomas Nagel, *What Does It All Mean?* (New York: Oxford University Press, 1987).
9. See W. T. Stace, *Religion and the Modern Mind* (New York: HarperCollins, 1952); Harry Frankfurt, "Freedom of the Will and the Concept of a Person," *Journal of Philosophy* 68, no. 1 (January 14, 1971): 5–20. Both of these philosophers view psychological states as the locus of freedom of the will, although they both acknowledge there are constraints on that will.
10. W. Gunther Plaut, ed., "Expulsion from Eden," *The Torah: A Modern Commentary*, rev. ed. (New York: URJ Press, 2005), 37–39.
11. *Gates of Repentance*, 345.
12. Plaut, "Commitment for the Future" in *The Torah: A Modern Commentary*, 1378.
13. Plaut, *The Torah: A Modern Commentary.*
14. Plaut, "Commitment for the Future."
15. My daughter made a full recovery and has grown into a beautiful independent woman in her own right who has also brought another generation of Jews into the world.

Viewing *Un'taneh Tokef* through a New Lens

Amy Scheinerman

Let us now relate the power of this day's holiness . . . Behold, it is the Day of Judgment . . . Who will live and who will die, who will die at his predestined time and who before his time?

These words from *Un'taneh Tokef* danced hauntingly through my mind twenty-two years ago, just at the time Jews in synagogues all around me were chanting *Kol Nidrei*. Tears welled in my eyes. The surgeon looked down at me and said, "You will be alright." I fell into anaesthetized slumber.

I had started bleeding that morning. How would I fit in an unscheduled trip to the OB/GYN the morning before Yom Kippur? But the doctor said: "You have an ectopic pregnancy. You have one hour to get to the hospital." By the time I was wheeled into the operating room, the sun was dipping below the horizon. At a time when I sought comfort, the Yom Kippur liturgy delivered cold judgment. In the place of assurance, it delivered guilt. Or so it seemed. I had not yet found a theological fit that permitted me to understand *Un'taneh Tokef* as anything more than an artifact of an ancient theology to which I didn't subscribe.

The tears that spilled out in the operating room were not for me or for my husband; we were exceedingly blessed to already have three healthy children. I knew my children, who had been campaigning for another sibling, would be sorely disappointed, but we would try again. My tears were not for them either. My tears were for all the people who suffer real tragedies, far greater losses, genuine adversity and calamity, and come to synagogue on the High Holy Days to hear *Un'taneh Tokef* tell them that their suffering is God's just judgment.

RABBI AMY SCHEINERMAN (NY84) does Jewish hospice, chaplaincy, teaching, writing, and public speaking. She is president of the Baltimore Board of Rabbis and the Greater Carolinas Association of Rabbis.

Un'taneh Tokef paints a picture of God as a Being who controls and manages the world, abrogates the laws of physics, and determines the length and quality of our lives. It is far from the only prayer that reflects a theology of judgment and retribution; it is merely the most graphic.

In *The Foreskin's Lament*, Shalom Auslander, who grew up in Monsey, New York, writes:

> When I was a child my parents and teachers told me about a man who was very strong. They told me he could destroy the whole world. They told me he could lift mountains. They told me he could part the sea. It was important to keep the man happy. When we obeyed what the man had commanded, the man liked us. But when we didn't obey what he had commanded, he didn't like us. He hated us. Some days he hated us so much, he killed us; other days, he let other people kill us . . . We called these days "holidays" . . . The people of Monsey were terrified of God, and they taught me to be terrified of Him, too . . . And so, in early autumn, when the leaves choked, turned colors, and fell to their deaths, the people of Monsey gathered together in synagogues across the town and wondered aloud and in unison, how God was going to kill them:—Who will live and who will die, they prayed—who at his predestined time and who before his time, who by water and who by fire, who by sword, who by beast, who by famine, who by thirst, who by storm, who by plague, who by strangulation and who by stoning.

Auslander describes how this theology can shape the soul of a child and instill fear and guilt. In fact, it eventually drove him out of Monsey, and far from his family of origin. Those of us raised in far different Jewish communities, if we had any Jewish education growing up, were probably exposed to a similar theology: God is omnipotent and omniscient, controlling and commanding. God loves and rewards, to be sure, but also becomes enraged and punishes. Auslander missed the loving and rewarding side of God and absorbed only the angry and punishing messages. On the High Holy Days, with *Un'taneh Tokef* taking liturgical center stage, we might too.

Structurally, *Un'taneh Tokef* is comprised of three parts:

1. The prayer opens with the assertion that each year we all stand trial for our deeds and failures to act in the past year. Will we be judged worthy to live another year, or will we be

found to lack merit? In the courtroom on high, so much is at stake that even the heavenly angels are gripped by fear and trembling. God, the cosmic Shepherd, herds us all before the divine throne for review; not a single one of us can escape judgment. God is Judge, Prosecutor, Witness, and Jury. (But aren't shepherds supposed to protect, not judge? And in what sense is a court where Judge, Prosecutor, Witness, and Jury are all the same "just?")

Then the terrifying litany begins: "How many shall leave this world and how many shall be born into it, who shall live and who shall die, who shall live out the limit of his days and who shall not, who shall perish by fire and who by water, who by sword and who by beast, who by hunger and who by thirst. . . ." Were this prayer being penned today, perhaps it would say, "Who by Hurricane Katrina or the Indian Ocean earthquake, tsunami, and floods? Who at the hands of terrorists in Israel or Mumbai? Who by violent car crashes on our highways? Who by brain cancer? Who by heart disease? Who by depression that drives them to suicide?"

The prayer continues: "Who shall rest and who shall wander, who shall be at peace and who shall be tormented, who shall be poor and who shall be rich, who shall be humbled and who shall be exalted?" Perhaps our twenty-first-century version might say, "Who will enjoy job security and who will be unexpectedly unemployed mid-career? Who will prosper and who will watch the bottom drop out of their 401(k)? Who will retain peace of mind, and who will suffer unending anxiety?"

2. The climax and turning point comes when we say, "*U't'shuvah u't'filah u'tzedakah maavirin et roa hag'zeirah*" ("repentance, prayer, and righteousness temper the severity of the decree"). In the ancient world, royal decrees were irrevocable. King Ahasuerus cannot retract the decree Haman issues with his imprimatur authorizing the wholesale slaughter of the Jews of Persia; at best he can issue an additional decree permitting the Jews to defend themselves. Given this understanding, what does it mean that we can *temper* the divine decree?

3. *Un'taneh Tokef* finishes with the assertion that God does not want to slam a guilty verdict down on us and consign us to the rubbish heap of history. God wants us to repent and

merit life. Yet the rock bottom reality is that we are ephemeral, mortal creatures. However long our lives, they are limited because we are like "fragile clay vessels, withering grass, fading flowers, passing shadows, fleeting clouds, vanishing dreams." God, in contrast, is boundless, timeless, and eternal. So the best we can do is to attach ourselves to God and ride God's coattails into eternity.

Un'taneh Tokef takes us on the yearly trip into the Forest of Frustration and Confusion. If God is both omnibenevolent and omnipotent, why is there such evil in the world? Why doesn't God prevent it? And if God is omniscient and omnipotent, in what sense can we say that God is good? Suffering is not reserved only for those who are "deserving." What is more, living in the twenty-first century, we are grounded in science: the laws of physics, biological processes of disease, and consequences of human choice. *Un'taneh Tokef*, long a theological conundrum, strikes the twenty-first-century mind steeped in science and rationalism minimally as straining credulity, generally as archaic and meaningless, and maximally as cruel and sadistic.[1]

What if we read the prayer not through the lens of rabbinic theology, but through the lens of process thought, as a process theology? Process theology is built on the foundation of Alfred North Whitehead's Process-Relationship Philosophy.[2] Alfred North Whitehead was a British mathematician and philosopher. After finishing *Principia Mathematica*, he turned to philosophy, seeking a cogent and comprehensive philosophy based on the one thing we know to be real: our experience. In the last analysis, it is all we "know." Whitehead sought to formulate a philosophical framework that is not at odds with science and, in particular, the revolutionary new ideas emerging from quantum theory about the nature of the universe and matter and their implications for human perception and experience. In a sense, Whitehead crafted a metaphysics of quantum physics. Whitehead believed that philosophy, and by extension theology, should work in concert with the discoveries of science to explain our universe and help us make meaning of our lives. Even more, he believed that his philosophical framework should be able to accommodate future scientific discoveries and "truths" without having to wholly revamp its notion of God and human existence.

The terms "process theology" or "process relational theology" first came into usage in 1950s in the Protestant world. They emerged from a debate between "Biblical-religious" thinkers and philosophical theologians. The former emphasized that the God of the Bible interacts with his creatures. The latter held that God is unchanging, absolute, and unconditioned, and hence unaffected by the universe. Whitehead, along with Charles Hartshorne, a theologian from the University of Chicago, sought a third way. Classical medieval theology, taking its cue from ancient Greece, saw the world as composed of forms and substances. Under the influence of quantum mechanics, Whitehead and Hartshorne described the world as composed of *events* and *processes*: occasions of experience. Our lives are a composite of experiences; when strung together we see that our lives are not static, but rather processes. We are not "beings," which are static and unchanging, but rather "becomings," continuously changing and evolving.

Process theology is panentheism: The world is in God, and God is in everything in the world. As *B'reishit Rabbah* 68:9, commenting on Psalm 90:1, expresses it: "God is the dwelling place of the world, but the world is not God's dwelling place." Put another way: Everything in the universe is part of the "body" of God, but God is also beyond the universe. God saturates and interpenetrates every part of the natural universe. God is the sum total of all of our experiences, and the experiences of the entire universe, but God is also beyond the universe.[3] God, who encompasses the entire universe, experiences all that we experience, including our pain and suffering. When we suffer, God suffers. This is not a God who judges and metes out punishment; this is God suffering with us, sharing our pain. *This* is the God I needed to meet in the operating room that Yom Kippur eve; this is the God I need in my life.

With this in mind, imagine for a moment that God is not as Shalom Auslander was taught: not a powerful, commanding, coercive, punishing Being who waits for us to slip up. Imagine that God is not a being at all, but rather that everything is contained within God and God is also beyond the universe. God is not immutable, unchanging, and wholly separate from our world but rather continuously changing and becoming because the universe is always in flux, always changing. God is as near and as intimate as our breath, our cells, the DNA that animates us and makes us who we are, the divine spark in each of us that makes us little lower than the angels. We, who are saturated with God are the hands, feet, eyes, ears, and mouths of God: We are the body of God. God cannot be omnipotent, because then we would be utterly powerless. God is not omniscient, knowing what we will choose before we decide, because then we would not have free will. Rather, God is the ethical lure that draws us to make the right choices, but does not force or coerce our choices. God is present at every decision and offers us the best choice, but we are completely free to decide. Because God is *within* us, as well as *beyond* us, God changes because we change. Perhaps it might help to think of God as the cosmic mind of the universe—always in flux, dynamic, rippling, changing. God knows each of us as we are—every decision we have made and how it is affecting the universe—but does not direct, control, reward, or punish. It is we who place that layer of interpretation on our experience of the world and ascribe it to God.

For the process theologian, rather than seeking to direct, control, reward, or punish us, God seeks to engage with us and empower us to align our lives with God and recognize the unity of all being and our place in the universe.

Through this lens, *Un'taneh Tokef* conveys a wholly different message. It is not about judgment, condemnation, and punishment, as Shalom Auslander hears it. Rather:

1. *Un'taneh Tokef* reflects the frightening and stark reality that our lives are finite may end prematurely. Our ancestors imagined that there is a God separate from the universe who is in charge. For a process theologian, the universe is in God, and only in that sense does God bring floods, earthquakes, and disease: They are part of the natural world. In the words of science fiction writer Robert Heinlein, "The supreme irony of life is that hardly anyone gets out of it alive."[4] But it is more than the knowledge of our mortality that haunts us. Novelist and essayist Joan Didion watched her husband die of a heart attack one evening at dinner. In her memoir of the year following his sudden and tragic death, *A Year of Magical Thinking*, she wrote, "Life changes fast. Life changes in the instant. You sit down to dinner and life as you know it ends."[5] Even if our lives do not end in sudden violence or illness, they will end because we are by nature, "like withering grass, a fading flower, a passing shadow, a fugitive cloud. . . . " It is only

when we stand in the stark, blinding light of our mortality that we can fully appreciate the immeasurable, incalculable *value* of our own lives. When we come to that realization—as Rosh HaShanah invites us to stop and do each year—we are faced with questions, the very asking of which can open doors to immense change for the better: **What am I doing with my life? How am I using my time? How am I spending my love? This is the power of *Un'taneh Tokef*.**

2. *Sefer HaZichronot* (the Book of Remembrance) is indeed written with our deeds. It is the totality of our universe—all that has ever been and all that is. Our decisions and actions have had their effect on the world, and in that sense *Sefer HaZichronot* is signed and sealed with our deeds. *Un'taneh Tokef* reminds us—at the moment we feel *most* vulnerable and powerless, and perhaps even inconsequential—that we have *genuine power*. We cannot change the fact of mortality and we cannot always avoid misfortune. But we can *temper its severity*. Consider our effect on the environment and how we have changed the landscape of our world. Consider how our decisions, individually, and nationally, affect the lives of people suffering in our backyard and around the world. Consider how your behavior—your attitude, your mood, your willingness to give and receive love—affects those nearest you on a day-by-day basis. ***Un'taneh Tokef* reminds us that we have real and meaningful power and must therefore use it with caution and in the cause of good. This is the power of *Un'taneh Tokef*.**

3. *U't'shuvah u't'filah u'tzedakah maavirin et roa hag'zeirah* ("repentance, prayer, and righteousness temper the severity of the decree") is the climactic statement and turning point of the prayer. As *Un'taneh Tokef* is the lynchpin of the High Holy Day liturgy, *u't'shuvah, u't'filah u'tzedakah* is the lynchpin of *Un'taneh Tokef*. While it may be the case that King Ahasuerus's decree is immutable, in God's real universe the future does not exist because it hasn't happened yet. The laws of nature limit the possibilities, and the past suggests probabilities, but we are not automatons responding to innate programming. We are more than our biology, more than massively complex chemical factories. We are not slaves to our instincts. We are endowed with free will, a divine spark, and

the capacity to cultivate our thoughts, choose our words, and make moral choices: Repentance is about our thoughts and intentions. Prayer is about our words. *Tzedakah* is about our deeds. Repentance, prayer, and righteousness are the avenues by which we exert our constructive will and influence on the world. They are how we *"maavirin et roa hag'zeirah,"* how we influence the direction of our lives and the life of the world. Where there is choice, there is hope and possibility. At every moment, God meets us and offers us a moral choice and the freedom to choose. **Un'taneh Tokef reminds us to use our freedom purposefully, carefully, and deliberately. This is the power of Un'taneh Tokef.**

Un'taneh Tokef reminds us where our immortality lies. Not in biology, but in having lived, learned, loved, and left our footprint on this world. Everything we do brings change to the world—and to God. Everything we do sends ripples out into the universe that continue to be felt by others—and by God. We are part of the cosmic mind of the universe, forever part of God. Therein lies our immortality, and it is indeed meaningful. As *Un'taneh Tokef* expresses it: "Your years have no limit. Your days have no end. Your mysterious name is beyond explanation. . . . And You have linked our name with Yours."

Interpreted through a process theology lens, *Un'taneh Tokef* is deeply comforting. Rather than imparting an ancient warning from a coercive, commanding, punishing God, it says: While there is much that is entirely beyond my control, and mortality is a reality I must face, I am not powerless: vulnerable yes, powerless no. The facts are the facts, but how I *respond* to them is entirely up to me. In every moment, with every breath, I have the opportunity to make choices that nurture life and cause goodness and righteousness to flow into the world. *Un'taneh Tokef* is a reality check that empowers us to live our lives with greater integrity and courage. What better message to hear on the High Holy Days?

Viktor Frankl was a neurologist and psychiatrist in Vienna when Hitler came to power. In 1942 he was deported to Theresienstadt along with his wife and parents. In Theresienstadt, Frankl treated both the medical and psychological needs of inmates overcome with shock and grief. He worked alongside Rabbis Leo Baeck and Regina Jonas. Frankl's wife was transferred to Bergen-Belsen and his parents were sent to Auschwitz. All three perished. Frankl survived the war, and from his experiences and observations he crafted the psychological theory of Logotherapy. In his pioneering book, *Man's Search for Meaning*, published in 1946, Frankl wrote, "We who lived in concentration camps can remember the men who walked through the huts comforting others, giving away their last piece of bread. They may have been few in number, but they offer sufficient proof that everything can be taken from a man but one thing: the last of the human freedoms—to choose one's attitude in any given set of circumstances, to choose one's own way."[6]

Un'taneh Tokef reminds us, when we feel powerless in the face of our mortality, that we have enormous strength: First, an inner power to ascribe meaning to our experiences and to decide for ourselves the purpose of our lives. Second, moral power to take charge of our lives and respond to the ethical lure God holds out to us by making the right choices. And third, a power that comes from knowing that as we do, we are changing the world and leaving our mark on it for all time. *U'sh'meinu karata vish'mecha.* (You have linked our name with Yours.)

Notes

1. The inverse problem also exists. Those for whom God is altogether absent resonate to the words of the Psalmist in the psalm of repentance recited from Rosh Chodesh Elul through Sh'mini Atzeret: "*Et panecha Adonai avakeish. Al tasteir panecha mimeni.*" (O Lord I seek You. Do not hide from me.) (Ps. 27:9).
2. An excellent introduction to process theology was published in these pages last year, authored by Rabbi Toba Spitzer: "Why We Need Process Theology," *CCAR Journal* (Winter 2012): 84–95.
3. Process theologians describe that differently. For some, it is *existence* itself: the very possibility of existence (which we usually take for granted). Ralph Waldo Emerson spoke of the Oversoul. Alfred North Whitehead himself described God as the Ultimate Source of possibility and potentiality in the universe. Torah describes God as "*Ehyeh-Asher-Ehyeh*" (I will become what I will become) (Exod. 3:14)—God is also becoming.
4. Robert A. Heinlein , *Job: A Comedy of Justice* (New York: Ballantine Books, 1984), 93.
5. Joan Didion, *A Year of Magical Thinking* (New York: Alfred A. Knopf, 2006), 3.
6. Viktor Frankl, *Man's Search for Meaning* (Boston: Beacon Press, 2006), 65–66.

Mystical Journeys and Magical Letters: The *Y'rushalmi*'s Cosmology in the *Machzor*

Judith Z. Abrams

So much of Judaism is clearly put together by contentious committees that it can be difficult to discern any coherent theology underlying it all. For example, our calendar is clearly a compromise between the solar and lunar factions, which led to the unwieldy nineteen-year, solar-lunar cycle we have today. Such negotiations, and their results, can be seen throughout our texts and traditions, including our prayer book and *machzor*. Both are pastiches of different schools of worship, and to understand them we must untangle the interwoven "genetic" strands so that we can see what different groups of Jews contributed to our worship. Then we can consider what is important to us and emphasize those elements.

Of course, we have at least two schools duking it out: the scribes and the priests. The scribes' voice is heard in the recitation of the *Sh'ma* and Its Blessings with the "choreographical" element of wearing *t'fillin*. If you think about it, there is nothing terribly prayerful about the recitation of the *Sh'ma* itself unless it is simply to proclaim one's love of the text.

The priests managed to get their prayer in as well: the *Amidah*, which replaces the sacrifices and gives almost no airtime to the scribes. Once we are into the body of the weekday *Amidah* and we pass the personal petitions, we have a step-by-step plan of action for the restoration of the Temple cult: God will return, punish the wicked, reward the righteous, and rebuild Jerusalem and the Temple and the sacrifices—normal, thanksgiving, and peace offerings—will begin again. (It is telling that in the *Y'rushalmi*'s version of the weekday

---

RABBI JUDITH Z. ABRAMS, Ph.D. (C85) is founder of Maqom: A School for Adult Talmud Study (www.maqom.com) and is the author of many books and liturgies.

Amidah [JT *B'rachot* 2:4], the House of David is not mentioned. Apparently the priests felt no great love for the political leaders that caused their business to crash.)

Now, if there are three crowns—the crowns of the priesthood, the Torah (scribes), and royalty (*Avot* 4:13)—where do we find the prayers of the kings in the prayer book? It seems unlikely that their voice would be silenced altogether. So where is it? It is in the prayers of *Heichalot* mysticism, created in the land of Israel between 70 and 500 C.E. Royalty is there; it's just changed its address. Earthly kings had failed the Jewish people too many times. Only God could be king. But a heavenly king must have a palace, guards, retinues, and court procedures, just as an earthly one did. To come before a king was a risky business on earth; all the more so, approaching one in heaven.

Let us imagine making a journey to meet our closest approximation to a king: the president. One doesn't simply knock on the White House door and say, "Yoo hoo, I'm here!" You have to make the journey to Washington, going through airport security, which might stop you from getting on your plane. Once in Washington, you'd have to petition your congressman or some other official to get you an audience with the president. You'd encounter roadblocks, inspections, and unhelpful guardians during that process. Then you'd have your background thoroughly checked by the Secret Service. There is a gatehouse before you can approach the White House. There is another guard inside who would wand you and there are further Secret Service agents ready to arrest you should you even sneeze incorrectly. There is an undersecretary who might block your approach to an actual secretary, who might block you before you get to an actual presidential aide, who might inform you that, unfortunately, the president is busy today and won't be able to see you and that you'll have to come back tomorrow. And if you actually met the president, you'd probably sing *Hallel* for actually having made it—or at least taken out your iphone and have your picture taken with the president to prove you'd actually visited the Oval Office. Afterward, you might jump up and down and grin, saying, "Wow! That was cool!" The prayers that embody this experience are the prayers of the *Heichalot* mystics, and they are part of our standard prayer service, too. In this essay, we'll explore parts of our weekly and High Holy Day prayers from this school.

Early Mysticism in the Land of Israel

When the Temple was destroyed, the place for our direct connection with God, our private line, so to speak, vanished. But the corresponding "telephone" still existed in the place it had always been—in heaven. The Sages of Israel sought to rebuild the connection to heaven, untethered to one physical location. That meant that the worshiper, instead of using the Temple's "direct line," would have to make the trip to meet God in heaven. But how could we go and visit God in heaven without staying there permanently? The journey would be almost unimaginably long and arduous and we would have no guarantee of a safe return to our world. So the Sages outlined the journey, and its dangers, by casting it as a trek through seven heavenly halls in early mystical works (70–500 C.E.) such as *Maaseh Merkavah* and *Heichalot Rabbati*.

Rhythmic Prayers and *Kaddish*

Prayers from these schools of worship have their own unique rhythms and rules of composition. So, for example, we learn that: "Second and third-person, imperfect hitpa'el verbs praising God are used as a form of opening for prayers . . . The accumulation of such verbs in series is . . . a feature of Heikhalot hymnology."[1]

Kaddish, of course, in all its permutations, would be the parade example of this sort of prayer. Each word, therefore, is a step up a steep ladder to meet God. Each set of steps (i.e., each new recitation of *Kaddish* throughout the service) signals us that we are moving higher and closer to God. This renders repetition of *Kaddish* meaningful instead of boring.[2] By the time we reach the Mourner's *Kaddish*, then, we are not only in God's presence, we are in the presence of our deceased relatives, who, presumably, are in heaven. (The video of Gershwin's "I'll Build a Stairway to Paradise" from *An American in Paris* can be an effective teaching tool here. As each stair lights up as he ascends, so each word of *Kaddish* is a step that leads us higher and higher.)

The rhythm of the *Kaddish* also can induce a meditative state, as can other *Heichalot* prayers that find voice in the *machzor*, for example, this acrostic:

> Excellence and faithfulness—are His who lives forever.
> Understanding and blessing—are His who lives forever.

Grandeur and greatness—are His who lives forever.
Cognition and expression—are His who lives forever.
Magnificence and majesty—are His who lives forever.
Counsel and strength—are His who lives forever.
Luster and brilliance—are His who lives forever.
Grace and benevolence—are His who lives forever.
Purity and goodness—are His who lives forever.
Unity and honor—are His who lives forever.
Crown and glory—are His who lives forever.
Precept and practice—are His who lives forever.
Sovereignty and rule—are His who lives forever.
Adornment and permanence—are His who lives forever.
Mystery and wisdom—are His who lives forever.
Might and meekness—are His who lives forever.
Splendor and wonder—are His who lives forever.
Righteousness and honor—are His who lives forever.
Invocation and holiness—are His who lives forever.
Exultation and nobility—are His who lives forever.
Song and hymn—are His who lives forever.
Praise and glory—are His who lives forever.[3]

The rhythmic, repeated descriptions of God, as well as the acrostic form are forerunners to the *piyutim* that mark so much of the High Holy Day liturgy.

The King

While earthly kings come and go, and even dynasties arise and fade, God as King in the *Heichalot* literature is untethered to history. In this literature, we enter a realm outside of history, even fictional history. If we think of Israel at this time, this is logical. Human history for the Jews in Israel from 70 to 500 C.E. is tough at best and tragic at worst. The kings are Roman emperors who, unlike their Persian predecessors, do not allow the Temple to be rebuilt. It is no accident, then, that these mystics sought out a different sort of king.[4]

For the High Holy Days, prayers systematically draw attention to God as King; whether it be in the *K'dushah* (...*hamelech hakadosh*) or in *Avinu Malkeinu*, changes in the liturgy for the High Holy Days emphasize God's kingly aspect. This is another feature of *Heichalot* mysticism. "The repetition of the word *melekh*, 'King' followed by an adjective or noun as a construct pair forms the basis for several hymns found in Heikhalot literature, particularly in Heikhalot Rabbati."[5] Thus, whenever we refer to God as King in the *machzor*, we can direct worshipers to experience this as a step upward in their spiritual quest to come as close to God as possible.

Unfriendly Spirits

On the High Holy Days, our sins and merits are marshaled as prosecuting and defending witnesses against us or in our behalf. Our sins loom large as we see them assembled in full. God remembers, counts, and weighs all our sins, and they pile up to the heavens. When taken in their aggregate, they form threatening, monstrous obstacles to the gates of redemption. This sense of impending danger is the counterpoint to the *Heichalot*'s experience of ecstatic union with God and it, too, is given voice in the *machzor*. In *Heichalot* mysticism, obstacles guard the seven levels of heaven. For example, each gate into the palace is defended by eight guards:

> At the gate of the seventh palace, the guards stand angry and war-like, strong, harsh, fearful, terrifying, taller than mountains and sharper than peaks. Their bows are strung and stand before them . . . Their swords are sharpened and in their hands. Bolts of lightning flow and issue forth from the balls of their eyes, and balls of fire [issue] from their nostrils, and torches of fiery coals from their mouths. They are equipped with helmets and with coats of mail, and javelins and spears are hung from their arms. (*Pirkei Heichalot* 17:8)

These are "killer angels" in the most literal sense. They have all the violence that is the hallmark of the Big Bang. They may also be echoes of the guards that were likely to be in an earthly court, surrounding the king. (A visual aid here might be the Terra Cotta warriors guarding the king's tomb.)

It is no accident, then, that when the journeyer finally reaches the seventh heavenly hall, and stands before God's footstool, s/he says, "*Alai l'shabeiach la-Adon hakol.*" The origin of the *Aleinu* is this early mysticism and we place it at the end of our services not to signal that we're mopping up, but to signal final, ecstatic union with the Divine. And it is an individual achievement, not a team effort, in this liturgy.

Counting as Mystical Practice

Another feature of this kind of mysticism is its penchant for counting as a way to comprehend God's vastness and one's own smallness. So, here, we see how long and dangerous the journey to heaven is:

> Rabbi Yishmael said: I asked Rabbi Akiba: What is the distance between one bridge and another? He said to me: Between one bridge and another [the distance] is 12,000 parsangs. At their ascent 12,000 myriad parsangs and their descent 12,000 parsangs.
> Between the rivers of fire and the rivers of awe 21,000 parsangs
> Between the rivers of awe and the rivers of fear are 22,000 parsangs.
> Between the rivers of hail and the rivers of darkness there are 36,000 parsangs.
> Between the chambers of thunder and the cloud of consolation there are 42,000 parsangs.
> Between the clouds of consolation and the Merkavah there are 84,000 parsangs.
> Between the cherubim and the Ofanim there are 24,000 parsangs.
> Between the Ofanim and the chamber of chambers there are 24 myriad parsangs.
> Between the chambers of chambers and the Holy Creatures there are 4,000,000 parsangs.
> Between one wing and another there are 12,000 parsangs, and such was their width.
> Between the Holy Camps and the Throne of Glory to the place where the Holy, high and exalted King, God of Israel is seated upon it there are 40,000 parsangs and his Great name is sanctified there. (*Maaseh Merkavah* para. 559, p. 234)[6]

The distance to the goal *increases*, rather than decreases, as the journey wears on. This is one of the counterintuitive truths of the spiritual quest: the more you learn, the less you know.

Counting and measuring all sorts of things is a feature of this school of mysticism. For example, Shiur Koma measures God's physical form. Obviously, the actual measurement of God is not the point; the point is contemplating numbers so large that they make us aware of our own Lilliputian dimensions.

The *K'dushah* as an Organizing Principle Underlying Services

Part of the liturgy that marks the seeker's progress through the heavenly halls is the *K'dushah*. The third blessing of the *Amidah* is a simple form of the prayer that is recited during the silent saying of the *Amidah*. It is not automatically logical that it should change into the *K'dushah* in the *Amidah*'s repetition. So why is it there? It is a post marker along "heaven's highway" through the seven heavenly halls. As you progress through the heavenly halls, the *K'dushah* is recited:

> In the first Hekhal, Merkavot of fire say: Holy, Holy, Holy is the Lord of Hosts, the whole earth is His glory and their flames spread out and gather together to the second Hekhal and say, "Holy, holy, holy . . ." (Maaseh Merkavah, 232)

The *K'dushah* is repeated in various ways until, in the seventh *heichal*, they say:

> Blessed be the King of Kings, Adonai, Lord of all power.
> Who is like God, great and enduring?
> His praise is in the heaven's heaven,
> The holiness of His Majesty in the highest heaven,
> His might is in the inner chambers,
> From this one, "holy" and from that one "holy"
> And they present song perpetually pronouncing the name . . .
> and say, "Blessed be the name of His majesty's Glory forever and ever from the place of His Shekhinah." (*Maaseh Merkavah*, 232–33)

If you think about the number of *K'dushah*s in a standard (non-Reform) Shabbat service you have a total of seven (including the *K'dushah*s in the *Amidah*s as repeated).[7] Thus, we see that the journey through the seven heavenly halls and the seven heavens underlies our liturgy.

Other Mystical Heroes and Democratizing Heaven

We are used to thinking of Rabbi Akiba as the mystical journeyer par excellence. However, the *Y'rushalmi* emphasizes Rabbi Elazar ben Arach's spiritual acumen. When Rabbi Elazar ben Arach and Rabban Yochanan ben Zakkai learn the works of the chariot together:

> Fire fell from heaven and surrounded them, and the ministering angels skipped before them like wedding guests rejoicing before the bridegroom. An angel answered from the midst of the fire

and said: According to your words, Elazar ben Arach, is the Work of the Chariot. (JT *Chagigah* 2:1, 77aV)

In other words, though some occupants of the heavenly halls mean the journeyer harm, there are also some who rejoice when we successfully make the trek.

Rabbi Elazar is joined in his spiritual excellence by Rabbi Yose haCohen and Rabbi Shimon ben Netanel:

> Rabbi Yose the priest and Rabbi Shimon ben Natanel . . . began to discourse on the Work of the Chariot. They said: it was a day in the summer season, and the earth shook and a rainbow appeared in the cloud. And a heavenly voice (*bat kol*) came forth and said to them: "Behold the place is vacant for you and the dining couches laid out for you. You and your disciples are destined for the third heaven." This corresponds to what is said, "In Your presence there is fullness of joy (Psalm 16:11)." There are *seven* classes of righteous in the time to come. (JT *Chagigah* 2:1, 77aV)

This passage lends a democratizing bent to the spiritual quest. We need not be great sages to attain a place in the heavenly spheres. There is room in these halls for seven whole classes of souls with sufficient righteousness.[8]

Heavenly Gates and a Midrash on Jonah

The idea of gates to each heavenly hall is a memory and reflection of the gates within the Temple compound. In this "midrash" on the story of Jonah, the mystics tell us that the Temple gates were also miraculous (and the heavenly ones, all the more so):

> Miracles occurred to Nikanor's doors and he was remembered with praise. He was bringing them to Israel on a ship to Israel and a great storm came upon them on the Mediterranean Sea.
>
> They threw one of his doors overboard, then they sought to throw the second door overboard, too. But Nikanor hugged the door and said to them: If you throw this door into the sea, you will have to throw me overboard with it. The storm subsided but Nikanor continued crying and mourning for the door that was lost until they landed in Jaffa. And some say a giant sea creature swallowed the door and spit it up onto the land at Jaffa port.
>
> Once they docked in Jaffa, the door popped up from under the boat.

And this is what we learn (in *Mishnah Midot* 2:3): All the gates were changed from copper to gold except for Nikanor's gates because a miracle occurred with them.

And some say that their copper shone so brightly that they looked like gold.

And it was taught in Rabbi Eliezer's name that the copper shone and was more beautiful than gold [so there was no need to change these doors to gold]. (*Tosefta Yoma* 2:4; JT *Yoma* 3:8, 25a2; BT *Yoma* 38a)

Nikanor's gates in the Second Temple were in a central place, figuratively and literally. They were the gates through which worshipers passed from the waiting area to the place where they offered their sacrifices. It would have been before these gates that people would wait and through these gates that atonement and salvation awaited via the sacrifices. In a very real sense, they were the physical gates of prayer to which the Reform Movement so often referred metaphorically.

Even the Letters of the Alphabet Give Us Courage

This democratization of heaven is even built into the letters that recount the creation of the world:

אֵלֶּה תוֹלְדוֹת הַשָּׁמַיִם וְהָאָרֶץ בְּהִבָּרְאָם בְּיוֹם עֲשׂוֹת יְהֹוָה אֱלֹהִים אֶרֶץ וְשָׁמָיִם:
Two worlds were created with two letters—with the yud and the hey—this world and the world-to-come. From where do we know this? "Trust in the Lord for ever and ever, for in Yah you have an everlasting rock. (Isaiah 26:4)"

בִּטְחוּ בַיהֹוָה עֲדֵי־עַד כִּי בְּיָהּ יְהֹוָה צוּר עוֹלָמִים:
But from this verse we still do not know which of the two was created with the yud and which with the hey. However, we know what is written, "These are the generations of the heaven and of the earth *b'hibaram*, i.e., with a hey and a yud they were created. (Genesis 2:4)"

"With hey He created them." This world was created with the hey and the next was created with the yud. As the hey is open be-

> neath, this indicates that all the inhabitants of the world shall go down to Sheol. As the hey has an upward projection, after they have gone down to Sheol they shall go up [to heaven]. As hey is open on every side, so a door is open to all who repent. As the yud is bent, so all the inhabitants of the world shall be bent low [with shame], as it is written, "All faces are bent low with pallor. (Jeremiah 30:6)"
>
> When David saw the significance of the letters, he began praising the Holy One, blessed be He, with the two letters, with the yud and with the hey, as it is written, "Halleluyah! Praise God in His sanctuary. . . . Let every thing that has breath praise Yah. Halleluyah (Psalm 150:1, 6)" (JT *Chagigah* 2:1; *P'sikta Rabbati Piska* 21:20; *B'reishit Rabbah* 12:10)[9]

In the *Y'rushalmi*, this midrash immediately follows the story of Elisha ben Abuya who won't repent because he is sure he will never be forgiven. So this playful midrash is a counterbalance to that story. The implication is that *everyone* is forgiven in the end.

Conclusion

We can think of our prayer services as living, breathing entities. Beneath the "skin" are layers of muscle and fascia, organ systems, and circulation mechanisms. And underlying all of these is the skeleton. One important part of that skeleton, which gives structure to our prayers, is *Heichalot* mysticism, which leads us higher and higher. Through the imaginings of mystical journeys, fanciful midrash, counting and meditative prayer, our services form a great, rising arc toward holiness.

Notes

1. Michael D. Swartz, *Mystical Prayer in Ancient Judaism: An Analysis of Ma'aseh Merkavah* (Tübingen: Mohr, 1992), 201.
2. "The composers of Ma'aseh Merkavah were evidently not content to sublimate their longing for the direct presence of God in this manner. They wished to experience the heavenly worship directly. To this purpose, they marshaled the affective powers of prayer and incantation." Ibid., 223.
3. *Pirkei Heichalot* 28:1; David R. Blumenthal, *Understanding Jewish Mysticism: The Merkabah Tradition and the Zoharic Tradition*, trans. Lauren Grodner (Jersey City, NJ: KTAV, 1978), 86.
4. "In *Heichalot* literature, historical allusions of any kind, accurate or fictional, are rare." Swartz, *Mystical Prayer*, 216.

5. Ibid., 205.
6. See BT *Chagigah* 12b–13a for more on the contents of the seven levels of heaven. "From the earth until the first heaven is a 500-year journey. And from one heaven to another is a 500-year journey. And the thickness of a heaven is a 500-year journey. And the same is true of each and every heaven . . . Even to traverse the hooves of the Chayyot [heavenly beings] is a 515-year journey . . . equal to the numerical value of the word yesharah [shall dwell, covering, straight, or unified; see Ezek. 1:7]. See how high God is above His world, yet when a person enters into a meetinghouse (beit k'neset) and stands behind the pillar and prays in a whisper, the Holy One, blessed be He, listens to his prayer." BT *Chagigah* 12b.
7. *P'sukei D'zimrah*, *Yotzer*, *Amidah* (2), Torah Service, *Musaf* (2).
8. A parallel text tells us about the organization of the righteous in heaven: "In Your presence is fullness of joy, at Your right hand there are pleasures for evermore." Ps. 16:11. "The companies of the righteous will be arrayed in the form of the candlestick of the Temple . . . Which of these companies is the most excellent and best loved? The one standing upon the right side of the Holy One blessed be He." Midrash Psalms 16:11.
9. In *P'sikta Rabbati* this midrash is part of a commentary on the Ten Commandments.

The *Machzor* before the *Machzor*: Interpreting the High Holy Days during the Second Temple Period

Aaron D. Panken

The little-known Second Temple period (586 B.C.E. to 70 C.E.) represents one of the most exciting periods of literary development in the early phases of our people's history. Heady interactions with Persian, Greek, Roman, and other external cultures created a potent brew of intellectual foment that resulted in experiments with new forms of writing, the potential for broad reinterpretation of extant literature, and the expansion of the activities of the literate class in highly creative ways. While there was certainly no authoritative, written assemblage of prayer texts (let alone a developed *machzor*) in this pre-Rabbinic era, much fascinating activity took place that shaped the course of later developments during the Rabbinic period, influencing far later impressions of the High Holy Days. Best of all, many of the issues that pervade the literature around the High Holy Days from this period are remarkably parallel to our own situation in contemporary North America. In this article, I hope to provide a glimpse into just a few of the uniquely creative interpretive developments of this period and briefly consider what lessons it might have for *machzor* reform in our own time.

Philo

Philo Judaeus of Alexandria (c. 10 B.C.E. to 45 C.E.) provides us with the High Holy Day phenomenological standout of his time. His *De Specialibus Legibus* (*The Special Laws*) takes on the momentous task of explaining the manifold laws and customs that make

---

RABBI AARON D. PANKEN, Ph.D. (NY91) has served as dean and vice president of HUC-JIR and has taught Rabbinic and Second Temple Literature at HUC-JIR/New York since 1996. He thanks the students in his Advanced Second Temple Literature class at HUC-JIR/New York of Fall 2011 for their helpful insights and musings on these texts as they studied them.

Judaism different from other religious systems. In his discussion on Yom Kippur, we find words describing the situation in first-century Egypt that feel as if they were written yesterday:

> On the tenth day [of the seventh month] is the fast, which is carefully observed not only by the zealous for piety and holiness, but also by those who never act religiously in the rest of their life. For all stand in awe, overcome by the sanctity of the day, and for the moment the worse vie with the better in self-denial and virtue. The high dignity of this day has two aspects, one as a festival, the other as a time of purification and escape from sins, for which indemnity is granted by the bounties of the gracious God Who has given to repentance the same honour as to innocence from sin.[1]

Here, Philo grapples with themes still prevalent in contemporary *machzorim* and the congregations reading them: bringing close those normally distant from religious practice and piety, the uniquely universal feeling of awe Yom Kippur evinces, and the tension between the experience of the "worse" sinners and once-a-year attendees who stand right next to the "better" regulars among the multitudes swelling a normally smaller congregation. The two overall aspects Philo delineates (festival versus purification) also parallel our own experience. Our observance is so often a mélange of binary oppositions: haute couture versus humility; the festive dinner before *Kol Nidrei* and the sumptuous post-*N'ilah* breakfast versus the headaches, halitosis, and hunger of the day's purification; the unified duality of *avinu* (the loving, celebrating parent) versus *malkeinu* (the harsh, judging sovereign); and so on. Notably, in this definitively pre-Christian document, Philo also presents a Jewish concept of salvation by grace—God does not forgive us because we are worthy of forgiveness, rather it is God's gracious equating of repentance with innocence that creates even the possibility that we might be forgiven. Such eschewing of God's harsh judgment and concomitant privileging of divine mercy recurs regularly in the words of the *machzor*.[2]

Earlier in this same work, Philo offers an imaginative reinterpretation of the Temple ritual on Yom Kippur. Beginning with a physical description of the Temple precincts in Jerusalem, he explains:

> Right in the very middle stands the sanctuary itself with a beauty baffling description, to judge from what is exposed to view. For

all inside is unseen except by the high priest alone, and indeed he, though charged with the duty of entering once a year, gets no view of anything. For he takes with him a brazier full of lighted coals and incense, and the great quantity of vapour which this naturally gives forth covers everything around it, beclouds the eyesight and prevents it from being able to penetrate to any distance.[3]

Amidst the sublime beauty of the most sacred place of Jewish worship, Philo implies that it is not actually the physical surroundings that make High Holy Day worship especially sacred. In fact, it is the unseen, unknowable reality that exists just beyond our eyes, inaccessible even to the High Priest, which elevates us beyond the mundane. This is so often the case at the High Holy Days: the unseen—long-past deeds and long-gone loved ones and those with whom we interact infrequently—loom somehow larger as we muster and number and consider on this sacred day. Likewise, God's presence seems enlarged and fortified not because of any particular physical space, but because of our special sense of focus. Cloaked in invisibility there exists a *mysterium tremendum*, a powerful, unknowable presence that bespeaks, in Rudolf Otto's felicitous terms, "awfulness," "overpoweringness," and "urgency."[4] Long before modernity, Philo's outlook anticipates this important concept of the power of the unseen at Yom Kippur.

The Book of Jubilees

Beyond Philo's evocative descriptions of contemporary celebrations and celebrants, much of the additional creative output of the Second Temple period turns its gaze toward the past, building upon a firm foundation of biblical texts to imbue the High Holy Days with innovative meanings. Second Temple authors often chose to link Rosh HaShanah and Yom Kippur back to various biblical characters and occurrences, reconstructing these holy days into annual commemorations of specific pivotal occasions in the lives of revered ancestors. This served two purposes: first, it rooted the observance of these holidays more firmly into our people's cherished folk history. Second, it allowed later authors to reshape the valence of particular elements of the holidays to stress the values and ideals they held dear, allowing for the redirection of tradition in new and continuously relevant ways.

We find some fine examples in the Book of Jubilees, an early interpretive parallel to the Book of Genesis, likely written in Hebrew during the second century B.C.E. in Palestine. While it often follows Genesis quite closely, it reinterprets and adds freely to the biblical tradition, opening a fascinating entrée for understanding the exegetical and improvisational trends of this period. In Jubilees, the date of Rosh HaShanah is set alternately against a backdrop of activity by Noah and Abraham. In Noah's case, Jubilees defines the first day of the seventh month (Tishrei) as the moment when "the mouths of the abysses of the earth were opened, and the waters began to descend into them."[5] That is to say, God's primordial Flood began to drain away from the earth on the day of Rosh HaShanah, a potent reminder that though those who engage in injustice will face God's penalty, the punishment meted out will not be arbitrary or endless: rather, only the righteous will be saved by God. Linking Noah with Rosh HaShanah in this manner reinforced *midat hadin* (the judgmental aspect of the holiday), crafting it as a time when the righteous (read: Noah and his family) will choose to abandon their sins, even as they watch the sinners (read: everyone else) pay dearly for their sinful actions. Jubilees, then, marshals the Flood story as an impetus toward *t'shuvah*, goading those who can act righteously to do so and raising the specter of horrid punishments to bring the sinner back in line.

Contrast this punishing reminder of judgment with Jubilees' longer depiction of Rosh HaShanah as a signpost along the way on Abraham's journey to monotheism:

> Abram sat up during the night on the first of the seventh month, so that he might observe the stars from evening until daybreak, so that he might see what the nature of the year would be with respect to rain. And he was sitting alone and making observations; and a word came into his heart saying: "All of the signs of the stars, and the signs of the sun and the moon are all in the hand of God. Why am I seeking?
>
> If God desires, God will make it rain morning and evening, and if God desires, God will not send [it] down; and everything is in God's hand."
>
> And he prayed on that night, saying:
> "My God, the Most High God, you alone are God to me,

And You created everything,
And everything which is was the work of Your hands,
And You and Your sovereignty I have chosen.
Save me from the hands of evil spirits,
Which rule over the heart of humanity,
And do not let them lead me astray from following you, O my God,
But establish me and my seed forever,
And let us not go astray henceforth and forever."[6]

Jubilees provides, here, a very early explicit linkage between Abram and Rosh HaShanah, one that will eventuate in the reading of the *Akeidah* as one of the Rosh HaShanah Torah portions many years later. It also anticipates the various annual judgments of agriculture we find later in *Mishnah Rosh HaShanah* 1:1. At a deeper level, for Jubilees' Abram, Rosh HaShanah was his first day of repentance and change—the moment when he ceased to see the world through idolatrous eyes and acknowledged, instead, God's providence and ultimate control of the world. This realization led him to leave his pagan homeland and family and begin the famous trek described in Genesis 12 to a new land and the founding of a new people. Read thus, Rosh HaShanah becomes the initial point for the personal spiritual journey from that which is prohibited—idolatry and the worship of stars and constellations—to that which is endorsed—the proper worship of the one God behind it all. Rosh HaShanah stands as an opportunity for each of us to walk in the footsteps of our ancestor Abram—to journey to a better place through the abandonment of misplaced personal religious faith and the taking on of more appropriate belief and practice. Such actions have the potential to build the future of our people in powerful, meaningful and long-lasting ways, as they once did for Abram.[7]

Read together, Jubilees' utilization of Noah and Abram encourages a useful combination of carrot and stick. The connection to Noah's Flood reminds readers of the punishment that awaits sinners as a stick that will inspire the unmotivated penitent to action (not unlike God's withholding inscription in the Book of Life or some of the scarier death sentences so prominent in *Un'taneh Tokef*). The more self-motivated penitent may simply look to Abram's carrot, the compelling prospect of many offspring and a life well-lived in service to God and the Jewish people.

Jubilees' author proceeds to create new understandings of Yom Kippur as well. Jubilees reorients the background for Yom Kippur by tying it to the ongoing strife between Joseph and his brothers. After paraphrasing Genesis 37, in which Joseph's brothers throw him into a pit and sell him to passing Ishmaelites, Jubilees states:

> And the sons of Jacob slaughtered a kid and dipped Joseph's garment into the blood and sent (it) to Jacob, their father, on the tenth of the seventh month. And he lamented all of that night, because they had brought it to him in the evening. And he became feverish in lamenting his death, and said that, "A cruel beast has eaten Joseph." And all of the men of his house lamented with him on that day. And it happened as they were mourning and lamenting with him all that day that his sons and his daughter rose up to comfort him but he was not comforted concerning his son.[8]

On Yom Kippur, Jubilees suggests, Jacob received the bloodied clothing of his beloved Joseph, along with the fabricated story of Joseph's jealous brothers, and he commenced intense mourning without any possibility of being comforted. One could certainly read this as a plea for honesty and integrity to other human beings. After all, nearly the entire family knew that Joseph's death had been faked and that Jacob's grief was unnecessary at best, or misdirected at worst. This primordial moment of mourning sets the scene for Jubilees' next interpretive act, which reads Yom Kippur as a communal day of mourning:

> Therefore it is decreed for the children of Israel that they mourn on the tenth [day] of the seventh month—on the day when that which caused him to weep for Joseph came to Jacob, his father— so that they might atone for them[selves] with a young kid on the tenth [day] of the seventh month, once a year, on account of their sin because they caused the affection of their father to grieve for Joseph, his son. And this day is decreed so that they might mourn on it on account of their sins and on account of all their transgressions and on account of all their errors in order to purify themselves on this day, once a year.[9]

This represents a significant excursion from the text of Genesis 37, which certainly never ties Yom Kippur to this incident. While this sort of insertion is not unusual for the Book of Jubilees, one has to ask what provoked the editor to make such an addition? A few possibilities come to mind. First, since the Jewish people are defined initially as children of Jacob (*B'nei Yisrael*), their actions in this story represent the first significant *communal* sin for which they can be held accountable as a corporate body. Such communal sin makes this incident well-suited for introducing the concept of the Day of Atonement for *all* the people of Israel.

Second, the appearance in Genesis 37:31 of the term *seir izim* (he-goat) creates a compelling intertext with identical language to the two goats of the Yom Kippur ceremony in Leviticus 16. There, the entire Israelite community provided two male goats for the Yom Kippur observance. Aaron (the High Priest) offered one goat, selected by lot, as a sin offering, ensuring its immediate death. Aaron then confessed the communal sins of the Israelites over the other goat, now designated the "scapegoat," and drove this sin-bearing goat out to the wilderness, to carry away the people's sins and make expiation for them.[10] Such an uncanny and uncomfortable resemblance with the story of Joseph (designated for God, and sent to his death) and his brothers (carrying sin, but living on) is hardly an accident. Jubilees reengineers the symbolic goats of Yom Kippur into reminders and atonement vessels not only for the community's current sins, but also for its earliest sin, assuaging leftover communal guilt from this troubling piece of our ancestral story. Tying Yom Kippur to these behaviors holds a mirror up to the brothers and demands their repentance, even as it warns future generations to avoid such cruelty.

The Dead Sea Scrolls

An obscure text from the Dead Sea Scrolls known as the Words of Moses (1Q22), likewise, proffers an interesting reinterpretation of biblical precedent with respect to Yom Kippur. This short work parallels parts of Deuteronomy and is preserved on thirty-two small fragments found at Qumran.[11] Unfortunately, the extant text is quite fragmentary, as can be observed in this excerpt about Yom Kippur:

Column III
7 [Go]d will bless you, forgiving you your] sin[s…] …
8 […] in the year […] of the month of
9 […] … […] on this day [… For] your [father]s wandered
10 [in the wilderness] until the [te]nth day of the month{the […on

the te]nth [day] of the month}
11 [You shall] refrain [from all work]. And on the te[nth] day [of the] month, atonement shall be made…

Column IV
1 in the congregation of the gods [and in the council of the ho]ly ones and in their […, in favour of the sons of Isra]el and on behalf of the la[nd]
2 [And] ta[ke] from [its blood and] pour (it) on the earth […] … […]
3 [and atone]ment [shall be made] for them by it…[12]

If we accept the reconstructions in brackets above, we find, unsurprisingly, the standard trope of Yom Kippur as day of atonement. Yet Yom Kippur is also aligned with a variety of notable moments in our people's mythic history. Yom Kippur comes, this Qumran text posits, at the time of the cessation of our people's wanderings (column III, lines 9–10). That is to say, our people stops their nomadic way of life and becomes settled in their land (presumably the land of Israel, though the text is not explicit) specifically on the day we celebrate Yom Kippur. Further, in column IV, line 1, when atonement is made, it is not only for the *people* of Israel, but for the *land* as well.[13] Atonement, then, becomes an act linked with landedness—a time of proper settling when one finds one's rightful, righteous place in this world. Yom Kippur represents the time of coming into a new and better home and keeping that home properly ordered and free of sin.

Intriguing, as well, is the reference in the same line to "the congregation of the gods [and in the council of the ho]ly ones," which certainly causes the mind to drift to thoughts of the introductory lines of *Kol Nidrei*, where both the *yeshivah shel maalah* and *yeshivah shel matah* participate in the courtroom setting established for the purpose of judging sinners. These words have preceded *Kol Nidrei* only since the thirteenth century, when they were added by Rabbi Meir of Rothenburg (1215–1293), but the ideas they express have a much older provenance, based in divine councils of the Ancient Near East[14] and echoed here in the Dead Sea Scrolls.

Another text from the unique genre of Qumranic *pesharim* constructs Yom Kippur as the day of a critical battle between the representatives of good and evil. Similar to midrash, but earlier and less developed, a *pesher* is a "type of biblical interpretation found in the

Qumran scrolls in which selected biblical texts are applied to the contemporary sectarian setting by means of various literary devices."[15] *Pesharim* begin with a *lemma* (a biblical statement quoted verbatim) from the book at hand[16] and follow it with an interpretation that is specific to the contemporary situation of the sectarians. This allows *pesharim* to apply older biblical texts to the present-day, retrojecting interpretations to create biblical support for the ideology of the sect. Pesher Habakkuk, one of the first scrolls to be found at Qumran, applies this method to the Book of Habakkuk with intriguing results:

> Column XI
> 2 (Hab. 2:15) "Woe to anyone making his companion drunk, spilling out
> 3 his anger, or even making him drunk to look at their festivals."
> 4 Its interpretation concerns the Wicked Priest who
> 5 pursued the Teacher of Righteousness to consume him with the heat
> 6 of his anger in the place of his banishment. In festival time, during the rest
> 7 of the day of Atonement, he appeared to them, to consume them
> 8 and make them fall on the day of fasting, the sabbath of their rest.[17]

Pesher Habakkuk understands Habakkuk 2:15's use of the term "their festivals" (*mo'adeihem*) as referring specifically to one manifestation of Yom Kippur in its contemporary world. The festival becomes the specific occasion for attacks on the sect by the Wicked Priest, a standard Qumranic character who works against the accepted sectarian leadership. Having this evil individual act against the Teacher of Righteousness (apparently one of the sect's most revered leaders) on the most sacred day of the year creates a nexus of heinous actions, far beyond any sectarian's possible acceptance. Such a scenario further valorizes the Teacher of Righteousness as a warrior for good, even as it completely vilifies the Wicked Priest. The interpreter's goal seems to be to personify the battles between good and evil that take place within each of us during Yom Kippur and expand them to have greater cosmic significance as they play out on the axis of sect versus world. In this way, it structures a world in which there are two very distinct poles in a grand struggle between the righteous and the sinners. Such a structure motivates listeners to consider carefully where they sit and to place themselves in the right corner through their deeds and through proper atonement.

In these few examples, we have begun to garner a sense of the active, innovative minds that were at work on our tradition during this early period of biblical interpretation and literary innovation. We noted some remarkable similarities between Philo's vision of his congregation and its rituals and those of our own time; we saw the exciting redeployment of biblical characters and scenes for new effect; and we saw how the agglomeration of ideas affiliated with Yom Kippur has served as a flexible symbol set with room enough for our people's nomadic wandering, our ancestors Noah, Abram, and Joseph, and even the battle of a Wicked Priest and Teacher of Righteousness. Such broadly meaningful symbolism was well-prepared to stand the tests of time and supplied useful precedents for themes that inhabit our *machzorim* still centuries later.

A Brief Closing Thought

Aside from reveling in the exciting ingenuity of these texts, there is also a meta-message to those who would engage in new acts of Jewish creativity as the editors of any new *machzor*: Second Temple texts suggest that editors not be afraid to rework, reconsider, and redirect understandings of prior material, for this is a healthy and natural part of the enduring Jewish interpretive process. Such literary creators must look to respond to the needs of the contemporary community in each new time and place, as the generations before always have. At the same time, though, they ought to note how their predecessors valued what came before them: rather than wantonly discarding challenging texts and ideas, they redeployed earlier models with sensitivity, respect, and love for their inherited tradition. That, surely, is the balance, the challenge, and the joy inherent in confronting any traditional text and remaking it for new meaning, whether before there was a *machzor* two millennia ago or before our movement's new one right now.

Notes

1. F. H. Colson, trans., *Philo*, vol. 7 (Cambridge, MA: Harvard University Press, 1937, repr. 1998), Special Laws 1:186.
2. See, for example, *Avinu Malkeinu* and the closing paragraphs of *Un'taneh Tokef* for just two examples of this tension between God's mercy and God's judgment.

3. Colson, *Philo*, Special Laws 1:72.
4. Rudolf Otto, *The Idea of the Holy* (London: Oxford University Press, 1923; repr. 1958), 12–30.
5. Adapted from Jubilees 6:26–27 in James H. Charlesworth, *The Old Testament Pseudepigrapha*, vol. 2 (New York: Doubleday, 1985), 68.
6. Adapted from Jubilees 12:16–20 in ibid., 81.
7. Compare, also, elements of the story in Genesis 15, when God takes Abram outside at night to count the stars and states that his offspring will be as numerous as they are. Rashi, ad loc., reads this as a call to give up his astrological speculation and see that with his new name (Abraham instead of Abram) comes an entirely revised celestial fate, also a sign of God's power over celestial happenings.
8. Jubilees 34:12–14, in Charlesworth, *Pseudepigrapha*, vol. 2, 121.
9. Jubilees 34:18–19, in ibid.
10. The Mishnah and Gemara also depict this ceremony in great detail, in chapter 4 of tractate *Yoma*.
11. Lawrence H. Schiffman and James C. VanderKam, eds., *The Encyclopedia of the Dead Sea Scrolls* (Oxford: Oxford University Press, 2000), s.v. "Moses"; Eibert J.C. Tigchelaar, "A Cave 4 Fragment of Divrei Mosheh (4QDM) and the text of 1Q22 1:7–10 and Jubilees 1:9, 14," *Dead Sea Discoveries* 12, no. 3 (2005): 303–12.
12. The English translation is from Florentino García Martinez and Eibert J.C. Tigchelaar, *The Dead Sea Scrolls Study Edition*, vol. 1 (Leiden: Brill, 1997), 62–63. The text was originally published in J.T. Millik, *Qumran Cave 1* (*DJD* 1; Oxford: Clarendon Press, 1955), 91–97.
13. Some scholars locate the origins of the High Holy Days within an ancient temple purification ceremony, observed in Sumerian, Babylonian, and Assyrian cultures. For a useful bibliography see David Noel Freedman, ed., *Anchor Bible Dictionary* (New York: Doubleday, 1992), s.v. "Akitu." The biblical account of Yom Kippur in Exodus 30:10 appears to preserve the concept of an annual purification of the altar in a similar vein, and the purification of the High Priest himself is a main focus of Leviticus 16's understanding of the holy day. These factors bolster the idea presented in this text of a land- or temple-centered festival.
14. See Marc Zvi Brettler, "The Heavenly Assembly," in *All These Vows—Kol Nidre*, ed. Lawrence A. Hoffman (Woodstock, VT: Jewish Lights, 2011) for a short review of the ancient precursors to the concept of *yeshivah shel maalah*.
15. Schiffman and VanderKam, *Encyclopedia*, s.v. "Pesharim."
16. A *lemma* is not unlike the familiar *dibbur hamatchil* by which printed commentaries indicate the verse they are analyzing.
17. Martinez and Tigchelaar, *Dead Sea Scrolls*, vol. 1, 18–21.

Yom Kippur in Moab: Reflections on the Setting of the *Parashah*

Elsie R. Stern

The designation of new Torah portions for Rosh HaShanah and Yom Kippur was one of the signature innovations of the early Reform High Holy Day liturgy. Since at least the 1894 *Union Prayer Book for Jewish Worship*, Reform *machzorim* have designated Deuteronomy 29:9–14 and 30:11–20 as the Torah portion for Yom Kippur morning instead of the traditional readings from Leviticus 16 and Numbers 29:7–11. In addition, until the publication of *Gates of Repentance* in 1979, American Reform *machzorim* omitted the entire *Avodah* service.[1] When they were instituted, these liturgical innovations articulated key ideological principles of the Reform Movement. The traditional readings and the *Avodah* service promulgated both traditional Judaism's affirmation of the privileged role of the ancestral priesthood and its ongoing hope for the reestablishment of the Temple cult. The omission of these texts by the early Reformers signaled the movement's rejection of these doctrines; the choice of the Deuteronomy readings affirmed the movement's belief in "the doctrine of personal responsibility" and articulated the central Reform principle that Torah, rather than the Temple cult, was the primary tool in the quest for redemption.[2]

While their ideology may have been radical, the Reformers' choice to use the Torah service as an opportunity to express their convictions is a time-honored one. Since its origins in the Second Temple period, the ritual recitation of Scripture in the synagogue has provided an opportunity for communal leaders to articulate ideas that they feel are important for their communities. The earliest literary representation of the reading of a prophetic text in a synagogue, which appears in the New Testament in Luke 4:15–21, provides a case in point. In this scene, Jesus recites verses from

---

ELSIE R. STERN, Ph.D. is associate professor of Bible at the Reconstructionist Rabbinical College.

a scroll of Isaiah and then explains that "today this scripture has been fulfilled in your hearing." Similarly, the lectionary readings that emerge during the Rabbinic period often articulate, in biblical language, central Rabbinic tenets and perspectives.[3] In addition, Rabbinic *p'tichtaot*, medieval *piyutim*, and medieval and modern *divrei Torah* all testify to the ways in which the texts of the Torah service have provided material and vocabulary for reflection on contemporary concerns and experiences.

Before the standardization of the liturgy, some of these Torah-inflected reflections were woven into the liturgy itself through the composition and performance of *piyutim* that were keyed to parts of the liturgy but were specific to the language and themes of the lectionary readings for a particular Shabbat or festival. For example, in a synagogue that performed Eleazar Kallir's *k'dushtaot* for the weeks following Tishah B'Av, the generic *K'dushah* would have been replaced by a poetic composition that combined elements of the *K'dushah* rubric with themes and language drawn from the week's haftarah and the midrashim associated with it. After the liturgy became standardized, however, this porousness between the lectionary and liturgy disappeared; the statutory liturgy and the lectionary readings, along with their accompanying explication or reflection, became two discrete elements in the worship service. One of the affects of this change was the creation of a contrapuntal relationship between liturgy and lectionary that allowed the Torah service to function as a thematic and experiential "change of venue" within the worship service—a time for communal engagement with, and potential immersion in, images and themes distinct from those of the surrounding liturgy.

The traditional Torah portion for Yom Kippur morning provides a powerful example of this phenomenon. With the exception of the *Avodah* service, the liturgy specific to Yom Kippur morning is saturated with royal and forensic language and imagery. The confessions and petitions all situate the worshipers as supplicants in the divine court where they confess their sins and attempt to earn acquittal, or at least a reduced sentence, from the omniscient and omnipotent divine sovereign. While the characterization of God in the Yom Kippur prayers is awesome, the construction of the human experience is quite earth-bound and naturalistic. In the imaginary courtroom of the Yom Kippur liturgy, worshipers confess their sins, proclaim their insignificance and remorse, and pray for forgiveness. The results of these actions unfold in real time over the course of the day. If their repentance is sincere, and if God acts mercifully, by the end of the day, they will be absolved of their guilt.

This scene shifts radically during the Torah and *Avodah* services. The traditional Torah readings describe the rituals for the annual purification of the innermost shrine of the tabernacle (Lev. 16) and the offerings mandated for the day (Num. 29:7–11). The ritual described in Leviticus 16 in turn becomes a generative text for the *Avodah* service. BT *Yoma* 36b and 56b attest to the recitation of the Mishnaic tractate *Yoma*, which is a tannaitic description of the Yom Kippur ritual that took place in the Second Temple. By the Middle Ages, the *Avodah* service had developed into an extensive reflection on this ritual and its role as centerpiece in a cosmic narrative that begins with the creation of the world and continues to the present day. As a meditation on the Temple cult and a theologically charged review of cosmic history, the *Avodah* service provides the worshiper with an opportunity to take a break from the liturgical courtroom and engage with an array of ideas and images that are absent from the surrounding liturgy. The *piyutim* of the *Avodah* service invoke creation, angels, the privileges of Israel and the priests, and divine glory and grandeur. Poetically, they deploy tropes of beauty, mystery, and wonder that are absent from the confessions and petitions of the rest of the day.[4] As Lawrence Hoffman has noted, the *Avodah* service also places the issues of sin, repentance, and forgiveness, which are at the heart of the surrounding liturgy, into a cosmic perspective by identifying sin, repentance, and forgiveness as the engines that drive Israel's historical experience.[5] The traditional Torah portion then, serves as the doorway into the cosmic theater of the *Avodah* service. Reflection on the priestly ritual from Leviticus leads to reflection on the Temple and its Yom Kippur ritual and their respective roles in the geography and history of the cosmos. The worshipers' experiential sojourn in the world of the *Avodah* service has the potential to shape the surrounding work of *t'shuvah* by placing it in a cosmic perspective. The *Avodah* service potentially inflects the worshipers' experience with nostalgia for the glory of the Temple and an anxiety about the cosmic effects of its absence. At the same time, the dialogue between the surrounding liturgy and the *Avodah* service suggests that the results of the individual "trials" that are unfolding on Yom Kippur have the power to influence the history of the world.

As I noted above, the Reformers used the Torah service as an opportunity to "speak their truth" through biblical texts. However, they did not exploit the potential change of venue made possible by the relationship between the new lectionary text and the liturgy. In what follows, I will take up that task. What would happen if we used the Torah portion as the gateway to a sojourn in Moab, which is the setting of Deuteronomy 29–30? Where might this imaginative journey lead and what effects could it have, at least potentially, on the Yom Kippur experience?

Unlike "Egypt," "Jerusalem," and the "land of Israel," the mythic resonances of "Moab" have not survived in Jewish culture. Whereas the invocation of "Egypt" has the power to conjure images of slavery, plagues, and the "narrow places," the invocation of Moab has far less resonance. This fact belies the size of Moab's footprint in the Pentateuch and beyond. Within the Torah alone, Moab is mentioned thirty-one times and is the subject of two discrete narrative episodes: Genesis 19 articulates a myth of origin for the Moabites and Numbers 22–24 tells the story of Balak, the king of Moab, and his attempts to get Balaam to curse the Israelites. In addition, Deuteronomy 2 and 23 refer to a prior encounter of the Israelites with the Moabites. Finally, the entire book of Deuteronomy is set in the steppes of Moab on the boundary of Canaan. Because it is the setting for Deuteronomy, in terms of pure page count, more of the Torah takes place in Moab than in any other single locale. Outside the Pentateuch but still within the *Tanach*, Moab and the Moabites continue to appear. Ruth is a Moabite and the beginning of the book of Ruth takes place in Moab; there are narratives of battles with the Moabites throughout the Deuteronomic history and oracles against the nation appear in several prophetic books.[6] Among this array of texts, a significant cluster deal with concerns about the boundaries and stability of Israelite identity—suggesting that, in the postexilic period at least, Moab and Moabites provided loci for anxiety over, and reflection on, these concerns.[7]

While communal identity is often a concern of contemporary Jewish communities, it is not the primary focus of Yom Kippur. In the context of the holiday, a different cluster of Moab texts emerges that resonate with the process of *t'shuvah*. In the spirit of the theatrical metaphor I used above, I will present these texts as different scenes that the worshiper might experience during a Yom Kippur sojourn in Moab.

Scene 1: Deuteronomy 29–30—If Only It Were So (Part 1)

[15]See, I set before you this day life and prosperity, death and adversity. [16]For I command you this day, to love the LORD your God, to walk in His ways, and to keep His commandments, His laws, and His rules, that you may thrive and increase, and that the LORD your God may bless you in the land that you are about to enter and possess. [17]But if your heart turns away and you give no heed, and are lured into the worship and service of other gods, [18]I declare to you this day that you shall certainly perish; you shall not long endure on the soil that you are crossing the Jordan to enter and possess. [19]I call heaven and earth to witness against you this day: I have put before you life and death, blessing and curse. Choose life—if you and your offspring would live— [20]by loving the LORD your God, heeding His commands, and holding fast to Him. For thereby you shall have life and shall long endure upon the soil that the LORD swore to your ancestors, Abraham, Isaac, and Jacob, to give to them. (Deut. 29:15–20)

Our first Moab text, the Torah reading for Yom Kippur morning, asserts that its hearers inhabit a world that is marked by moral clarity (v.15), free will (v.19), and clear and consistent consequence (vv.15–18). When stated so baldly, the utopian nature of this vision becomes apparent. Any worshiper engaged seriously in the work of *t'shuvah* knows that each aspect of this assertion is subject to nuance, if not outright rejection. The clarity assumed by the assertion of an accessible divine will contradicts much contemporary experience of real moral ambiguity. Similarly, the unnuanced assertion of free will resonates naively for many contemporary people. Even within its ancient Israelite context, the assertion of a clear and simple choice was part of Deuteronomy's rhetorical strategy, rather than a worldview shared by all members of its audience. In all probability, the choice to worship only *YHVH* in the central shrine in Jerusalem was not a simple one. It would have demanded the abandonment of ancient and traditional practices including the worship of other long-venerated gods as well as *YHVH* in ancient and holy shrine sites. Any thoughtful Israelite would have experienced this as a difficult choice in which the pull of tradition and traditional authority came into conflict with newer forms of authority allied to the king and Jerusalem priesthood. By describing the choice of *YHVH*-only worship as a starkly simple one, Deuteronomy denies the validity of the alternatives it outlaws and denies the complexity of the choice that it demands. Like its vision of moral clarity, the Torah portion's unequivocal assertion of free will may also strike contemporary Jews as an idealized vision, out of synch with lived experience. While many contemporary Jews still adhere to a theoretical doctrine of free will, most also recognize that our choices are rarely, if ever, unfettered. Gender, race, class, and DNA all place constraints on our freedom in ways that make the reality of choice far more complicated than Deuteronomy's clarion call admits.

Perhaps the most wishful part of Deuteronomy's worldview is its assertions that all our actions have consistent and predictable consequences. Like the doctrine of free will, the belief that human experience is an unalloyed meritocracy in which good is rewarded and bad is punished rarely sustains extensive scrutiny. Here, too, factors of power and privilege as well as luck come to bear, making it far from certain that good will be rewarded and evil punished. By spending time in Moab on Yom Kippur, worshipers can take a break from the complexities of the moral world they inhabit and both recognize and engage with the powerful fantasy of moral clarity, free choice, and consistent consequence that the Torah portion asserts. Just as the traditional Torah portion serves as a gateway into longer imaginative sojourns in the Temple, so, too, can the portion from Deuteronomy serve as a gateway to other Moab experiences that lie outside the bounds of the lectionary reading.

Scene 2: Numbers 22–24—If Only It Were So (Part 2)

And now that I have come to you, have I the power to speak freely? I can utter only the word that God puts into my mouth. (Num. 22:38)

The story of Balaam offers a fantasy that is diametrically opposed to, but equally as poignant as, that of Deuteronomy 29–30. Numbers 22–24 recounts the story of Balaam, a seer who reluctantly agrees to the king of Moab's request to curse the Israelites. Despite his eventual acquiescence, Balaam states clearly from the outset that he can only say what God wants him to say. In the ensuing scenes, Balaam repeatedly blesses the Israelites in more and more enthusiastic terms. After each oracle, Balak protests: "What have you done to me? Here I brought you to damn my enemies, and instead you have blessed them!" Balaam repeats: "I can only repeat faithfully what the Lord puts into my mouth." Thinking that a change of venue might improve the outcome, Balak suggests that Balaam try again from a different vantage point. However, the outcome is the same. Each time Balaam opens his mouth to curse the Israelites, he ends up blessing them, in total conformity to God's will. When read in its canonical context, this story functions as a testament to God's immense power. Like the story of the hardening of Pharaoh's heart, the Balaam story asserts that God is more powerful than even the most powerful gentiles. Within the context of the Book of Numbers, this assertion of power functions ironically in light of the ability of the Israelites to repeatedly resist God's will. On Yom Kippur morning, however, the Balaam story resonates in yet another way—as a wishful counterpoint to the work of *t'shuvah*. Unlike Yom Kippur worshipers who are grappling with the consequences of human agency and the ability to make good and bad moral decisions, Balaam presents us with the fantasy of the person who has no choice but to do the right thing. No matter how many times he tries, no matter how rich the reward, no matter the change of venue, Balaam cannot do other than what God wants. While Deuteronomy 29–30 asserts that we are totally free, the story of Balaam offers us the possibility of no choice at all—the only possibility is obedience to God.

When we consider these two texts together, Moab becomes the site for the articulation of two fantasies, diametrically opposed to one another, that give voice to two of the longings that the process of *t'shuvah* can bring: On the one hand is the longing for crystalline moral clarity, unfettered free will, and clear and consistent consequences for good and bad behavior. On the other is the desire for a world in which moral behavior did not require such vigilance—a world, like that which Balaam inhabits in Numbers 23, in which we are compelled to do what is right regardless of our self-interest or the interests of people more powerful than we are.

Scene 3: Deuteronomy 2:28–29, 23:4–5—*Ashamnu*, or Maybe Not

> What food I eat you will supply for money, and what water I drink you will furnish for money; just let me pass through—as the descendants of Esau who dwell in Seir did for me, and the Moabites who dwell in Ar—that I may cross the Jordan into the land that the LORD our God is giving us.
>
> (Deut. 2:28–29)

> No Ammonite or Moabite shall be admitted into the congregation of the LORD; none of their descendants, even in the tenth generation, shall ever be admitted into the congregation of the LORD, because they did not meet you with food and water on your journey after you left Egypt, and because they hired Balaam son of Beor, from Pethor of Aram-naharaim, to curse you.
> (Deut. 23:4–5)

Both of these references to the encounter between Israel and Moab during the Israelites' journey to Canaan are ascribed to Moses in his farewell addresses on the steppes of Moab. Despite their common attribution, the two versions are incompatible. The first implies that Moab did grant the Israelites safe passage; the second asserts that they did not. From a historical perspective, these two versions represent variant traditions about the encounter between the Israelites and the Moabites that were circulating in ancient Israel before the redaction of the book of Deuteronomy. For reasons that are now irretrievable, both versions made it into the textual tradition that became the backbone for the Masoretic text. During our Yom Kippur sojourn in Moab, however, this contradictory account provides a fruitful counter-narrative to the Deuteronomic worldview. Whereas Deuteronomy 29–30 asserts that human experience is marked by moral clarity and clear consequence, the conflicting accounts of the encounter with Moab offer a vision of a much muddier human experience where not only the moral valence of our actions is unclear but where even the very facts of the case are up in the air.

Scene 4: Deuteronomy—Remembering and Retelling

> These are the words that Moses addressed to all Israel on the other side of the Jordan.
> (Deut. 1:1)

Moab is the site of the Bible's most extensive recollection. In the beginning of the book, Moses remembers for the people what they have experienced since they left Egypt. In comparison to the wishful portrayals of moral action in Deuteronomy 29–30 and Numbers 20–22, the act of remembering attributed to Moses feels far more realistic. Like most memories, Moses' account is selective, self-serving, and purposeful. He "remembers" and retells those episodes that are relevant to the moment of remembering—his farewell to the Israelites on the brink of their entrance into the land of Canaan. He also "remembers" in a way that serves his own interests. In Numbers, Moses is forbidden from entering the land of Canaan on account of his own actions. In Moses' account, he is not allowed to enter because of the transgressions of the Israelites (Deut. 3:26). Finally, Moses' retelling is purposeful. He tells a version of the wilderness experience that testifies to God's power and to the allegiance that the Israelites owe God as a result both of their gratitude for God's saving actions and of their covenantal agreement. On Yom Kippur, this distinctively human portrayal of memory can come into conversation both with the portrayal of divine memory in the *Zichronot* section of the Rosh HaShanah liturgy as well as with the acts of memory that are necessary to the work of *t'shuvah*. On Rosh HaShanah, worshipers remind God of God's role as "remember-er" and urge God to remember those elements of the past that will work in the community's favor. On Yom Kippur, worshipers echo this act by searching their memories for the sins that they have committed and the webs of habits and circumstances that led to these misdeeds. In the *Zichronot*, God's memory is cosmic, flawless, and magisterial. Deuteronomy's portrayal of memory reminds us that ours is not. Rather the act of remembering is as personal and as purposeful as the remembered deeds with which we grapple.

A Yom Kippur sojourn in Moab then provides worshipers with the opportunity take a break from the nuts and bolts of *t'shuvah*: the cataloguing of transgressions, the work of true repentance, and the quest for alternative ways forward. Just as the sojourn in the Temple provided by the *Avodah* service situates the rest of Yom Kippur in a larger cosmic perspective, so, too, does the sojourn in Moab offer a wider perspective. Imaginative reflection on the Moab texts allows us to engage with the larger context of memory, morality, and agency that frame our understanding of our actions and their consequences. Whereas the traditional *Avodah* service might well lead participants to regard their transgressions with even greater rigor and dread and to mourn for the absent Temple with greater fervor, a sojourn in Moab has the potential to lead worshipers to do the work of *t'shuvah* with greater compassion and gentleness as it strikes poignant notes of both contrast and penitence with the experience of the day.

Notes

1. *Gates of Repentance* includes an *Avodah* service that explicitly reflects a modern myth of history and does not rely on the Temple and Temple service as central or generative symbols. For an analysis of this service, see Lawrence Hoffman, *Gates of Understanding*, vol. 2 (New York: CCAR Press), 138–44.
2. Ibid., 129.
3. Elsie Stern, "Concepts of Scripture in the Synagogue Service," in *Jewish Concepts of Scripture: A Comparative Introduction*, ed. Benjamin D. Sommer (New York: NYU Press, 2012), 19-26.
4. Michael Swartz and Joseph Yahalom, *Avodah: An Anthology of Ancient Poetry for Yom Kippur* (University Park: Pennsylvania State University Press, 2005), 30–39.
5. Hoffman, *Gates of Understanding*, vol. 2, 142.
6. Isa. 15:1–16:14, 25:10–12; Jer. 48:1–47; Ezek. 25:8–11; Amos 2:1–3; Zeph. 2:8–11.
7. Deut. 23:4–5 prohibits the admission of Moabites into the congregation of *YHVH*. This prohibition is invoked in Neh. 13:1–3 as support for the radical endogamy policy of the book's protagonists. The characterization of Ruth as a Moabite in the book of Ruth is likely a polemical response to exclusionary policies like that advocated by Ezra-Nehemiah. As Regina Schwartz has observed, even Gen. 19, which ascribes Moab's origins to the incestuous union between Lot and his daughters, can be seen as part of this conversation. Regina Schwartz, *The Curse of Cain* (Chicago and London: University of Chicago Press, 1997), 99. As quintessential foreigners, Moabites symbolize forbidden exogamy; as products of incest, they also stand in for prohibited radical endogamy. Appropriate Israelite marriage resides between these two extremes. It is not surprising that Moab became a flashpoint for these concerns. Moab was a close relation to Israel: The two entities probably came into being at about the same time; their languages, material culture, and religions were similar; and parts of the territory of Moab were sporadically under the control of the kingdom of Israel. It is often similar cultures, rather than radically different ones, that spark anxiety over communal identity and boundaries.

Maayanot (Primary Sources)

Maimonides' *T'shuvah* to Ovadyah the Proselyte

Philip Matoff Posner

In 1993 I had the honor of receiving my honorary D.D. and my D.H.L. on the same day. As I submit this translation[1] and commentary based on the chapter from my dissertation, *Sympathy and Empathy—The Stranger and Proselyte—As Seen in Maimonides' T'shuvah to Ovadyah the Proselyte,* I feel especially grateful to Professors Bob Katz[2] and Stanley Cheyet, *aleichem hashalom*.[3]

It is my thesis that Rambam's sensitivity to Ovadyah is primarily motivated by his empathy for the complex position of the proselyte. His *t'shuvah* exemplifies some of the major criteria of empathy, "the focus of attention is clearly on the feelings and the situation" of the proselyte who has asked for his help; it exhibits a "keen, almost vivid sense of closeness or sameness with the other person," and he writes to his respondent "in a manner sensitive to the other person's actual ongoing emotional world and context."[4]

In addition to Maimonides' empathy, this *t'shuvah* reflects a wonderful blending of tradition and innovation: True faith is manifest in one's personal relationship with God. And for Rambam, to use two modern terms, a "Jew-by-choice" precisely because he had chosen Judaism, merits far more "personal autonomy" in his prayer than that normally accorded a native Jew.

At this time in the history of the Jewish people when our survival may well come down to the numbers of Jews who assimilate away from versus those who convert to Judaism, Maimonides'

RABBI PHILIP MATOFF POSNER (C68) is semiretired; lives half the year in Mexico and half in Santa Cruz, California, with his partner, Louise; and is the author of *Food for Thought, Character and Soul—Recipes and Blessings Included.*

Mencouraging and empathic words to a proselyte of his time is especially meaningful and timely.

Not only is it a relevant text for our students who are studying for conversion, Maimonides' empathy and understanding of the position of the convert is an enlightening dynamic for the rabbi as well. Practically some sections of this *t'shuvah* may be used as a beautiful addition to a conversion ceremony.[5]

Like many others, this responsum does not bear the date of its composition, though there is scholarly consensus that it was written sometime between Maimonides' arrival in Egypt in 1167 and "a little before his death" in 1204. Franz Kobler is probably correct that the letter was written in the "last quarter of the 12th century"[6]— after Maimonides had written the *Mishneh Torah*.

Below is the text in **bold** and the commentary in roman.

Thus said Moshe the son of Rabbi Maimon, [a descendant] of the children [of those] "exiled from Jerusalem, a Spaniard," may his righteousness be remembered. We have received questions from Rabbi Master Ovadyah, the learned and intelligent righteous proselyte. May God reward his accomplishment(s) and may a perfect recompense be bestowed upon him by the Lord, the God of Israel, since he came to take refuge beneath His wings.

While it is unclear whether Ovadyah's "accomplishments" are more a matter of literary rhetoric than of substance, what is clear is that Maimonides, "usually a terse and concise writer," goes out of his way to instruct Ovadyah that he has a providential relationship with the God whose "wings" provide "refuge" to all proselytes who seek Him.[7] In so doing, Maimonides not only sets the theological stage for Ovadyah's specific liturgical concern, but illustrates his real understanding of a proselyte's "needs," which, according to Heinz Kohut, the psychotherapist who most favored empathy as a therapeutic tool, is crucial to the ability to empathize.

You have raised practical questions concerning the blessings and the prayers:[8] When you are all alone, praying by yourself or praying with the community, are you allowed to recite "Our God and God of our fathers," and "who sanctified us by his commandments," and "who has distinguished us," and "who has chosen us," and "who has bequeathed our ancestors an inheritance," and "who brought us out of the land of Egypt," and "who performed

miracles for our fathers," and any other relevant prayers or blessings that are derived from these?

These are "practical questions," as they deal with specific prayers and blessings of action, but as the next paragraph suggests they also relate to the proselyte's relationship with God and the Jewish people. Even though Ovadyah, judging by Maimonides' description of him, is a Jew of stature and wisdom, nevertheless he feels the need to ask serious questions regarding his status as a Jew."Obadiah," writes Menachem Lorberbaum, had ample reason to be anxious especially as he was attempting to enter a community whose "readings and declamations of the prayers were a daily reaffirmation of communal identity.[9]

One of the accepted psychological definitions of "empathy" is that it involves "other-oriented feelings of concern, compassion, and tenderness experienced as a result of witnessing another person's suffering."[10] But perhaps, because "it is the well-nigh unanimous verdict of the ages that Rabbi Moshe ben Maimon is the greatest authority in the realm of Halakha,"[11] there is the mistaken view that his rationalism, his elitist preference for the philosophers and the scientists, caused him to be devoid of feeling for others, especially the *amei haaretz* (masses). In his *Guide,* that cultural distance from the masses is expressed in this well-known passage:

> When . . . I see no other way of teaching a well-established truth except by pleasing one intelligent man and displeasing ten thousand fools—I prefer to address myself to the one man and to take no notice whatsoever of the condemnation of the multitude.[12]

"However, with that rational purposefulness there was also a deep humanity and compassion for his fellow man . . . a part of the generous qualities of his soul."[13] As seen in his *t'shuvah,* Maimonides' halachic genius has to be understood not only on the basis of "his own rationale of Judaism," but in his ability to remember and reflect on "his own actual experiences and critical situations."[14]And in that sense we need to remember that Maimonides personally experienced feelings of loss and deprivation: the loss of a homeland, the loss of a beloved brother, and the constant knowledge that he was the religious adversary.

Our Torah commands: "And you shall remember that you were a slave," elsewhere it says, "a stranger in Egypt!" Maimonides remembered that he was if not a slave then a servant in Egypt. And he knew how to live in his adopted land without feeling a stranger himself. The psychotherapist Alice Miller writes:

> A person who has consciously worked through the whole tragedy of his own fate will recognize another's suffering more clearly and quickly. He will not be scornful of other's feelings, whatever their nature, because he can take his own feelings seriously.[15]

Maimonides, although he called it *"rachamim,"* or *"rahma,"*[16] felt empathy intuitively, and bequeathed it to humanity as part of his legacy. He wrote his son:

> The passage of days impregnated me with variegated experiences and the trials of life made me wise. The lapse of time chastened me. He blessed and spared me until now and endowed me with an empathic understanding toward others.[17]

This same "empathic understanding toward others" reached across age and place to Jerusalem, to comfort and succor "a troubled, sensitive and vulnerable soul."[18]

You are expected to say everything in the standard way and should not change a single word. Furthermore it is proper for you whether you are reciting a prayer or a blessing, whether you are praying alone, or acting as the *sh'liach tzibur* (community prayer leader) to pray and bless as would any [other] native Jew.

Clearly, Maimonides' response to Ovadyah is an unequivocal affirmation of the proselyte's right to feel connected not only to God, through his private prayer, but equally connected to the Jewish community; so much so that Maimonides reminds Ovadyah that in our religion the proselyte is not only equal to every other "native Jew," but he may even serve as the *sh'liach tzibur*.

As suggested earlier, an individual's participation in community prayer and ritual is the heartbeat of religious affirmation, and the exact opposite of affirmation is the feeling of rejection. It is as if a Jew were to come to a rabbi and say: "At services whenever all of you say 'God of our ancestors' I feel as if I am standing outside, watching everyone else in the sanctuary connected in a prayerful embrace. I want to feel a part of the circle, but instead I feel like an uninvited guest."

Maimonides justified his legal decisions in this *t'shuvah* by casting Abraham as not only the embracing father, but as the first teacher and missionary of "the true faith"—a veritable warrior against idolatry.

And the basis [for this] statement is that it is Abraham our father who taught all the people, and enlightened them and informed them of the true faith and of the unity of the Holy One, blessed be He; spurning idolatry and inhibiting its practice he brought many children under the wings of the Divine Presence, and taught them the significance [of monotheism] and commanded his children and his household after him to observe the way of the Lord, as is written in the Torah [Gen. 18:19]: "For I have known him [to the end][19] that he may command his children, and his household after him that they may keep the way of the Lord."

Maimonides' genius is also seen in his ability to write a response that mandates the proselyte's inclusion in every prayer drawn by the Jewish community—one originally drawn by our father Abraham—so that all who choose to stand in that circle will never feel excluded. Maimonides' description of Abraham as the spiritual father of all who embrace monotheism suggests that Abraham, as the first proselyte, would understandably have a special empathy for all future proselytes. No wonder in the Jewish tradition the proselyte is *ben* or *bat* Avraham.

Just how universal is Maimonides' approach is seen in contrast to the particularistic and less empathic position of Judah Halevi, who in his *Kuzari* writes: "Those, however, who become Jews do not take equal rank with born Israelites."[20] Elsewhere, he writes, "Any Gentile who joins us unconditionally shares our good fortune . . . ," though again, "without, however, being quite equal to us."[21]

What makes Maimonides' position so different is that for him, our election is connected to our existence as a Jewish community that shares beliefs and truths—made sacred because of our covenantal relationship with God. For Halevi, the uniqueness of being a Jew is seen in our history—a history that, while certainly connected to belief, is distinctive because of our biological choosiness. Halevi writes:

> If the Law were binding on us only because God created us, the white and the black man would be equal, since he created them all.

But the Law was given to us because He led us out of Egypt, and remained attached to us, because we are the pick of mankind.²²

It is significant that both Maimonides and Halevi cast their theories of revelation in the framework of personality and history. But for Maimonides, Abraham's understanding of God is inclusive from the very beginning. Therefore, Maimonides holds, unlike Halevi, that those who convert to Judaism are of "equal rank" because monotheism is grounded not in God's election of a particular people, but in the possibility of all people believing in a God whose message, monotheism, and whose messenger, Abraham, are eternally valid, whether one is a Jew by birth or by choice.

Maimonides' brilliance is also seen in his emphasis that Abraham's invitation to the faith is redemptive throughout history—an eternal invitation—whose acceptance entitles that individual to full equality, for all time.

Therefore whoever converts, to the end of all generations, and whoever declares the oneness of the name of the Holy One, blessed be He, as is written in the Torah, is a disciple of Abraham our father, peace be upon him, and they are children of his household—all of them. For just as he turned them to [God's] right path, as he turned the people of his generation by [the words of] his mouth and his teachings, so he turned all the future [generations] that were to be converted by his mandate which he had commanded [to] his children and their household after him. [Thus] it is established that it is Abraham our father, peace unto him, who is the progenitor of his trustworthy descendants who walk in his ways, the father of his disciples and of every stranger who converts.

In Maimonides' portrayal of Abraham as the universal teacher, he not only undermines the community's possible claim of an election based on ethnicity as Halevi would have it, but he brilliantly sets the stage for the importance of belief and the idealization of the proselyte as an ideal member, in that the proselyte emulates the steps of the first spiritual father.²³

Therefore you are obligated to say "Our God and God of our fathers" for Abraham, peace unto him, is your father. And you are obligated to say "who has given our fathers an inheritance," for

the land was given to Abraham, as it says: [Gen. 13:17] "get up, walk through the land, its length and its width, for I will give it to you." However, [as for the blessings] "who brought you out of Egypt" or "who did miracles for your fathers," if you want to change [them] you may say: "who brought Israel out of Egypt," and "who did miracles for Israel."[24]

Maimonides' decision to allow the proselyte the right to include himself in the community of prayer by saying "our fathers," has an important provision that differs from the unequivocal inclusivism of "you are expected to say everything in the standard way and should not change a single word."

The proselyte has every right to recite a blessing that reads "our God and God of our fathers," because Abraham is also his father, but for blessings that say "your fathers," or blessings involving historical events such as the Exodus from Egypt at which the proselyte was not present, Maimonides (unlike other halachists) believes the proselyte ought to be given a choice as to whether he wants to say them or not.

This decision to grant an individual the personal freedom to change or not to change a prayer appears to be without liturgical precedent and reflects just how much, on the one hand, Maimonides identified with the proselyte's relationship to the community and, on the other, idealized the proselyte's autonomous relationship with God.

But if you do not change [them] it is of no consequence whatsoever. Since you have entered [the Covenant] under the wings of the *Shechinah* [Divine Presence], and are joined to it, there is no difference whatsoever between us and you. For all the miracles that were done, it is as if they were done for us and for you. And so it says in Isaiah [56:3]: "Neither let the son of the stranger, that hath *joined* himself to the Lord, speak saying, 'The Lord will surely separate me from His people.'"

Maimonides' adroit use of this Isaiah quotation suggests that the "stranger" who has become a part of the community and his son need to know that their personal covenant is exemplary of "join[ing oneself] to the Lord" through the *z'chut* (merit) of father Abraham. It is a merit that ought to mitigate any feeling of inferiority caused by a community's possible discrimination.

[Thus] there is no difference whatsoever between us and you. And certainly you have the obligation to say the blessing: "Who has chosen us," and "who has given us" [His Torah],[25] "who has bequeathed unto us an inheritance," and "who has distinguished us [from all the people]." For the Creator, may He be exalted, has already chosen you, and separated you from the [other] nations, and has given you the Torah—the same Torah he gave to us and to [you] the proselytes. As [Numbers 15:15–16] says: "As for the community, there shall be one statute for you and the stranger; it shall be a law for all time throughout the ages. You and the stranger shall be alike before the Lord; the same ritual and the same rule shall apply to you and to the stranger that resides among you."

It is fascinating to note that even after citing the above verse of Torah to support equality of treatment for the proselyte, Maimonides feels the need to blunt any chance that Ovadyah might still feel inferior. It is almost as if the Rambam had Halevi's statement in front of him, "but the Law was given to us because He led us out of Egypt, and remained attached to us, because we are the pick of mankind," and was all the more moved to "identify" with Ovadyah, lest Ovadyah might feel ashamed that his ancestors were not monotheists. Hence, Maimonides lessens that possibility by declaring that "our ancestors" had also worshiped "false gods."

And you should know that our ancestors who came out of Egypt—the majority of them had been worshiping false gods. In Egypt they were intermingled with non-Jews and were learning their way of life until the Holy One, blessed be He, sent Moses our teacher, peace be upon him, the teacher of all the prophets, and he separated us from the [other] peoples and gathered us under the wings of the *Shechinah*, us and all the proselytes, by giving all of us one law.

However, as much as the Rambam found a view like Halevi's strong ethnicity detrimental to a proselyte's Jewish self-esteem, it is especially Maimonides' commitment to monotheism that is the ideological basis for the above paragraph. True faith is not a derivative of history—whether it be redemption from bondage or even creation[26]—but comes through one's own personal knowledge of

God. Further, Maimonides suggests that in one's personal discovery of God, there is less likelihood that one will be led astray by community, as was the case for "our ancestral fathers," who had they remained attached to their non-Jewish beliefs would have remained polytheists.

At this point, Maimonides "utters the boldest theological statement"[27] of his responsum. Indeed, it is such an audacious statement that it is easy to assume it is unrelated to what has preceded it. However, as with all great deliberations, every word of Maimonides' *t'shuvah* has a purpose and a connection with previously stated thoughts. Implicit in the preceding is his view that our "ancestral fathers" are meritorious for their willingness to be "gathered under the wings of the *Shechinah*." Had they not accepted monotheism, their "merit" could not possibly encompass future proselytes.

Thus, the ancestors not only set the stage for a pluralistic concept of revelation, they also set in motion a revelation that included the corporate nation at Sinai with one that moves the individual proselyte to a personal acceptance of God. Further, by suggesting that "our ancestral fathers" had also once been "worshiping false gods," the proselyte "becomes a full-fledged member of this historic group, sharing its experiences, remembrances ... expectations and hopes."[28]

"As important as are history and community, man's ultimate relationship to God cannot be the exclusive experience of any particular historical community":[29] "Not only the tribe of Levi,[30] but every single individual from among the world's inhabitants whose spirit moved him and whose intelligence gave him the understanding to withdraw from the world in order to stand before God—to serve and minister to Him, to know God ...behold! this person has been totally consecrated and God will be his portion and inheritance forever and ever."[31]

Psychologically, the next paragraph again gives succor to the proselyte's requirement of Jewish self-esteem, although it also seems to be based as much on Maimonides' "role taking." Ovadyah's right to feel that having gained a new spiritual connection should not mean that he has to abandon his own familial ties. Also, because his individual decision to embrace Judaism cannot be separated from the Universal God, to whom he has claimed allegiance, the proselyte must never deprecate his genetic family whose existence is the result of God being the universal creator.

It is almost as if we may hear Maimonides saying to himself, "It is not fair that this Ovadyah, who has labored so hard, has sacrificed so much to be a Jew; who has every right to enjoy all the fruits of his Jewish vineyard with his Jewish family, should feel that he has to abandon his own genetic family."

But you must never view your own ancestry as unimportant; if we are related to Abraham, Isaac, and Jacob, behold you are related to the One who said and the world came into being.[32] And that is the way it is explained by Isaiah: "This one may say: I am the Lord's, and another may call himself by the name of Jacob."[33]

And everything that we have expressed to you concerning the blessings that you should not change [God of our fathers] and so forth, we already have proof for this from the tractate *Bikurim* (first fruits). There we learn: "The proselyte brings the [offering of first fruits] but does not recite [the proscribed] proclamation: My father was a wandering Aramean for he is not able to [literally] say: '[the land] which the Lord swore to our fathers to give to us,' but when he prays in the synagogue he should say: 'God of our fathers,' [and when he prays at home he should say 'God of our fathers'] and when he prays privately by himself he should say: 'My God, and the God of the fathers of Israel.'" And this in general is the Mishnah,[34] and it is according to Rabbi Meir, but it is not [accepted as] the halachah.

Maimonides' statement that "it is not the halachah," is radical indeed, not just because the viewpoint of the Gemara in the *Y'rushalmi* Talmud differs from this mishnah, but amazingly the mishnah text Maimonides quotes is not the Mishnah that we have today, either in the Babylonian or Jerusalem versions of the Talmud. This is particularly interesting, given the fact that he concludes the above statement by saying, "and this is *s'tam* the Mishnah," words which suggest that "he has the Mishnah in front of him."[35] In fact, although the mishnah Maimonides cites and the Mishnah we have both begin with the same view that "the proselyte brings the [offering of first fruits] but does not recite the [proscribed proclamation] . . .," they differ from then on. The Mishnah we are familiar with continues: "but if his mother was an Israelite he may bring them and make the avowal. And when he prays in private he should say, 'O God of the fathers of Israel'; and when he is in the Synagogue he should say, 'O God of your fathers.' But if his mother was an Israelite he may say 'O God of our fathers.'"[36]

However in the Kiva manuscript and in each of the eight texts, we read that when the proselyte prays in the synagogue he should say, "God of our fathers," and when he prays privately, he may say, "My God, and the God of the fathers of Israel." And six of the texts add an opportunity for him when he prays at home to say "God of our fathers."

For Maimonides, the proselyte, to use a contemporary term, was a Jew-by-choice, whose personal decision "to cast in his lot with the people Israel" also mandated that he be given the freedom to choose when and where to say "my God," and "God of the fathers of Israel."

Not only is Maimonides' wording different from the actual Mishnah, but allowing the proselyte to say "my God" in private prayer instead of the usual collective formula "our God" is unique, as the only prayer similar to it in the prayer book is the personal prayer of Rabbi Judah: "May it be thy will, O Lord my God and God of my fathers, to deliver me from. . . ."[37] Apparently, "Originally, personal prayers like this one were added before and after the A'midah...Eventually this one was added to the preliminary prayers (Birchot Ha shachar)."[38] It is possible, therefore, that Rabbi Judah's prayer served as the model for the blessing Maimonides composed for the proselyte to use while reciting the *Amidah*.

A question that cannot be ignored is: Did Maimonides use a variant Mishnah, one that is not available to us today, or as I believe possible, he purposely changed the Mishnah in order to include this blessing. I have two reasons for my view. The first is he has no alternative but to reject the position of the Mishnah as exclusionary and antithetical to his already stated position ("that there is no difference whatsoever between us **and** you...and certainly you have the obligation to say the blessing: 'Who has chosen us, and who has given us [His Torah], who has bequeathed unto us an inheritance, and who has distinguished us people . . .'"), all of which moves Maimonides to assure all proselytes explicitly of their right to feel included—part of the "us" in the praying house of all Israel.

Hence in the synagogue it would be inappropriate for the proselyte to have to say, "God of your fathers." With other Jews he should be able to say what all Jews say: "God of our fathers," whether "his mother was an Israelite," or he "entered the Covenant under the wings of the *Shechinah*" as "a son of Abraham." Otherwise the proselyte would feel like a stranger in his newfound spiritual home. But even in his own residence, he should have the opportunity to feel connected to the "God of our fathers."[39]

Secondly, perhaps as a way of indicating his real opposition to the exclusivism of the Mishnah statement, Maimonides gave the proselyte a choice given no other Jew—to say silently or in private: "my God, and the God of the fathers of Israel." Again this innovation reflects not only Maimonides' universalistic view, but it is a brilliant theological and liturgical rubric. Allowing the proselyte to say "my God" personalizes his relationship with God, which is fundamental to Maimonides' conviction that covenant is grounded in the Jew's relationship with God more than it is in community or history. Liturgically, the proselyte's opportunity to connect privately "and the God of the fathers of Israel" to the previous "my God" allows the proselyte the integrity of maintaining the covenant to the "fathers of Israel" without having to abandon the bond to his or her own genetic fathers. It also reinforces the previously stated, empathic "but you must never view your own ancestry as unimportant." It is a major change in the liturgy, but evidently not the only one he had made: "Maimonides made various changes in liturgical custom, the most radical of which was the abolition of the repetition of the Amidah in the interests of decorum."[40]

Further, the difference between the Mishnah itself as we know it and Maimonides' reading of it is made all the more intriguing and significant by the fact that in the Rambam's code, the *Mishneh Torah*, he seems to contradict himself. In *Mishneh Torah, Bikurim* his ruling differs with the Mishnah, and is therefore consistent with his position in this *t'shuvah*, as he states:

> A proselyte must bring first fruits and recite the confession, since Abraham was told, the father of a multitude of nations have I made thee [Gen. 17:5], implying that he is the father of everyone who enters under the wings of the Presence; and the Lord's oath was given first to Abraham that his children shall inherit the land.[41]

However in the *Mishneh Torah* of *Maaseir Sheini* (Second Tithe) he states:

> Israelites and bastards may make confession but not proselytes and freedmen, because the latter [too] have no share in the land, since it is said, and the land which Thou hast given us [Deut. 26:15].[42]

Is it conceivable that Ovadyah the proselyte sent his question to the greatest legal mind of the medieval period because he knew of this dichotomy in Maimonides' code? After all, Maimonides tells us that Ovadyah was a "learned and intelligent righteous proselyte." If he was indeed so "learned," then his anxiety may have been increased all the more by his knowing that the Babylonian Talmud also suggests that it is not appropriate for a proselyte to recite the proclamation with the first fruits:

> Said R. Ashi: since first fruits were also brought to the Temple by proselytes and they ought to have recited the [prescribed] wording "that I am come into the land which the Lord swore to our fathers to give us" and could not. . . .[43]

But even if Ovadyah was unaware of the contradiction between the two positions in the Code, and the view of the Babylonian Talmud, Maimonides certainly knew of the discrepancy, and that the halachah usually agrees with the Babylonian Talmud. He also knew that the contradiction between the two Talmudic positions was irreconcilable, which, parenthetically, might suggest that his ruling in this *t'shuvah* was especially significant because he wrote it after he had already stated the two different positions in the Code. Thus, as we shall see, his way out of the dilemma was to ignore the *Maaseir Sheini* statement in the Babylonian Talmud and cite the Jerusalem Gemara on first fruits, thus clarifying two issues—an explication of his contradictory statements in the Code, and an emendation of the Mishnah—all with one brilliant proof text:

Rather [the halachah] is as interpreted by the Jerusalem [Talmud] [*Bikurim*, end of ch. 1]. There we learn as taught in the name of Rabbi Judah, A proselyte brings his own [offering] and recites

[God of our fathers . . .] Why? Because [God said to Abraham] a father of a multitude of nations have I made you [Gen. 17:5]. Formerly he was the father to Aram, from then on he [Abraham] became the father to all humanity.[44] Rabbi Joshua the son of Levy says the law is according to Rabbi Judah. Then the matter came up for a decision before Rabbi A'vahoo, and he taught the matter according to Rabbi Judah.

Behold, now it has been clarified for you that you have the obligation to say: "which the Lord, the God of our fathers swore to give to us," for Abraham is your father and ours, and is father to all the righteous who walk in his ways. And the same [principle] applies to any of the other blessings and prayers, so that you should not change anything at all.

It was Maimonides' genius not only as a legalist, but as a psychologist-philosopher, which nurtured his empathy for a guest who, as if returning to the home of his host lost the key and worried he would be locked out—a stranger once more. In that sense Maimonides, still in Egypt, and Ovadyah, in Jerusalem, each a stranger in his own land, accomplished for each other what divinely inspired empathic dialogue always does: conditions the door to our hearts to be open, motivates us to truly listen to one another, and prompts us to feel another's pain as our own.

So it was for the student and the teacher. Ovadyah's question inspired an empathic answer from Maimonides, which strengthened them both; no doubt encouraging more mitzvot of compassion as they sought to imitate their Creator, saying forever in the words of this greatest of teachers: "Therefore, if he cries out to Me, I will pay heed, for I am compassionate."[45]

And so wrote Moses the son of Maimon, may his righteous memory be for blessing.

Notes

1. Unlike the other translations by Solomon Freehof, Isadore Twersky, and Franz Kobler that are based on the "critical edition" of Joshua Belau, from a manuscript called Ms. Aleph, my translation is based on a manuscript called Ms. Kiva, which I personally obtained from the Hebrew University in Jerusalem in November 1992. I have edited it down to three quarters the size of the original chapter in my dissertation.

My comparison of the two manuscripts leads me to believe that there are other manuscripts that are missing and that Ms. Kiva and Ms. Aleph reflect the more extreme positions, especially regarding the *Avot* blessings, than what we might see if other manuscripts were discovered.

2. Dr. Katz taught human relations at the Cincinnati campus to my generation of rabbis. It was his book, *Empathy: Its Nature and Uses* (in therapy) that influenced my conviction that empathy is also a significant catalyst to pro-social behavior.
3. Stanley Cheyet was not only my D.H.L. advisor, with David Ellenson, but the two of them and others at the Los Angeles campus were the personification of empathic concern for this colleague who while serving Temple Beth El of Riverside had also entered into the exciting world of research and the writing of a dissertation.
4. Robert L. Katz, *Empathy: Its Nature and Uses* (New York: Free Press, 1963), 8.
5. "[Thus] there is no difference whatsoever between us and you. And certainly you have the obligation to say the blessing: 'Who has chosen us,' and 'who has given us' [His Torah], 'who has bequeathed unto us an inheritance,' and 'who has distinguished us [from all the people].' For the Creator, may He be exalted, has already chosen you, and separated you from the [other] nations, and has given you the Torah—the same Torah he gave to us and to [you] the proselytes ... But you must never view your own ancestry as unimportant; if we are related to Abraham, Isaac, and Jacob, behold you are related to the One who said and the world came into being. And that is the way it is explained by Isaiah: 'This one may say: I am the Lord's, and another may call himself by the name of Jacob.'"
6. Franz Kobler, *A Treasury of Jewish Letters*, vol. 1 (Philadelphia: JPS, 1953), 194.
7. "Maimonides took pains to write at length when leadership and pedagogic abilities were called for." Abraham Halkin and David Hartman, *Crises and Leadership: Epistles of Maimonides* (Philadelphia: JPS, 1985), intro.
8. The question that Ovadyah raises relates to "practical" matters of personal worship and the observance of ritual. In the order that Maimonides enumerates them, these blessings refer to the *Amidah*; various blessings of action, including the *Kiddush*; the Torah; Passover and other festivals, including Chanukah.
9. Menachem Lorberbaum, "Maimonides' Letter to Obadya: An Analysis," Shalom Hartman Institute, Jerusalem, 1985, 2.
10. Nancy Eisenberg and Janet Strayer, "Critical Issues in the Study of Empathy," in *Empathy and Its Development*, ed. Nancy Eisenberg and Janet Strayer (Cambridge: Cambridge University Press, 1990), 3.

11. Aryeh Newman, ed., *Six Talks on Maimonides* (Jerusalem: World Zionist Organization, 1955), 14.
12. Moses Maimonides, *The Guide for the Perplexed*, trans. M. Friedlander (New York: Hebrew Publishing Co., 1881), 22.
13. Leon D. Stitskin, *Letters of Maimonides* (New York: Yeshiva University Press, 1977), 10–11.
14. Ibid., 31.
15. Alice Miller, *The Drama of the Gifted Child: The Search for the True Self* (New York: Basic Books, 1997), 112–13.
16. In Arabic, *rahma* means "compassion, human understanding, sympathy, kindness." J. Milton Cowan, ed., *A Dictionary of Modern Written Arabic* (Ithaca, NY: Cornell University Press, 1961), 332. Also in the more classical Arabic of the Turkish, *rahmi* means "merciful [and] compassionate." *New Redhouse Turkish-English Dictionary* (Isanbul: Redhouse Press, 1968), 946. Depending on the context, both *rachamim* and *rahma* express the idea of empathy as well as compassion.
17. Stitskin's translation is "endowed me with a sympathetic understanding." Stitskin, *Letters of Maimonides*, 142.
18. Halkin and Hartman, *Crises and Leadership*, intro.
19. The Soncino *Chumash* and other translations of the Torah add "to the end," as does Rashi. For Maimonides these words are an important part of the Genesis proof text as they optimistically predict an eternity of future converts.
20. Judah Halevi, *The Kuzari*, trans. H. Hirschfeld (New York: Schocken Books, 1964), 79.
21. Ibid., 47.
22. Ibid.
23. Lorberbaum, *Maimonides' Letter*, 4.
24. Ms. Kiva reads, "who did miracles *l'yisrael* (for Israel)," whereas Ms. Aleph reads "who did miracles *im yisrael* (with Israel)." Obviously the Kiva makes more sense.
25. Freehof's translation inexplicably ignores the whole phrase: "*va-asher natan lanoo [torato]*" (and who has given us [His Torah]), which is clearly an omission as Maimonides' central point is that Torah belongs to all Jews.
26. Yeshayahu Leibowitz, *The Faith of Maimonides* (New York: Adama Books, 1987), 52.
27. Lorberbaum, *Maimonides' Letter*, 5.
28. Isadore Twersky, *Introduction to the Code of Maimonides* (New Haven, CT: Yale University Press, 1980), 485.
29. Halkin and Hartman, *Crises and Leadership*, 53.
30. Maimonides points to "the tribe of Levi," as exemplars of monotheism, because not only is Moses of the tribe of Levi, but in the

Mishneh Torah he tell us that in Egypt this was the only tribe that did not relapse into polytheism. Nahum N. Glatzer, *The Jewish Tradition* (New York: Behrman House, 1969), 314..

31. Ibid., 53, from *Mishneh Torah*, Laws of the Sabbatical Year and the Jubilee, XIII, 13.
32. Maimonides reinterprets Gen. 1:3. In the Torah, God creates not the world but the light of the world by merely saying it into existence.
33. Maimonides' beautiful use of this paraphrase of Isa. 45:5 is likely taken from the *M'chilta* to Exodus, Tractate *N'zikin* 45: "Among the four groups who respond and speak before Him by whose word the world came into being: One shall say: 'I am the Lord's', that is: 'all of me is the Lord's and there is no admixture of sin in me.' And another shall call himself by the name of Jacob, these are the righteous proselytes." Twersky and Kobler inexplicably conclude their translations with this Isaiah quote.
34. Freehof reads: "This is the anonymous Mishnah and is the opinion of Rabbi Meir (this according to the general principle stated in the Talmud [*Sanhedrin* 86a] that all anonymous parts of the Mishnah are to be ascribed to Rabbi Meir)."
35. Discussion with Dr. Mark Washofsky, HUC Cincinnati, February 1990.
36. Herbert Danby, trans., *The Mishnah* (London: Oxford, 1933), 94. The Freiman/Blau reading of the Mishnah reads: "and when he prays privately by himself he says, 'our God, and the God of the fathers of Israel.' And when he prays in the Synagogue he says, 'our God and the God of our fathers.'"
37. *Shiloh Siddur* (New York, 1931), 16.
38. Hayim Halevy Donin, *To Pray as a Jew* (New York: Basic Books, 1980), 197.
39. The Freiman/Blau texts, following Ms. Aleph, read that in the Synagogue the proselyte should say, "Our God and God of our fathers," while Ms. Kiva and its texts read: "God of our fathers." Ms. Kiva's reading is more logical because it corresponds with the actual wording of the Deuteronomic proclamation.
40. *Encyclopaedica Judaica* (Jerusalem: Keter, 1971), 11:765.
41. Isaac Klein, trans., *The Code of Maimonides*, book 7, *The Book of Agriculture* by (New Haven, CT: Yale University Press, 1979), 303–4.
42. *Ma-a'ser Sheini*: Moses Maimonides, *Mishneh Torah: The Book of Knowledge*, trans. Moses Hyamson (Jerusalem: Jerusalem Pulishers, 1962), 287.
43. *The Babylonian Talmud*, vol. 4, *Seder Nezikin, Makkot* 19a (London: Soncino Press, 1952),133.

44. As Dr. Blau states in personal correspondence of March 5th, 1990: "As to the variant readings, av l'adam, av l'avraham, av l'aram, there is in my mind no doubt that av l'aram is the correct reading being a pun on Avram = av aram. See also BT *B'rachot* 13:1. As Rashi says, both in his bible and Talmud commentaries: "Avram was the father of Aram because his place of living was Aram." Clearly, the fact that Av l'aram is the correct reading, is another reason for the authenticity of the Kiva text.
45. Halkin and Hartman, *Crises and Leadership*, 169, quoting Maimonides, chap. 28 of *Hilchot Y'sodei HaTorah* of the *Mishneh Torah*.

Responses to the Fall 2012 Symposium

I feel compelled to comment on Jodie Gordon's article, "Emerging Rabbis," in the Fall 2012 issue of the *CCAR Journal* ("Gender and Judaism in Conversation"). Two aspects of what she wrote actually sadden me.

First, she indicated that "Gender was a lens, a way in which I understand the world around me" (p. 9). Except the way she presented her case, gender is *the* lens by which she understands the world. It seems to me that there are a number of other "lenses" by which we rabbis perceive reality, although gender is undoubtedly among them. For example, what about Jew and non-Jew, Israeli and Arab, member and nonmember, Reform or Liberal Jew and Traditionalist? When I approach any situation, I try to look for the "lens" that is particularly relevant and helpful to those circumstances, not one that is predetermined by some ideological preference. To proceed in this manner is little different than to use the equivalent of a Procrustean bed in which all issues are reduced to the same measure.

I also question her assertion that "'Rabbi' is a static and unchanging noun" (p. 14). My experience over the last fifty-plus years suggests that to be a rabbi is to engage in a constant process of development and evolution. I would be enraged at myself if I were the same today, static, as it were, as I was on June 4, 1966, when I was ordained. I know that I have changed in many ways and often as a person and as a rabbi, and for that I am immensely grateful.

P.S. I suppose I sound like a superannuated, antediluvian male, and in some ways I probably am, but I also point out that one of the proudest days of my life was when I stood on the pulpit of Plum Street Temple in 1972 and had the great honor as dean of HUC-JIR in Cincinnati to present Sally Priesand to Alfred Gottschalk for ordination.

KENNETH D. ROSEMAN, Ph.D. (C66) is the rabbi of Congregation Beth Israel in Corpus Christi, Texas.

RESPONSES TO THE FALL 2012 SYMPOSIUM

Reading Rabbi Geela Rayzel Raphael's paean to *Shechinah* ("*Shechinah*: The Divine Feminine," Fall 2012) made me feel I was in a time warp; transported back to the '70s and '80s when *Shechinah* became an essential part of Jewish feminist consciousness. While the enthusiastic welcome accorded Her over thirty years ago was understandable for women seeking to recast a masculine-defined and -dominated Judaism, Raphael's uncritical approach to *Shechinah* today, seems to me to be, at best, naïve and, at worst, simply uninformed.

First, her "feminine-is-nurturing-and-kind" thesis is too simplistic. Have we not gained the insight from depth psychology that everything casts and carries a shadow? Thirty years after the rediscovery of *Shechinah*, with women occupying positions of influence and control in government, business, and academia, have we not learned that feminist power also has a dark side? Though Raphael does mention *Shechinah*'s involvement with the destruction of Sodom and Gomorrah, she ignores its implications. If *Shechinah* is "nurturing, the Mother who suckles her children" how exactly then, is She also the force who destroys the children of Sodom and Gomorrah? How is She the one who turns Lot's wife, Edith, into a pillar of salt as she looks backward to see what has become of her daughters?[1] While Raphael rhapsodizes that "*Shechinah* is the earth, and nature is her robes," she focuses solely on the flowers and ignores the darker aspects of nature.

Add to this Raphael's muddled equation of Asherah with *Shechinah*. Middle Eastern studies have, for some time, made clear that these ancient pagan goddesses were not only nurturing earth mothers but were violent warriors, as well.[2] Raphael, again, however, ignores this shadow side. (I will not treat, here, her specious argument that Asherah worship is acceptable today because she was once worshiped in Ancient Israel.)

Second, though over forty years (!) have passed since the beginning of women's liberation and though women today have, indeed, come into power, Raphael wants to focus, instead, on how masculine energy, imagery, definitions, and teachers still dominate Judaism. She is quick to assert that "the patriarchy is alive and well" but the only evidence she musters is "the dearth of professional women in leadership in the central organizations of the

---

RABBI JEFF MARX (NY83) is rabbi of The Santa Monica Synagogue in California.

American Jewish community." (I wonder if that is a useful criterion, given the general decline in influence and power of national organizations.) She is silent about the influx, these last thirty years, of Jewish women into congregational and communal life and the influence that they have. Last I looked, women from Reform, Conservative, and Reconstructionist seminaries are featured prominently in the Jewish press, and are leading the way in "senior positions" in the creation of new worship forms.[3] My shelves are filled with brilliant insights from female Jewish scholars in Bible, liturgy, Chasidic studies, and history that are recognized authorities in these fields.

The serious question that we should be asking today is: How has the *Shechinah* archetype worked as a political, spiritual, communal guide in the hands of Jewish women? How has the awareness of *Shechinah* influenced the lives of Jewish men? Rather than Raphael spending time setting up the patriarchal straw man, we would have been better served by her taking a hard, critical look at what her sisters have accomplished or failed to do with this feminine aspect of divinity.

Third, Raphael seems unaware that the past thirty years have wrought changes in our definitions of masculine and feminine. From queer theory, we've learned to approach with caution the notion there are only two ways of defining gender and sexual orientation, and that what we assumed were fixed ways of being masculine or feminine are, in reality, quite fluid.[4] Nor does she seem cognizant of the admixture of masculine and feminine found in medieval Kabbalah. *Shechinah's* feminine *s'firah*, for example, also known as *Malchut*, is associated with the masculine, David! This is not explained by her assertion that "gender is a continuum between masculine and feminine poles" but rather by Jay Michaelson's notion that Kabbalah involves a far more radical kind of gender bending.[5] (And exactly how will Raphael illustrate her deck of "*Shechinah* Oracle Cards" in light of Elliot Wolfson's thesis that the *Shechinah* is the manifestation of the *b'rit*, the circumcised phallus?)[6]

Finally, rather than engage in the more challenging kabbalistic task of *coincidentia oppositorum* (unification of opposites), Raphael simply posits that masculine energy is sexist, domineering, and earth-polluting; consigning the masculine aspects of God to, as it were, the *Sitra Achara* (Dark Side). Yet, as she knows, kabbalistic thought teaches that divine energy flows through the world when the feminine *and* masculine aspects of God are brought face to face with one another.[7]

A mystical approach that is unwilling to consider the positive aspects of masculine energy, that glosses over the shadow aspects of the feminine, and that ignores the elaborate interplay of these two forces with one another, does not seem to me to be ultimately useful in helping to heal our broken world.

Notes

1. Gerald Friedlander, trans., *Pirke de Rabbi Eliezer* (Skokie, IL: Varda Books, 2004), chap. 25.
2. Samuel H. Dresner, "Goddess Feminism," *Conservative Judaism* 46 (Fall 1993): 3–23.
3. I am mindful, here, that there still exist disparities in salaries between male and female clergy and that full equality has not yet been reached, but it seems to me that, today, Jewish professional women are in a very different world than existed in the 1970s.
4. Margaret Moers Wenig articulates this well in "Male and Female, God Create Them?" *CCAR Journal* (Fall 2012): 130–42.
5. Jay Michaelson, "I'm Just Not That Kind of God: Queering Kabbalistic Gender Play," in *Queer Religion*, ed. Donald L. Boisvert and Jay Emerson Johnson (Santa Barbara: Praeger, 2012), 51–68.
6. Elliott Wolfson, *Through a Speculum That Shines* (Princeton: Princeton University Press, 1994), 355–72.
7. Paganism also embraces this concept but even when Raphael champions the return of the goddess, she banishes the masculine side from her discourse. Does not Asherah have a consort? Where is he in her neo-pagan equation?

Poetry

Stretching toward *S'lichot*

Ruth Lerner

The last angel arrived at midnight to take me home.
I did not want to go with her.

I did not want to put on my soft black ballet shoes
to begin my annual practice at the barre.

I did not want to begin the lengthy limbering up
the slow stretching of mind muscles
moving in time to ancient melodies.

I did not want to begin the sacred *pliés* or *relevés*
the well-disciplined risings and descendings of the soul
struggling to return to the Source.

I did not want to begin the silent conditioning of the body:
the bending and the bowing
the pushing and the pausing
the stretching and the searching within.

I did not want to begin peering over the past year's
lapsed practiced sessions:
the ones where I had failed completely
the ones where I had erred half-way
the ones where I had done the bare minimum
or the ones where I did more than the bare minimum,
but did them with a stony detachment.

RUTH LERNER has been writing poetry for the High Holy Days for more than twenty years. Every year her poetry is integrated into the High Holy Day services at her synagogue, Kehillat Israel in Pacific Palisades, California.

All these holy loosening-up exercises
I did not want to begin.
But it was *S'lichot* and I had no choice.

The last angel arrived at midnight to take me home.
I held her hand, clasped my black ballet shoes to my breast
and began beating them into my heart.

POETRY

Rosh HaShanah in the Pines, 2011/5772

Hara E. Person

Darkness settles, slowly, across the horizon.
The new year rises before us,
its fragile moon awaiting our embrace.

Heaven and earth entwine
in their annual dance of re-creation.
A fissure appears in the firmament tonight,
an entranceway into new beginnings.

Out beyond the swales
the sea expands and contracts,
keeping time to the thrumming of the universe.

Under this Rosh HaShanah sky
the path before us is uncertain.
All we can do is hold each other tight
as we make our way home.

RABBI HARA E. PERSON (NY98) is the publisher and director of CCAR Press and the managing editor of the *CCAR Journal*. She also serves Congregation B'nai Olam in Fire Island Pines as the High Holy Day rabbi.

POETRY

What if . . .

Donald B. Rossoff

What if each of us was like a drop of rain
forming weightless in the clouds,
having made our ascent from the great ocean below,
in ways that were us but not yet,
coming into being as separate selves,
spending our time in a great journey
back to where all are one again?

And what if some of us were soft and gentle
like the soothing showers of spring,
barely noticed
as we brought life to the earth?

And what if some of us were hard and strong
like the raging summer storms,
spending our journey midst thunderous tumult
that never finds peace?

And what if God were like that great ocean,
teeming with life and its potential
where we each begin
      and end
      and begin again
      and again?

Together we would be forever
But I would not be I
and you would not be you
but together we would be in that greater I
dancing to the rhythm
of rising and falling

DONALD B. ROSSOFF (C81) has been a rabbi at Temple B'nai Or in Morristown, New Jersey, since 1990. He is the author of *The Perfect Prayer* (URJ), the composer (with Cantor Bruce Benson) of *Adonai Li* (Transcontinental), and has contributed chapters to several books.

dissolving and transforming
being and becoming,
never missing a step
even when we thought we had.

What if each of us was like a raindrop
and God were like the ocean
and life was the journey
of leaving and coming home?

Would my heart not still be shattered?
Would the seas not be filled with my tears?

POETRY

Kol Nidrei

Jenni Person

Kol Nidrei's streaming live
chanting
from a bedside laptop;
Game Seven
is muted on TV;
kids are nestled between us
"Sssssssh, listen to the rabbi."
They fall asleep at the mention of her name
too bad they don't do that in shul.

Now some guy is being interviewed on the tube
"Hey, he's cute, is he a Jew?"
David pulls out his iPhone Wiki app
and discovers: Jew/Half-Jew
"He did what Sandy Koufax
swore he'd never do
But never needed to
hey, I'd play Game Seven on Yom Kippur too
and I'm the seminarian!"

Because baseball is a faith.

Marlins fans meet at a third inning minyan.
And the Jew/Half-Jew in question
shares the last name
of Sandy Koufax's mom before she married.
And his grandfather lived in a house previously owned
by Hank Greenberg.
So the lineage is long

and *Kol Nidrei* is live online.

JENNI PERSON is a literary artist and the director of Next@19th, a Jewish Culture Center in Miami. She received her MFA in Interdisciplinary Arts from Goddard College.

POETRY

Yom Kippur, The Essence Does Not Change

Yehoshua November

Isn't this why, though he knew little Torah,
Sandy Koufax gave up what is unthinkable to give up?
Isn't this why, a century earlier,
young Jewish boys—
kidnapped from the *cheder* and raised
in the Russian army—
took off their shirts
at the last hour of Yom Kippur?
Revealing their whip marks, they said,
"God, we did not forget you, please bless us."

YEHOSHUA NOVEMBER is the author of *God's Optimism,* which won the MSR Poetry Book Award and was selected as a finalist for the *L.A. Times* Book Prize in Poetry. He teaches writing at Touro College and Rutgers University.

The Ankle of the High Priest

Joseph R. Black

The cord is thick: silky soft
Belying its macabre purpose.
They tie it tight—to remind him of his holiness
And his mortality.

Once a year he crosses the threshold of that sacred, musty site.
He leaves behind his glory, his splendor, his pretense.
Accompanied by the sound of bells
He is hampered in his forward progress
By the tautness of his tether.

He limps toward the place that only he and his fathers before
   him have seen.

      A year of dust covers the altar—
          Spilling over like so many unanswered prayers—
          That someday, in a different time, will be
          Gathered together,
          Hastily scribbled, and
          Shoved between the cracks of massive stones.

He hesitates while walking—
Dragging his rope,
Hoarding the hope of his people
He knows he cannot remain silent for long
Lest those outside the entryway grow nervous.

And yet, he yearns to be still:

      To remember
      To reveal
      To rule

JOSEPH R. BLACK serves as senior rabbi of Temple Emanuel in Denver, Colorado. In addition to his work in the pulpit, he also is a poet, singer/songwriter, and author of two children's books, several CDs, videos, and a songbook.

For what shall he ask?
Two goats have already died.
Shofars have sounded.
Souls afflicted.
What's left to do?

He carries the dreams and fears of all who wait outside:
Petitions for health and healing
For wealth and feeling
For babies to be born
And loved ones who are mourned
For enemies defeated
And lovers entreated

He is the one
Who speaks to The One

Jumbled pleas and petitions
Swirl round his head
As the knot grows tighter round his foot.
He opens his mouth in prayer:

> Return, O Israel, to your God
> Return, O God, to your Israel

We are pulled towards one other
In an ancient game of tug of war.

He falls, prostrate at the foot of the altar.
Digging in his fingers, he holds tight
Until, drawing ten straight lines in the dust,
He emerges into the light of a new day.

POETRY

The Wilderness of Tishrei

Barbara AB Symons

Two goats, brothers perhaps.

One has the honor of being
sacrificed
Becomes *tahor*
postmortem.

One touched with sin
is led out to the wilderness
Becomes *tamei*
for life.

How did he choose the fate?
He, author of the Book of Life volume II
Did he see which goat was strong enough
to live with sin
to die without sin
Did he look into eyes as human as can be without being?

We are in the wilderness of Tishrei.
What does it mean to live with sin?
What does it mean to die without?

BARBARA AB SYMONS (NY94) has served congregations in New York, Connecticut, and Massachusetts and is currently serving as rabbi and director of education at Temple David in Monroeville, Pennsylvania, where she lives with her husband, Rabbi Ron Symons, and three children.

Call for Papers: *Maayanot*

The CCAR Journal: The Reform Jewish Quarterly is committed to serving its readers' professional, intellectual, and spiritual needs. In pursuit of that objective, the *Journal* created a new section known as *Maayanot* (Primary Sources), which made its debut in the Spring 2012 issue.

We continue to welcome proposals for *Maayanot* —translations of significant Jewish texts, accompanied by an introduction as well as annotations and/or commentary. *Maayanot* aims to present fresh approaches to materials from any period of Jewish life, including but not confined to the biblical or Rabbinic periods. When appropriate, it is possible to include the original document in the published presentation.

Please submit proposals, inquiries, and questions to *Maayanot* editor, Daniel Polish, dpolish@optonline.net.

Along with submissions for *Maayanot*, the *Journal* encourages the submission of scholarly articles in fields of Jewish Studies, as well as other articles that fit within our Statement of Purpose.

Since 1889

CENTRAL CONFERENCE OF AMERICAN RABBIS

איגוד הרבנים המתקדמים

NEW FROM CCAR PRESS!

Birkon Artzi: Blessings and Meditations for Travelers to Israel

Edited by Rabbi Serge Lippe
Preface by Rabbi Rick Jacobs, President, Union for Reform Judaism
Introduction by Bruce Feiler, author of *Walking the Bible*

Birkon Artzi seeks to create spiritual opportunities and responses for the thousands of Jews who journey each and every year to visit, study in, and get to know the State of Israel.

Mishkan R'fuah: Where Healing Resides

Edited by Rabbi Eric Weiss
Consulting Editor, Rabbi Shira Stern

This beautiful compilation contains contemplative readings and prayers for many different moments of spiritual need, including illness, surgery, treatment, chronic illness, hearing good news, transitions, addiction, infertility, end-of-life, and more.

Also through Kindle, Nook, and iBooks.

**Visit us online for more books, including back-in-print classics and new releases
Follow the CCAR at RavBlog.org**

   For more information and to order, go to: www.ccarpress.org or call 212-972-3636 x243
CCAR | 355 Lexington Avenue | New York, NY 10017

The *CCAR Journal: The Reform Jewish Quarterly*
Published quarterly by the Central Conference of American Rabbis.

Volume LX, No. 3. Issue Number: Two hundred thirty-seven.
Summer 2013.

STATEMENT OF PURPOSE

The *CCAR Journal: The Reform Jewish Quarterly* seeks to explore ideas and issues of Judaism and Jewish life, primarily—but not exclusively—from a Reform Jewish perspective. To fulfill this objective, the Journal is designed to:

1. provide a forum to reflect the thinking of informed and concerned individuals—especially Reform rabbis—on issues of consequence to the Jewish people and the Reform Movement;

2. increase awareness of developments taking place in fields of Jewish scholarship and the practical rabbinate, and to make additional contributions to these areas of study;

3. encourage creative and innovative approaches to Jewish thought and practice, based upon a thorough understanding of the traditional sources.

The views expressed in the Journal do not necessarily reflect the position of the Editorial Board or the Central Conference of American Rabbis.

The *CCAR Journal: The Reform Jewish Quarterly* (ISSN 1058-8760) is published quarterly by the Central Conference of American Rabbis, 355 Lexington Avenue, 18th Floor, New York, NY, 10017. Application to mail at periodical postage rates is pending at New York, NY and at additional mailing offices.

Subscriptions should be sent to CCAR Executive Offices, 355 Lexington Avenue, 18th Floor, New York, NY, 10017. Subscription rate as set by the Conference is $100 for a one-year subscription, $150 for a two-year subscription. Overseas subscribers should add $36 per year for postage. POSTMASTER: Please send address changes to CCAR Journal: The Reform Jewish Quarterly, c/o Central Conference of American Rabbis, 355 Lexington Avenue, 18th Floor, New York, NY, 10017.

Typesetting and publishing services provided by Publishing Synthesis, Ltd., 39 Crosby Street, New York, NY, 10013.

The *CCAR Journal: The Reform Jewish Quarterly* is indexed in the *Index to Jewish Periodicals*. Articles appearing in it are listed in the *Index of Articles on Jewish Studies* (of *Kirjath Sepher*).

© Copyright 2013 by the Central Conference of American Rabbis.
All rights reserved.
ISSN 1058-8760

ISBN: 978-0-88123-199-1

GUIDELINES FOR SUBMITTING MATERIAL

1. The *CCAR Journal* welcomes submissions that fulfill its Statement of Purpose whatever the author's background or identification. Inquiries regarding publishing in the CCAR Journal and submissions for possible publication (including poetry) should be sent to the editor-elect, Rabbi Paul Golomb, Rabbi@Vassartemple.org.

2. Other than commissioned articles, submissions to the *CCAR Journal* are sent out to a member of the editorial board for anonymous peer review. Thus submitted articles and poems should be sent to the editor with the author's name omitted. Please use MS Word format for the attachment. The message itself should contain the author's name, phone number, and e-mail address, as well as the submission's title and a 1–2 sentence bio.

3. Books for review and inquiries regarding submitting a review should be sent directly to the book review editor, Rabbi Laurence Edwards, at LLE49@comcast.net.

4. Inquiries concerning, or submissions for, *Maayanot* (Primary Sources) should be directed to the *Maayanot* editor, Rabbi Daniel Polish, at dpolish@optonline.net.

5. Based on Reform Judaism's commitment to egalitarianism, we request that articles be written in gender-inclusive language.

6. The *Journal* publishes reference notes at the end of articles, but submissions are easier to review when notes come at the bottom of each page. If possible, keep this in mind when submitting an article. Notes should conform to the following style:
   a. Norman Lamm, *The Shema: Spirituality and Law in Judaism* (Philadelphia: Jewish Publication Society, 1998), 101–6. **[book]**
   b. Lawrence A. Hoffman, "The Liturgical Message," in *Gates of Understanding*, ed. Lawrence A.Hoffman (New York: CCAR Press, 1977), 147–48, 162–63. **[chapter in a book]**
   c. Richard Levy, "The God Puzzle," *Reform Judaism* 28 (Spring 2000): 18–22. **[article in a periodical]**
   d. Lamm, *Shema*, 102. **[short form for subsequent reference]**
   e. Levy, "God Puzzle," 20. **[short form for subsequent reference]**
   f. Ibid., 21. **[short form for subsequent reference]**

7. If Hebrew script is used, please include an English translation. If transliteration is used, follow the guidelines abbreviated below and included more fully in the **Master Style Sheet**, available on the CCAR website at www.ccarnet.org:

   "ch" for *chet* and *chaf* "ei" for *tzeirei*
   "f" for *fei* "a" for *patach* and *kamatz*
   "k" for *kaf* and *kuf* "o" for *cholam* and *kamatz katan*
   "tz" for *tzadi* "u" for *shuruk* and *kibbutz*
   "i" for *chirik* "ai" for *patach* with *yod*
   "e" for *segol*

   Final "h" for final *hei*; none for final *ayin* (with exceptions based on common usage): *atah*, *Sh'ma*, <u>but</u> *Moshe*.

   Apostrophe for *sh'va nah*: *b'nei*, *b'rit*, *Sh'ma*; no apostrophe for *sh'va nach*.

   Hyphen for two vowels together where necessary for correct pronunciation: *ne-eman*, *samei-ach*, <u>but</u> *maariv*, Shavuot.

   No hyphen for prefixes unless necessary for correct pronunciation: *babayit*, *HaShem*, *Yom HaAtzma-ut*.

   Do not double consonants (with exceptions based on dictionary spelling or common usage): *t'filah*, *chayim*, <u>but</u> *tikkun*, Sukkot.

www.ingramcontent.com/pod-product-compliance
Lightning Source LLC
Chambersburg PA
CBHW071621170426
43195CB00038B/1673